Redeeming Nietzsche

On the piety of unbelief

Giles Fraser

London and New York

First published 2002
by Routledge
11 New Fetter Lane, London EC4P 4EE

Simultaneously published in the USA and Canada
by Routledge
29 West 35th Street, New York, NY 10001

Reprinted 2002

Routledge is an imprint of the Taylor & Francis Group

Typeset in Garamond by
The Running Head Limited, Cambridge
Printed and bound in Great Britan by The Cromwell Press,
Trowbridge, Wiltshire

British Library Cataloguing in Publication Data
A catalogue record for this book is available
from the British Library

Library of Congress Cataloging in Publication Data
Fraser, Giles.
    Redeeming Nietzsche: on the piety of unbelief/Giles Fraser
        p. cm.
    Includes bibliographical references and index.
    1. Nietzsche, Friedrich Wilhelm, 1844–1900—Religion.
  I. Title.

    B3318.R4 F73 2002
    193—dc21   2001044459

ISBN 0–415–27290–4 (hb)
ISBN 0–415–27291–2 (pb)

Contents

Acknowledgements

The bulk of this project was written in Walsall during the 1990s while I was serving my curacy at All Saints, Streetly and at All Saints, Blakenall Heath. It was completed in the very different context of Wadham College, Oxford during my time as Chaplain of the College and of the University Church of St. Mary the Virgin. I thank both my training incumbents, Peter Hammersley and Brian Mountford, for letting me have the time to undertake this project when the immediate benefits to the parish seemed hard to justify.

My greatest debt is to Andrew Shanks. He has been mentor and friend throughout this work and one could not want for a better guide or stimulating conversation partner. I thank him very much. I want to thank Rowan Williams for early encouragement to undertake this project and James Alison, Daniel Conway, Philip Goodchild, Fergus Kerr, Paul Morris, Richard Roberts, Stephen Williams and Linda Woodhead who have made important interventions at various points along the way.

Much of this book has been sieved through endless late-night conversations with friends and students who have helped to shape its arguments in many ways. Thanks to Philip Bullock, Maria Critchley, Chris Insole, Jacob Knee, Elizabeth MacFarlane, Jane Shaw, and William Whyte.

But most of all thanks to my wife Sally who has had to put up with my absence – both literal and mental – as I became increasingly absorbed in the writings of a dead German philosopher.

1 Holy Nietzsche

I condemn Christianity, I bring against the Christian Church the most terrible charge any prosecutor has ever uttered. To me it is the extremest thinkable form of corruption . . . Wherever there are walls I shall inscribe this eternal accusation against Christianity upon them – I can write in letters which make even the blind see . . . I call Christianity the one great curse, the one great intrinsic depravity, the one great instinct for revenge for which no expedient is sufficiently poisonous, secret, subterranean, petty – I call it the one immortal blemish of mankind.

Nietzsche, *The Anti-Christ*, p. 62

In search of God?

In the last few months before his final mental breakdown Nietzsche wrote of his fear that some day he would be pronounced 'holy'. One could be forgiven for thinking this a strange fear from one who is remembered most of all for having broken the news of God's death and then for proceeding to dance at His wake. Nonetheless, there have been a considerable number of thinkers who have seen in this dance patterns of movement that remind them of the religion whose demise is being celebrated. Heidegger called Nietzsche 'that passionate seeker after God and the last German philosopher'[1] – a reference, no doubt, to the fact that the madman who proclaims God's death enters the market place crying out 'I seek God! I seek God!' Julian Young has gone as far as to suggest that Nietzsche's intellectual quest can be characterised as 'proving that God, after all, exists'. And yet, of course, Nietzsche was one of the most emphatic and militant of all 'atheists'. His condemnations of Christianity are, arguably, unrivalled in their ferocity and vitriol. One of the challenges facing those who seek to come to grips with Nietzsche's work is finding a way of making sense of these seemingly conflicting drives. Erich Heller, for instance, suggests the following:

He is, by the very texture of his soul and mind, one of the most radically religious natures that the nineteenth century brought forth, but is endowed with an intellect which guards, with the aggressive jealousy of a watchdog, all approaches to the temple.[2]

In what follows I will be proposing an answer to why it is that Nietzsche manages to come across simultaneously as both atheistic and pious. My basic argument will be this. Nietzsche is obsessed with the question of human salvation. It is an obsession that is formed in his childhood through the Pietistic upbringing given to him by family and teachers. And despite the fact that he becomes an atheist, he continues passionately to explore different ways in which the same basic instinct for redemption can be expressed in a world without God. He could well have had himself in mind when he wrote of European culture in general: 'it seems to me that the religious instinct is indeed in vigorous growth – but that it rejects the theistic answer with profound mistrust.'[3] Nietzsche's work, as I understand it, is a series of experiments in redemption. That is, Nietzsche's work is primarily soteriology: experiments to design a form of redemption that would work for a post-theistic age.

Having established the priority of soteriology in Nietzsche's thought I proceed to examine a number of his central doctrines as successive attempts to square the circle of post-theistic soteriology – that is, as experiments in redemption. First I will offer a reading of *The Birth of Tragedy* as an attempt to articulate salvation as art: 'life is only justified as an aesthetic phenomenon'[4] is the best known summary of this position. Next, I will look at Nietzsche's attack upon Christian soteriology as developed in *On the Genealogy of Morals* and *The Anti-Christ*. Here we begin to see Nietzsche advance the idea of the *Übermensch* as his own version of what redeemed humanity ought to look like. This leads on into an examination of what is arguably the pinnacle of Nietzsche's soteriological experimentation, the enigmatic eternal recurrence of the same. With the development of the eternal recurrence, Nietzsche believes himself to have given birth to an idea capable of offering genuine redemption, albeit to a very few, and those not yet born. In his thought of the eternal recurrence, Nietzsche imagines a doctrine sufficient to survive the death of God and capable of replacing the soteriology of the Christian past.

As I go along, reflecting upon these different experiments, I will seek to draw attention to the extent to which Nietzsche is involved in a complex and sophisticated process of theological sampling, repeating the patterns of thought that animated his early childhood faith. Although designed to be atheistic, Nietzsche borrows a great deal from the Christian past he eschews. This will be my answer to why there is a double textured quality to Nietzsche's attitude to Christianity, why the 'conflicting drives'. Nietzsche's a-theology may reject Christian soteriology, but it borrows substantially from it nonetheless.

In the last three chapters I will turn from interpretation to assessment. There I will seek to explore why Nietzsche's experiments in redemption come to fail. Furthermore, my aim is to assess these experiments in Nietzsche's own terms My overall point will be that Nietzsche fails to appreciate the full horror of human suffering. For although he envisions redemption as being achieved by some almost super-human act of heroic affirmation, 'Yes saying' to life in all its horrific fulness, the truth is that Nietzsche's conception of horror, of suffering and indeed of the nihil itself are the imaginings of the comfortably off bourgeoisie. 'An armchair philosopher of human riskiness' is what Martha Nussbaum has called him, and I, for somewhat different reasons to Nussbaum, will be claiming much the same.

So much for where the argument is going. Before I get on to the main part of the argument we need to do a certain amount of stage setting. The 'theological' Nietzsche has been misread from a variety of different perspectives and these threads need to be unpicked before further progress can be made. The rest of this chapter will be concerned to review something of the theological *Rezeptionsgeschichte* of Nietzsche's work with the aim of excavating the foundations of various misreadings, as well as indicating those readings which anticipate my own.

All of this, I hope, will be a long way from claiming Nietzsche himself to be 'holy'. Indeed those most in danger of constructing a holy Nietzsche are not those who claim that Nietzsche remained indebted to Christianity despite his 'atheism' but rather those who have come to construct hagiographies around his anti-Christianity. It is ironic that though Nietzsche insisted that he did not want 'believers' or 'followers', every subsequent generation has thrown them up; from the development of the various Nietzsche cults at the turn of the twentieth century to his becoming a fetish of post-modern credibility, Nietzsche is always in danger from those who most admire him. 'May your name be holy to future generations' pronounced Nietzsche's friend Peter Gast at his funeral.[5] In challenging the ideological purity of Nietzsche's 'atheism' one is not making Nietzsche holy. One may indeed be saving him from an unwanted secular saintliness.

Early appropriations of Nietzschean 'religiosity'

Early attempts to make sense of Nietzsche's 'religiosity' often had 'a crackpot, fringe quality about them'.[6] Though the vast majority of Christians who read Nietzsche saw a Nietzscheanised Christianity or Christianised Nietzscheanism as an impossible and monstrous idea, there were some, mostly Protestants, who sought to appropriate something of the energy of Nietzsche's philosophy as a way of re-invigorating what they perceived as a religion in decline. Albert Kalthoff (1850–1906), a reasonably well-known and influential Protestant pastor in Bremen, gave a series of what he called 'Zarathustra Sermons' in which he contrasted a Nietzschean Christianity of vitalism and will with an analysis of the sterile and life-denying theology inherent in the Church. Kalthoff's vision was of a world 'in which everything unliving, unfree, dying, weakly and sick in man is eliminated'.[7] It cannot pass without comment that an understanding of faith that had incorporated such clearly eugenic language in the search for a Christian *völkisch* revival was systematically weakening the capacity of Christianity to resist the holocaust which was to come. Kalthoff's free-floating 'radicalism' sought to establish that

Christianity and Nietzscheanism originated in the same impulse: as Jesus was to the Pharisees, so Nietzsche is to the contemporary Church; Nietzsche has 'more morality, this antichrist, more Christianity than those who blaspheme him'.[8]

Though Nietzschean ideas were equally attractive to left wing and right wing groups (Kalthoff was himself a Marxist), it was those who sought to promote nationalist ideology who were most successful in harnessing the cultural authority of Nietzsche's image. For thinkers like Arthur Bonus writing just before the First World War, a cross-pollination of Christianity and Nietzsche was seen to produce a specifically German Christianity centred not upon guilt and weakness but on power and strength. Nietzsche's German 'religiosity' became a lens through which Christianity was refracted into nationalism. Redirecting the Christian tradition meant breaking the power of the established Church as mediator of the Gospel message and linking the emergent spirituality with the history of the Volk itself. The feasibility of this transformation was, however, only apparent to a few; more commonly, Nietzschean religiosity was understood in opposition to Christianity. According to the influential Horneffer brothers, editors at the Nietzsche Archive, Nietzschean spirituality was pagan in origin, it expressed and celebrated the explosive potential of Nordic energy and individual heroism. It believed not in God but above all in itself, and in particular (following Nietzsche's dictum 'remain true to the earth') in the blood and soil of the German people. This particular use of Nietzsche was to find its fullest expression in the infamous Deutsche Glaubensbewegung, the German Faith movement. Avowedly Nietzschean and anti-Christian, the German Faith movement saw itself as the spiritual wing of the Nazi revolution. It was, according to its founding figure Jakob Hauer, 'an eruption from the biological and spiritual depths of the nation'. Increasingly Nietzsche's language of health and weakness was used as the moral basis of a movement keen to contrast its own strength with the weakness and decadence of the Christian past. 'Can there be a higher value than the health of a Volk which unconditionally demands the extermination of bad instincts and criminal drives?' asks Hauer ominously.

Dietrich Bonhoeffer

But just as Nietzsche was claimed by those who sought to provide the spiritual justification of Nazism, so too was he to have a significant influence upon one of the most celebrated Christian opponents of the Nazi regime, Dietrich Bonhoeffer. 'Bonhoeffer', his biographer and friend Eberhard Bethge writes 'read all of Nietzsche very carefully' and was clearly indebted to his thought.[9] In particular Bonhoeffer saw in Nietzsche's phrase 'beyond good and evil' an approach to ethics that he believed to be at the very heart of Protestant theology and central to a proper understanding of the Gospel. Thus in his Barcelona lecture of 1929 Bonhoeffer claims:

The Christian gospel stands beyond good and evil. Nor could it be otherwise; for, were the grace of God to be subordinated to human criteria of good and evil, this would establish a human claim on God incompatible with the uniqueness of God's power and honour. There is a profound significance in the Biblical attribution of the fall to human-ity's eating from the tree of the knowledge of good and evil. The original – one might say childlike – community of humans stands beyond their knowing of good and evil; it rests on the knowledge of one thing alone, God's limitless love for humanity. Thus it was by no means Fr. Nietzsche who first penetrated 'beyond good and evil', even though it was on this basis that he denounced the 'moral poison' of Christianity. But, however much it may have come to be obscured, this insight belongs to the patrimony of the gospel itself.[10]

Nietzsche himself seems to interpret Jesus' attitude towards good and evil in these terms when he writes in *Beyond Good and Evil*: 'Jesus said to his Jews: "The law was made for servants – love God as I love him, as his son! What do we sons of God have to do with morality!"'[11]

This aphorism does seem to suggest that Nietzsche is claiming an affinity with Jesus' teaching (both denouncing 'morality') – an affinity which is the basis of Bonhoeffer's Nietzscheanism. For Bonhoeffer the freedom and free-spiritedness of the *Übermensch*, a freedom that is made possible by the capac-ity of the *Übermensch* to operate beyond the dictates of morality, is remarkably similar the freedom of the Christian, who is likewise able to operate beyond conventional morality because of his or her life in Christ.[12] In this Bonhoeffer is simply seeking to restate what he takes to be 'orthodox' Lutheran theology; namely, that freedom is the very essence of salvation, and salvation is only possible 'beyond good and evil', beyond, that is, the devious delusions of ethical self-righteousness. Like Nietzsche, Bonhoeffer believes all ethics, and so-called Christian ethics no less, to be dangerous corruptions. For Bonhoeffer the knowledge of good and evil takes humanity further away from our original unity with God: 'The knowledge of good and evil shows that he [humanity] is no longer one with his origin.'[13] In a telling passage in *The Anti-Christ* Nietzsche himself tells of a pre-lapsarian community 'at one' with its God and with itself.[14] The 'fall' from this idyllic community is for Nietzsche co-temporal with the introduction of morality, and it is not too much of an oversimplification of Nietzsche's complex genealogy of Christianity to suggest that, for him, the transformation of Yahweh into a 'moral God' is the source of all the trouble. To this extent both Nietzsche and Bonhoeffer conceive of 'salvation' as some sort of reversal of the original 'moral' fall: both envisage salvation as looking something like the sort of life led by Adam and Eve before the fall; that is, before the introduction of good and evil. We will explore this particular 'experiment in redemption' in more detail later on.

Bonhoeffer is perhaps best known for his attempts to articulate what he calls 'Religionless Christianity'. 'We are moving towards a completely religionless time; people as they are now simply cannot be religious any more.'[15] Bonhoeffer thinks it is both foolish and unnecessary to resist changing attitudes towards religiosity. Just as St. Paul attacks the idea of circumcision being a precondition of salvation, so likewise Bonhoeffer attacks the idea of 'religiosity' being a precondition of salvation. Thus the central theological task, the task of articulating 'who is Jesus Christ for us today?' involves asking:

> How do we speak of God without religion, i.e. without the temporally conditioned presuppositions of metaphysics, inwardness, and so on? How do we speak (or perhaps we cannot now even 'speak' as we used to) in a secular way about 'God'? In what way are we 'religionless secular' Christians, in what way are we εκ-κλησια, those who are called forth, not regarding ourselves from a religious point of view as specially favoured, but rather as belonging wholly to the world.[16]

Too often Bonhoeffer's talk of 'God without religion' is interpreted as something like God without Church, or God without all the ecclesiastical paraphernalia of priests and rituals and so forth. This, however, is emphatically not what Bonhoeffer is going on about here. 'What does it mean to "interpret in a religious sense"?' he writes to Bethge, attempting to clarify his theme: 'I think it means to speak on the one hand metaphysically and on the other individualistically.'[17] What I want to argue is that the denominator that is common to 'metaphysics', 'inwardness', 'individualism' etc. — by which Bonhoeffer groups such phenomena together pejoratively as 'religion' — is that they are all attempts to deny or betray 'belonging to the world'. Christianity must, in the proper sense of the word, be 'secular'; that is it must be 'of the world'.

Throughout Bonhoeffer's writings the theme of 'belonging wholly to the world' is one that constantly recurs.

> The profound old saga tells of the giant Antaeus, who was stronger than any man on earth; no one could overcome him until once in a fight someone lifted him from the ground; then the giant lost all his strength which had flowed into him through his contact with the earth. The man who would leave the earth, who would depart from the present distress, loses the power which still holds him by eternal, mysterious forces. The earth remains our mother, just as God remains our Father, and our mother will only lay in our Father's arms him who remains true to her. That is the Christian's song of earth and her distress.[18]

Of course, one could argue that passages such as these do not necessarily suggest the specific influence of Nietzsche's call to remain true to the earth but rather reflect, for instance, a passionate and lyrical commitment to incarnational theology. On one level this is indisputable. What Bonhoeffer learns specifically from Nietzsche, however, is an acute sensitivity to the various subtle guises which disloyalty to the earth can take. That is, he learns to be on the look out for *ressentiment.*

Nietzsche's work can be read as a sustained meditation on the various forms in which, through weakness and cowardice, human beings betray their humanity, betray their body, betray the earth, etc. in the search for supposedly consoling (though, in fact, profoundly damaging) fantasies. Metaphysics is, for both Nietzsche and Bonhoeffer, the name for a particular genre of betrayal; for in as much as metaphysics attempts to locate what gives human life its ultimate value in some realm beyond the earth, it degrades and disparages earth-bound fleshly human existence. Of course, Nietzsche would insist that Christianity (with all its emphasis on heaven and eternal life) *necessarily* involves this sort of betrayal. But Bonhoeffer would argue that Nietzsche has misunderstood Christianity, in particular that he has misunderstood the Biblical attestation of 'otherness'.

> It is not with the beyond that we are concerned, but with this world as created and preserved, subjected to laws, reconciled, and restored. What is above this world is, in the gospel, intended to exist *for* this world; I mean that, not in the anthropological sense of liberal, mystic pietistic, ethical theology, but in the biblical sense of the creation and of the incarnation, crucifixion, and resurrection of Jesus Christ.[19]

Another form of betrayal Bonhoeffer explores in letters from his prison cell in Tegel is the betrayal of 'inwardness'. Like the betrayal of 'metaphysics', the betrayal of 'inwardness' shifts the focus of the Christian life out of the world, out of the public and everyday sphere of human life, but instead of shifting it, so to speak, upwards (metaphysics) it shifts it 'inside' or 'within'. The displacement of God from the world, and from the public part of human life, led to the attempt to keep his place secure in the sphere of the 'personal', the 'inner' and the 'private'. That is, the emphasis on one's inner life, an emphasis encouraged by 'existentialist philosophy and psychology', represents a retreat from 'belonging wholly to the world'. And Christian thinkers, in privileging the inner in this way, have become the spiritual equivalent of the gutter press, assuming that the truth is (a) always hidden and thus needs to be dug out and (b) always something shoddy and shameful – 'as if you couldn't adequately appreciate a good play till you had seen how the actors behave off-stage' as Bonhoeffer memorably puts it.[20]

What is distinctively Nietzschean here is the way in which Bonhoeffer understands the motivation behind this retreat into interiority as issuing from *ressentiment.*

> From the sociological point of view this is a revolution from below, a revolt of inferiority. Just as the vulgar mind is not satisfied till it has seen some highly placed personage 'in his bath', or in other embarrassing

situations, so it is here. There is a kind of evil satisfaction in knowing that everyone has his failings and weak spots. In my contacts with the 'outcasts' of society, its 'pariahs', I've noticed repeatedly that mistrust is the dominant motive in their judgement of other people . . . Anything clothed, veiled, pure, and chaste is presumed to be deceitful, disguised, and impure; people here simply show their own impurity. A basic anti-social attitude of mistrust and suspicion is the revolt of inferiority.[21]

The 'revolt of inferiority' is, for Nietzsche and Bonhoeffer, precisely what gives rise to slave-morality – the attempt to redefine what is of value from the perspective of those who cannot cope with the reality of 'belonging wholly to the world'. Bonhoeffer learns from Nietzsche that the Church is particularly prone to *ressentiment* and, through his theology, seeks to provide a basis upon which Christianity can affirm and celebrate a faith which does not originate in failure – the failure to affirm the human-ness of human life. The sort of faith Bonhoeffer seeks to portray is one that issues from 'strength' (the necessary strength to resist the Nazis effectively). And like Nietzsche, Bonhoeffer sees a magnificent example of this spiritual strength exhibited in the religion of the ancient Greeks:

I am at present reading the quite outstanding book by W.F. Otto, the classics man at Königsberg, *The Gods of Greece*. To quote from his clos-ing, it's about 'this world of faith, which sprang from the wealth and depth of human existence, not from its cares and longings'. Can you understand my finding something very attractive in this theme and its treatment, and also – *horribile dictu* – my finding these gods, when they are so treated, less offensive than certain brands of Christianity? In fact, that I almost think I could claim these gods for Christ.[22]

Karl Barth

The preoccupation of early twentieth-century German theologians with the idea of rejecting 'religion' is more commonly seen as a theological response to the crisis of faith articulated by Nietzsche as the death of God. Though clearly not prepared to admit that God is actually *dead*, many acknowledged that 'the death of God' did name a certain sort of death, the death of a certain way of doing theology, the death of a certain conception of the theological project. Perhaps the foremost representative of this approach was Karl Barth. Bonhoeffer acknowledges that 'Barth was the first theologian to begin the criticism of religion'[23] and he has surely been among the most influential. Indeed the impact of Barth's theological revolution could be said to have determined much of the agenda of subsequent theology in the century. Barth's revolution, articulated in the second edition of his *Roemerbrief* (1921), was founded upon a wholesale rejection of the possibility of human knowledge of God. It is this possibility which is the very foundation of 'religion'. According to Barth, God is so wholly other, our relatedness so emphatically disjunctive, that we can know nothing whatsoever about God – nothing, that is, unless that 'knowledge' originates in God and impacts on us as grace. Knowledge of God is, in a sense, impossible. It is made possible only by a miracle; only, that is, by and through the workings of God; hence what Barth calls the 'impossible possibility of faith'. And, strange to say, it is a precondition of this faith that we acknowledge first our God-forsakenness.

The proximity of 'God is dead' to Barth's dialectical theology is, for some theologians, quite unmistakable. Von Balthasar, for instance, puts it thus:

> In the fire of Overbeck, Nietzsche, Dostoyevsky and Kierkegaard (and the Reformers, who by now in this light look a bit strange), the gun-powder has been ignited . . . The second edition is like 'dynamite', com-ing dangerously close to Nietzsche; it 'revolutionises religion', it is the 'cry and the silence'. We have now truly fallen into the 'hell' of religion. We must smell 'the stench of death to the point of death that is wafted from the summits of religion'.[24]

Such is the extent of Barth's re-think of theological presuppositions that he is prepared to recognise and affirm a number of the instincts that make up unbelief: 'Indeed, a certain perception is betrayed when we begin to reject the non-God of unbelief.'[25] Genuine faith, therefore, must face the evaporation of meaning that Nietzsche called nihilism. It must renounce the comfort of human constructions and give up any residual assurance inherent within faith. Neither must it – nor indeed can it – seek out any other supposedly sound theological platform on which to ground itself.

> Just as surely as the recognition of the sovereignty of God overthrows all confidence in human righteousness, it sets erect no other ground of confidence. Men are not deprived of one security, in order that they may immediately discover for themselves another. No man can shelter him-self behind the triumphant will of God; rather, when it is once per-ceived, he comes under judgement and enters a situation of shattering confusion – from which he can never escape.[26]

In seeking to draw out continuities between Nietzsche and Barth, Karen Carr has argued that through Barth 'Nihilism was made holy as a part of the gracious act of God. Thus Nietzsche's uncanniest of guests became, for a brief period of time, a divinely bestowed gift.'[27] However fair this may be as an analysis of Barth's theology itself, it is clear that thinkers such as Barth and Bonhoeffer introduced into the theological imagination a sense that Nietzsche was not a theological road-block but, when properly understood, could be used as an aid in the search for an authentic voice in which to speak the Christian Gospel. Later on I will look specifically at Barth's criticisms of Nietzsche and will suggest that he correctly identifies the fundamental weakness of Nietzsche's position. Indeed Barth is, I think, one of the very few thinkers who seems to understand the nature of Nietzsche's attack upon Christianity. It is, I think, no coincidence that Barth, like Nietzsche, rejects what one might call the 'philosophical' approach to the question of God.

Death of God theology

Perhaps the most enthusiastic reception Nietzsche has received in theological circles is that from the so-called 'death of God' theologians, the most widely read of whom is probably Thomas Altizer. Altizer's theology is built upon the work of three great nineteenth-century religious radicals: Hegel, Nietzsche and Blake. Altizer's work seeks to re-interpret the 'death of God' as a fundamentally Christian event and argues that the proclamation of God's death is the authentic voice of radical Christianity.

> Once we recognize that radical Christianity is inseparable from an attack upon God, then we should be prepared to face the possibility that even Nietzsche was a radical Christian.[28]

Central to Altizer's theology is the idea of the kenotic, self-emptying God; a God who transcends His transcendence by becoming wholly immanent in the person of Jesus. Altizer understands the incarnation of God in Christ as a non-reversible kenotic self-emptying; a process whereby God 'negates himself in his own revelatory and redemptive acts'.[29] Through Jesus the sacred dissolves itself (without remainder) into the profane, thus redefining both, and thereby overcoming the distance between God and humanity.

For Altizer this process has to be understood as, in itself, a victory over 'Satan'. Like Blake, Altizer takes the sovereign creator-God, the God who reveals Himself to Job as the wholly other, to be none other than Satan himself. This is the God who represents 'the oppressive power of every alien reality standing over against and beyond humanity'.[30] This is the God who denies human flourishing. In this analysis Altizer sides with Nietzsche in a condemnation of 'traditional' Christianity.

> When Nietzsche understood the Christian God as the deepest embodiment of man's self-hatred and resentment, he unveiled the solitary and transcendent God of Christianity as the absolute antithesis of a total existence in history or what the new Zarathustra calls the 'body'. It is precisely because a primordial and religious deity is the antithesis of life and history that its sacred name can so naturally and spontaneously be evoked to sanction evil and injustice (e.g., The Book of Job).[31]

The 'death of God', however, represents the (self-)annihilation of this oppressive transcendent God and the birth of a reconstructed sense of God united with human beings in the person of Jesus. Altizer thinks that this 'death' should not surprise Christians, for after all the whole logic of the Christian proclamation is built around a pattern of death and resurrection.

> Christianity has always celebrated death as the way to redemption, proclaiming that Christ's death inaugurated a new reality of joy and forgiveness, and calling all men to a participation in his death as the way of salvation.[32]

So, likewise the 'death of God'. But how much is all of this really influenced specifically by Nietzsche? What would his theology miss if the Nietzschean element was subtracted? For surely Altizer's salvation schema, as I have described it, is explicable with reference to Blake and Hegel on their own. Simply put: from Blake Altizer derives the idea that a certain manifestation of God is evil, and from Hegel he borrows the logical machinery to reconstruct the Divine and a justification that this reconstruction is itself the defining feature of *Heilsgeschichte*. To put it another way: from both Blake and Hegel he derives his radical opposition of the true God of the gospel to the false God of the authoritarian 'unhappy consciousness'; from Blake specifically, a certain commitment to the truth-potential intrinsic to unfettered poetic creativity; from Hegel specifically, a sense of divine revelation pervading the whole of world history and climaxing in the present. What does Nietzsche add? Very little, I suggest. Indeed even the way Altizer uses the 'death of God' motif reveals that he is using it in a Hegelian rather than a Nietzschean way. For Nietzsche the 'death of God' is not a move within an overall negative theology, nor is it a part of some opposition waiting to be superseded. It may be that Gilles Deleuze overstates the difference between Nietzsche and Hegel – 'the dialectic is the natural ideology of *ressentiment* and bad conscience' (the thesis of his influential *Nietzsche and Philosophy*)[33] – nonetheless running together Nietzsche and Hegel, as Altizer is wont to do, is an unacceptable obfuscation.

Eberhard Jüngel

The influence of Nietzsche upon twentieth-century theology is not confined to radical voices that seek to instigate an intellectual revolution, a theological revaluation of all values, so to speak. Indeed it is arguable that Nietzsche's work has been just as significant, if not more so, for a whole range of much more conservative thinkers who have perceived in Nietzsche an unlikely ally in the attempt to overcome certain strains of theological thought that have their source in the Enlightenment.

Eberhard Jüngel in his *God as the Mystery of the World* seeks clearly to distance his use of Nietzsche from that of people such as Altizer.

The return to talk about the death of God to theology, which is going on currently, was prepared if not initiated in the remarks Dietrich Bonhoeffer wrote down in prison. It is no accident that the proponents of God-is-dead theology in all the world appeal to him. However, a clear distinction must be made between the special intellectual achievement of Bonhoeffer and the thoughts of those who appeal to him. The chief element of this distinction is that Bonhoeffer did not take modern atheism to be a reason to remove God from contemporary thought, but rather conversely took modern atheism as an opportunity to investigate anew a Christian concept of God in critical interaction with the theological tradition.[34]

Jüngel believes that in articulating 'the death of God' and in bringing to a head the subsequent theological crisis, Nietzsche has done Christian theology a great service, for, Jüngel insists, the God Nietzsche finds dead is a distinctly sub-Christian perversion of the genuine Christian God. Through Nietzsche the metaphysical/theistic concept of God is revealed as morally and intellectually bankrupt – and thus Nietzsche generates the conceptual space in which theology can ground itself solely upon the manifestation of God in the person of Jesus Christ. By appropriating Nietzsche's critique of 'God', Christianity can become more authentically itself. Jüngel is not alone in seeing things this way. For instance, Helmut Thielicke in *The Evangelical Faith* remarks:

> Thus Nietzsche is not just fighting decadence, he is also fighting a degenerate view of God. His arrogance in opposing God and proclaiming his death is not, to the best of our human judgment, guilty hubris but a prejudice induced by the empirical phenomena of Christianity, its institutions, its theology and its behaviour.[35]

Theism is a degenerate theology because it posits a notion of God which is self-sufficient, theoretically separable from the other persons of the Trinity. For Jüngel the identity of the Christian God is to be understood only in and through a proper appreciation of the subsistence of Father, Son and Holy Spirit in each other. There is no principal *causa sui* from which the Son and the Spirit are secondary derivations. Thus a-theism, in rejecting the idea of a God who is over and above human beings and who does not intersect with humanity at any point, is to be cautiously applauded. On Jüngel's account Nietzsche's atheism amounts to a rejection of the God of the metaphysicians, the God of Descartes especially, and as such is to be commended.

It is worth pointing out that Jüngel's account of Nietzsche's rejection of God is almost the complete opposite of Barth's. Whereas for Jüngel Nietzsche rejects a false God, for Barth, Nietzsche rejects the real thing. Thus, for instance, Barth opines that Nietzsche 'resolutely and passionately and necessarily rejected not a caricature of the Christian conception of humanity, but in the form of a caricature the conception itself'.[36] Nietzsche is foremost among the opponents of the Christian faith because he is an atheist who understands the logic (one might say, the 'depth grammar') of the Christian faith. My sympathies are with Barth on this. In the next chapter I will argue that Nietzsche's opposition to Christianity is not founded, as is too often presumed, upon a rejection of Christian theism. I will suggest that there is a disposition within a certain sort of typically analytic philosophy which misunderstands the nature of Nietzsche's opposition to Christianity because it fails to appreciate that one can reject Christianity without being all that interested in the philosophical question of God's existence. For just as it is very unusual indeed for people to become Christians because they have had the truth-claims of the Christian faith rationally demonstrated to them, so too it is unusual for people to lose their faith on the basis of any discovered argument. Generally speaking people do not commit themselves one way or the other on the basis of philosophical proof. Also, to invoke Wittgenstein's notion of depth grammar once again, one ought to notice that the language employed to describe the coming-to-be of faith is wholly different from that appropriate to proofs or rational demonstrations. Nietzsche is among the few atheists who genuinely understands that to attack Christianity, or, to be more specific, to attack the Christian faith, one operates on an entirely different level from that of rational/philosophical demonstration. Nietzsche knows that to be an effective (evangelising) atheist one does not need to bother much with being an a-theist. That is, atheism is a variegated phenomenon and not reducible to a hostility to 'theism'. Nietzsche, as Barth rightly notes, is not against theism, he is against God.

Jüngel, however, wants to use Nietzsche to have a go at theism, thus to generate space for God. Jüngel's failure is a failure to appreciate the diversity of atheisms, so struck is he with the idea that atheism = a-theism. Jüngel's basic strategy in *God as the Mystery of the World* (and note the subtitle: *On the Foundation of the Theology of the Crucified One in the Dispute between Theism and Atheism*) is to collapse all forms of atheism into a-theism or anti-theism, and then to condemn such approaches as failing to appreciate the properly Christocentric basis of the Christian faith. This move fails to account for, indeed it even fails to acknowledge, species of atheism which are indifferent to questions of metaphysics or philosophy (what, for instance, of Alasdair MacIntyre's comment that, following the process of European secularisation in the late nineteenth and early twentieth centuries indifference is the most common form of atheism?)[37] Such an acknowledgement would spoil Jüngel's attempt to by-pass the atheist and the theist at the same time. Because of this Jüngel has to be very careful how he characterises the 'death of God', for if Jüngel is to use Nietzsche in the way he wants he must create a strong association between 'God is dead' and a-theism. Jüngel is therefore keen to persuade us to fit the 'death of God' into an intellectual history which begins with the Enlightenment and which marks the end point of a process of metaphysical demystification. Thus for Jüngel the important question

Nietzsche asks is whether God is conceivable, and in answering 'no' Nietzsche thereby articulates the 'death of God'.

It is important to note how theologically influential this (mis)reading of Nietzsche has become. The source of the misreading is the allocation to Nietzsche of a part in the story of intellectual history in which he is understood as blowing the whistle on a conception of God generated by the Enlightenment. Consider the story as told by Michael Buckley.

Michael Buckley in his *At the Origins of Modern Atheism* has sought to demonstrate that in deferring responsibility to the philosophers, theologians set themselves up as hostages to a philosophical debate over which, increasingly, they had little control. Buckley's focus is on the sixteenth and seventeenth centuries, though he believes the same patterns are discernible throughout Christian history. He argues that, responding to the challenge posed by the Enlightenment, the Church tasked philosophers with the refutation of scepticism and the defence of God. Those philosophers who took up this challenge, most notably Descartes and Newton, did so within the same frame of reference of the scepticism they sought to refute. As a debate it was to be conducted wholly within the domain of natural reason. The Cartesian method in particular exemplifies the degree to which the defence of God was mounted upon the seemingly neutral ground of Enlightenment rationality. To begin from a *tabula rasa*, thence, from indubitable first principles, to proving God's existence was, it was assumed, the very ultimate in Christian apologetics. The Church, Buckley argues, made an enormous investment in the success of this whole enterprise, but in doing so conceded to a way of envisioning God which cut God off from those resources, Christological and Pneumatological, through which alone God is properly disclosed. Buckley's conclusion is a radical one: that theism, in seeking to generate a sense of God without recourse to Christian foundations, internally generated the atheism it set out to refute. That is to say, the origins of modern atheism, at least intellectually, are to be found in the abandonment by Christian thinkers of a God disclosed in and through Jesus Christ. In seeking to construct a notion of God from rational first principles alone, in separating God from his revelation through Christ or from religious experience, the question of God was posed in such a way that no answer could possibly support a properly Christian sense of God. Hence Buckley's understanding of the provenance of contemporary atheism:

> Religion abandoned the justification intrinsic to its own nature and experience, and insisted that its vindication would be found in philosophy . . . Atheism is not the secret of religion, as Feuerbach would have it, but it is the secret contradiction within a religion that denies its own abilities to deal cognitively with what is central to its nature. Atheism is the secret of that religious reflection which justifies the sacred and its access to the sacred primarily through its own transmogrification into another form of human knowledge or practice.[38]

A number of influential theologians adopt a similar position with respect to the Enlightenment and its influence; Colin Gunton, Lesslie Newbigin, as well as Jüngel, even (a very different thinker) Andrew Louth, all subscribe to this general view. I do not want to dispute the particular story told by Buckley and others (indeed I am personally quite sympathetic to its overall purpose); what I object to is placing Nietzsche and the 'death of God' at the end of this story as its conclusion, or rather, as its *reductio ad absurdum*. As Stephen Williams argues in his important book *Revelation and Reconciliation* Nietzsche's thought 'is ostensibly rooted in other, historically deeper and psychologically more fundamental strains of resistance to the Christian tradition'.[39] Indeed Nietzsche would surely regard himself far more as a child of the Renaissance than of the Enlightenment, far more an inheritor of the scepticism of the ancients than a spokesman for a society which finds the idea of God 'no longer conceivable'. Nietzsche claims, for instance, that 'The Italian Renaissance contained within it all the positive forces to which we owe modern culture . . . it was the golden age of the millennium.'[40] And 'there has been no more decisive interrogation than that conducted by the Renaissance – the question it asks is the question *I* ask – : neither has there been a form of attack *more* fundamental, more direct, and more strenuously delivered on the entire front of the enemy's centre!'[41]

Why then have so many Christian thinkers been persuaded to accept Nietzschean philosophy as the culmination of a specifically *Enlightenment* thought-experiment which reduced God to a certain sort of metaphysics (a tradition which then went on to dispose of metaphysics, thus finishing off God in the process)? Part of the reason Nietzsche has been so located is that many of the most influential theologians, including Jüngel himself, read their Nietzsche through Heidegger. Jüngel has spoken of meeting Heidegger when he (Jüngel) was still a young academic, and the decisive impression this meeting had upon him.[42] G.O. Mazur, in an article examining Nietzsche's influence upon Jüngel entitled 'On Jüngel's four-fold appropriation of Friedrich Nietzsche', makes precisely this link by situating Jüngel's appropriation of Nietzsche squarely within the context of Jüngel's own appropriation of Heidegger.[43] Perhaps other thinkers were not so directly influenced by actually reading Heidegger's writings on Nietzsche, but such was the theological popularity of Heidegger in the mid part of the twentieth century that he came to mediate Nietzsche's philosophy for a number of generations of influential theologians. Consequently the 'theological' Nietzsche is very often the Heideggerian Nietzsche: the problem being that it is now generally accepted that Heidegger's Nietzsche, specifically the lecture series Heidegger gave in the late 1930s and the consequent four-volume work on Nietzsche, is a great deal more about Heidegger than it is about Nietzsche.

Nietzsche, according to Heidegger, was 'the last thinker of metaphysics'; that is, though he emphatically attacks metaphysics, he was nonetheless wholly embroiled within its remit. Nietzsche reveals his metaphysical base precisely in and through the very act of criticising metaphysics. Nietzsche is upside-down Plato: if Plato is the great founding father of metaphysics, Nietzsche's work represents an inversion of that founding logic which, precisely because it is an inversion, is still governed by the original dimensions of the onto-theological tradition.

> The pronouncement 'God is dead' means: The supersensory world is without effective power. It bestows no life. Metaphysics i.e. for Nietzsche, Western philosophy understood as Platonism, is at an end. Nietzsche understands his own philosophy as the countermovement to metaphysics, and that means for him a movement in opposition to Platonism. Nevertheless, as a mere countermovement it necessarily remains, as does everything 'anti', held fast in the essence of that over against which it moves.[44]

For the purposes of my argument it is of little consequence that Heidegger's actual view of Nietzsche, or indeed of metaphysics, was much more sophisticated than this short quotation suggests. For, generally speaking, it was this *reading* of Heidegger's Nietzsche that gained popularity and came to exert so much influence over twentieth-century theologians.

What differentiates Heidegger's story from that of Buckley is that for Heidegger Nietzsche is seen as the ultimate consequence and nemesis of Platonism, for Buckley, Nietzsche's thought is a *reductio* of Cartesianism. Nonetheless, as we have already seen in Buckley's narrative – and it is a narrative shared by many – it is Descartes who is taken to be at the root of the trouble dubbed as 'metaphysical'. The following passage, for instance, would not be out of place (style aside) in Buckley's *At the Origins of Modern Atheism*, though in fact, it comes from Heidegger's *Nietzsche*:

> Descartes' principle that man's claim to a ground of truth found and secured by man himself arises from that 'liberation' in which he disengages himself from the constraints of biblical Christian revealed truth and church doctrine. Every authentic liberation, however, is not only a breaking of chains and a casting off of bonds, it is also a new determination of the essence of freedom. To be free now means that, in place of the certitude of salvation, which was the standard for all truth, man posits the kind of certitude by virtue of which and in which he becomes certain of himself as the being which founds itself on itself.[45]

This is precisely why, for many Evangelical theologians, Descartes is the enemy *par excellence*. On this account Nietzsche attacks the Cartesian self, only to reduplicate the same logic of self-founding, except not, as with Descartes, on the basis of some disengaged ego, but on the basis of a more holistic sense of the body and its conflicting drives. Nietzsche's anthropology remains an attempt to 'found itself on itself' nonetheless.

With this all the pieces are now in place for the 'contemporary Protestant theologian' to render Nietzsche's thought theologically innocuous. The great thing about Heidegger's Nietzsche, as far as the Christian theologian is concerned, is that he is like a dangerous agent employed to assassinate some foe and who, instead of staying around afterwards to cause trouble, is himself killed in the very process of finishing off his opponent. How very neat and tidy. The problem with hiring Nietzsche to assassinate the Cartesian God is that, if Heidegger's account of how the story ends turns out to be mistaken, then one is left to reckon with Nietzsche. And there can be little doubt that, released from the bonds of Heidegger's 'last metaphysician' narrative, Nietzsche will prove an embarrassment, indeed a fundamental danger, to his former employers.

The post-modern Nietzsche

Towards the latter part of the twentieth century the loose (European) consensus formed in theological circles around Heidegger's interpretation of Nietzsche began to break up under pressure from those who would read him as a forerunner to deconstruction. Derrida, for instance, has sought to demonstrate that Nietzsche's thought exceeds Heidegger's interpretation of it and that Nietzsche's attempt to wrestle with/against 'metaphysics' ought not to be bound to the restrictive logic of Heidegger's thesis.

> It is important in this context to take Heidegger's Nietzsche and show that there are other possibilities in Nietzsche which are not programmed by a history of metaphysics, that there are moves which are stronger, which go further than what Heidegger calls the history of the completion of metaphysics; moves which actually put in question Heidegger himself: his reading of Nietzsche in particular and his philosophical orientation in general.[46]

The practitioners of deconstruction tend to feel a strong affinity with Nietzsche; in particular with the strategies he adopts in seeking to combat traditions of thought within which he nonetheless recognises himself to be embroiled. Nietzsche is seen not to be attempting to reverse 'metaphysics' but to subvert it. He is a philosophical fifth columnist. As one commentator puts it:

> Criticism as reversal is rejected as inadequate, since it remains within the terms of an opposition set up by metaphysics, and criticism as displacement suggested in its stead. Criticism as displacement effectively recognizes that definitive escape from metaphysics is, in fact, impossible, and attempts to frustrate the recuperative logic of opposition-reversal by locally disrupting the identity of metaphysical concepts through the disclosure of their dependence on the differences which they suppress.[47]

Whereas for Heidegger, so it is argued, the internal contradictions between Nietzsche's desire to 'overcome metaphysics' and his complicity within it render Nietzsche's project ultimately unsuccessful (a failure Heidegger believes his own work manages to overcome), for Derrida these internal contradictions become the very engine of critical discourse.

This makes Derrida's methodology sound a bit too much like Hegelian dialectic: a process driven by the constant encounter and overcoming of oppositions. In fact, for both Nietzsche and Derrida, belief in binary oppositions is precisely what constitutes metaphysical thought. Thus Nietzsche claims 'The fundamental faith of the metaphysicians is the faith in antithetical values.'[48] Both Nietzsche and Derrida want to expose the belief in binary logic as responsible for shaping our fundamental attitudes, and seek to go 'beyond metaphysics' by dismantling a whole succession of foundational oppositions – truth/error, good/evil, being/becoming, speech/writing, etc. – upon which the metaphysical project is founded. It is not that Nietzsche and Derrida want simply to reverse the traditional valuations attached to either side of these polarities. It is not that they want to upturn the priority attached to truth or goodness, for instance, and instead found a discourse upon the prioritisation of error and evil, though this may constitute the first phase of any particular deconstruction. Such a move, of course, would be to leave untouched the faith in antithetical values. Rather the process of dismantling is more subtle and complex; it involves, for instance, the attempt to demonstrate that supposedly fixed opposites are, in fact, asymmetrical and blurred, neither fixed nor simple opposites. This, then, is the world made soft: concepts are not locked into a matrix of oppositions which themselves build up and reinforce each other in a whole architecture of thought. Deconstruction seeks out dimensions of meaning that exceed the matrix imposed upon them; it points us to the genealogy of concepts, the context within which concepts are employed, thus disrupting the clean logic of conceptual opposition. Deconstruction is to this 'architecture' what God was to those who sought to build the tower of Babel: it disrupts in order to liberate.

One of the most sustained attempts to demonstrate the theological usefulness of this sort of thinking has been undertaken by Mark C. Taylor. Taylor describes his own work as a/theology, the '/' being a 'permeable membrane [which] forms a border where fixed boundaries disintegrate. Along this boundary the traditional polarities between which Western theology has been suspended are inverted and subverted.'[49] A/theology thus suggests the collapse of a whole cluster of (supposedly fundamental) theological oppositions: belief/unbelief, theist/atheist, sacred/secular, etc. For Taylor this style of thinking is addressed to those who are '[s]uspended between the loss of old certainties and the discovery of new beliefs, these marginal people constantly live on the border that joins and separates belief and unbelief.'[50] It could also be said to be the logic of those who pray 'Lord I believe, help thou my unbelief.' Philippa Berry, introducing a collection of essays on *Postmodernism and Religion*, comments:

It now seems plausible that the deconstructive style of thinking which was initiated a century ago, in Nietzsche's twilight, has subtly and unobtrusively dissolved the clear-cut distinction between secular and religious thinking which Kant and the Kantian tradition had carefully secured. Hence the question which was implicitly asked by the conference where most of these papers were first presented: could an apparently nihilistic tradition of thought – a thought ostensibly shaped by that darkness of angst, of meaninglessness and abjection, which shrouds the 'end' of the modern era – paradoxically have acquired a new religious or spiritual dimension?[51]

More cautious Christian thinkers remain suspicious of deconstruction, suspicious that it carries with it a built-in hostility to the Christian faith. And Taylor's description of deconstruction as 'the "hermeneutic" of the death of God' might serve only to deepen such fears. For some the fashionable interest in deconstruction is the academic community playing chicken with nihilism. Carl Raschke is foremost among those who would blow the whistle on the theologian's attempt to romance the 'death of God': 'Theologians who might appropriate Nietzsche's great "myth" . . . are like children who have discovered some black and treacherous abracadabra. The madman is our reminder of the "price" of deconstruction.'[52]

A number of Christian thinkers, however, in seeking to claim that deconstruction is not a threat to Christianity (and may indeed prove some sort of unlikely friend), have wanted to claim that Nietzsche's slogan 'God is dead' has, in fact, nothing directly to do with theology or with an attack upon God. Rather the 'death of God' is Nietzsche's way of speaking of the absence of transcendental signification. Consider this passage by Graham Ward written in the introduction to his reader *The Postmodern God*:

> It is not a theological claim, as it is in Hegel where the death of God is the death of Jesus Christ, the Son of God and the second person of the Trinity. For Hegel, Christ's death is God's absolute deliverance of His transcendent being to the immanent movement of history and community. This is not Nietzsche's claim. Neither is Nietzsche making the claim that 'God does not exist' – an onto-theological claim made by an atheist. 'God' in Nietzsche's assertion is used metonymically. That is, it is a name which substitutes for and sums up a way of doing philosophy in which the highest principle is sought that grounds the possibility of all things. As 'the White House' is a name substituting for and summing up the American government under its presidential head of state, so 'God' is a metonymy for 'absolute truth', 'absolute Goodness', 'absolute reality', 'absolute reason', the origin and measure of all things (Being in modernity's understanding of metaphysics).[53]

I think this is quite wrong. It is surely clear that the phrase 'the death of God' has multiple resonances; Nietzsche speaks of many different deaths (murder, sacrifice, suicide, neglect, etc.) and indicates that there are many different candidates that can be cast as 'God'. Part of the problem with the phrase 'the death of God' is that it is hopelessly overloaded with meaning – it has been used (by Nietzsche as well as by subsequent thinkers) to describe too many different things and with every new interpreter a new level of meaning is laid down upon the old. It is of course such a wonderfully arresting *bon mot* and therefore thinkers can't leave it alone. Ward can, if he likes, set a meaning for it (there is no Nietzschean copyright on the phrase). He can let 'the death of God' stand for a carefully circumscribed denial of metaphysics. But this is not how it is with Nietzsche. Nietzsche is much more aware of the inter-relatedness of his multiple meanings, he is promiscuous and playful in generating new perspectives by the bringing together of differing ideas. Indeed it is because of this that Nietzsche is celebrated as a precursor to deconstruction. From this perspective Ward's attempt to fence off a 'metaphysical' reading is unconvincing. Nietzsche was obsessed with Christianity and certainly intended 'God', in 'the death of God' to be thought of, on one level at least, as the God of Abraham, Isaac and Jacob. How, for instance, can one substitute 'absolute reason' or 'absolute reality' for 'God' in a phrase such as: 'God died of his pity for man'?[54] In *Thus Spoke Zarathustra* God is said to have been murdered by the ugliest man because the ugliest man could not bear God looking at his ugliness. In explaining himself and his action the ugliest man speaks clearly of a 'personal' God and not of a category summing up a particular strain of metaphysics:

> But he, he had to die: he looked with eyes that saw everything, he saw the depths and abysses of man, all man's hidden disgrace and ugliness. His pity knew no shame, he crawled into my dirtiest corners. This most curious, over-importunate, over-compassionate god had to die.[55]

The God whose murder is being described here is not the G/god of 'absolute goodness' or 'absolute reason', but the God prayed to by Christians in Church; it is the same God described in the Collect for Purity of *The Book of Common Prayer* 'unto whom all hearts be open, all desires known and from whom no secrets are hid'. Or – the same God described in Psalm 139 from whose penetrating gaze the Psalmist seeks to hide (as Paul Tillich notes in his essay 'The Escape from God'.)[56] This God is not the God of metaphysics but something much more recognisably Biblical.

Ward is not alone in seeking to recommend Nietzsche as an aid to theological endeavour by suppressing his vociferous anti-Christianity, subtly disguising it as anti-onto-theology. Consider the way in which the opening of this essay by Merold Westphal locates (and implicitly commends) Nietzsche's critique of Christianity to a (presumably largely) Christian audience:

> Not every construal of the theological enterprise will be able to entertain the possibility of Nietzsche as a recourse, if not exactly an ally. For

example, if theology interprets itself onto-theo-logically, it will be unable to see any ambiguity or irony in his self-designations as immoralist and anti-Christ. They will simply be the literal confessions of a loathed enemy. The possibility of Nietzsche as *ancilla theologiae* presupposes at least an interruption of the interpretation of theology in onto-theological terms.[57]

Nietzsche's attack upon Christianity is completely underestimated by Westphal. Indeed Nietzsche's resistance to Christianity has a lot less to do with his attitude towards metaphysics than Westphal presumes. What Nietzsche hates, above all, is the cross and the Christian story of redemption. And what is particularly galling to Nietzsche about 'metaphysics' is the way Christian theologians have managed to score the shape of the cross into the basis of the European imagination – that is, he hates the way in which corrupt Christian values have become inscribed into the fabric of our world view, indeed into our very grammar. Nietzsche does not object to metaphysics 'as a philosopher', what he objects to fundamentally is the way in which a certain picture of how the world works has been used to *evangelise* a set of corrupt and corrupting values. Christianity is, for Nietzsche, some sort of plague. The source of the disease is the cross and the carrier of the disease, or at least, one of the carriers, is called 'metaphysics'.[58] Nietzsche berates his contemporaries for thinking that the disease has been eliminated through secularisation. He recognises that through metaphysics this disease re-emerges within our cognitive and linguistic 'genes'.

Thus I want to reply to Westphal: where is the 'ambiguity' or 'irony' of which he speaks in the following?

> Christianity has as its basis the rancune of the sick, the instinct directed against the healthy, against health. Everything well-constituted, proud, high-spirited, beauty above all, is hurtful to its ears and eyes. I recall again the invaluable saying of Paul: 'God has chosen the weak things of the world, the foolish things of the world, base things of the world and things which are despised': that was the formula, in hoc signo *décadence* conquered. – God on the Cross – is the fearful hidden meaning behind this meaning still understood? – Everything that suffers, everything that hangs on the cross is divine . . . We all hang on the cross, consequently we are all divine . . . We alone are divine . . . Christianity was a victory, a nobler disposition perished by it – Christianity has been up till now mankind's greatest misfortune?[59]

It would thus be wholly inappropriate to invoke *Nietzsche's* use of the death of God to provide support for the idea that one can head off the protest atheist by insisting that God takes suffering and death into himself upon the cross.[60] Nietzsche does indeed think that the Christian God is the crucified God, though he does not think that this makes the Christian God any more acceptable. On the contrary, it is precisely the crucified God that is the source of all the trouble. The popular idea that a God who suffers with and alongside humanity provides the best chance for theodicy – and one thinks here particularly of the use made by Christians of Eli Wiesel's story of the execution of the child caught stealing bread in *Night* – cannot be employed to circumvent Nietzsche's protest atheism. For it is exactly this sort of thinking that Nietzsche believes to be sick and sickening. Here then we see something of the significance of emphasising the important difference between an attack upon the metaphysical God and an attack upon the crucified God. For the instinct that operates in the above theodicy is that the metaphysical God is a source of genuine grievance with respect to its incapacity to engage with human suffering and that the crucified God, by taking upon itself the suffering and pain of humanity, demonstrates genuine compassion and not 'metaphysical' indifference. But it is the God of compassion Nietzsche is out to destroy. To use Nietzsche to undermine the 'metaphysical' God thus to make space for the crucified God is totally wrong-headed and promotes a wholly distorted impression of Nietzsche's priorities.

Now we can see more clearly how absurd it is for a conservative Protestant scholar such as Thielicke to claim that Nietzsche attacks a degenerate view of God. In *The Anti-Christ* Nietzsche makes it clear that he believes the principal agent of theological corruption was not Plato, or Aristotle, or St. Thomas, but St. Paul: 'On the heels of the "glad tidings" came the *worst of all*: those of Paul. In Paul was embodied the antithetical type to the "bringer of glad tidings", the genius of hatred, of the vision of hatred, of the inexorable logic of hatred.'[61] 'What he [Paul] divined was that with the aid of a little sectarian movement on the edge of Judaism one could ignite a world conflagration; that with the symbol "God on the Cross" one could sum up everything down-trodden, everything in secret revolt, the entire heritage of anarchist agitation in the Empire into a tremendous power.'[62]

One of the most extraordinary things about Nietzsche's reception by theologians in the twentieth century is how so few of them have a bad word to say about him. Barth attacks Nietzsche (though really only in a footnote, albeit a very long one) and so does Milbank (and we shall look at this later), but apart from these two it is hard to think of a major theological voice which seeks to rebut the charges Nietzsche makes against Christianity. Christian theology is not alone in offering so warm a welcome to one so hostile to its fundamental beliefs. Nietzsche wrote that 'When a woman has scholarly inclinations there is usually something wrong with her sexuality'[63] yet he has managed to become a fashionable figure in academic feminism. Nietzsche also had nothing good to say about democracy or socialism yet he has been appropriated by leftist movements from the very beginning. Nietzsche is a charismatic figure and everybody wants to be his friend.

Over the centuries Christianity has made a habit of appropriating the arguments of non-Christians and turning them to its own purposes. Given the powerful role Nietzsche has had in shaping twentieth-century thought it is unsurprising that Christian theologians have looked to use his work as a theological resource. The way in which this has been done has been to break up Nietzsche for his parts. The aspects of Nietzsche's work that are wholly incompatible with Christian theology are fenced off and (largely) ignored, or cleverly re-interpreted. Thus Christians can join in the general applause of Nietzsche's work. I have tried to suggest in this opening chapter that though there is much to learn from Nietzsche, these fences are not very secure. If Nietzsche is to be used as a theological resource I think the Christian theologian ought first to set about the task of refuting him (best of all, on his own terms). And in order to do this we must try to understand him better.

2 The orientation of Nietzsche's question of God

> I want to know you, Unknown One,
> you who have reached deep into my soul,
> into my life like the gust of a storm,
> you incomprehensible yet related one!
> I want to know you, even serve you.
>
> Nietzsche, *To the Unknown God*[1]

On style and seduction

It has become a familiar strategy when approaching Nietzsche to begin with a consideration of his notorious 'style'. As many have noted, there is in Nietzsche's work a great deal of self-consciousness about the relationship between what is being said and how it is being said; how 'style' and 'content' mutually inform each other. Indeed such is the extent of this mutuality that it becomes impossible to speak of style and content as wholly separate dimensions. Those who fail to register that Nietzsche's God-talk is constructed in the complex geometry generated by this mutuality are in danger of presenting a rather flat-footed Nietzsche, a Nietzsche whose attack upon Christianity is all too easily misunderstood and misrepresented.

Consider, first of all, an approach to philosophical writing as different as it is possible to get from that of Nietzsche. Consider what John Locke has to say about 'style':

> But yet if we would speak of things as they are, we must allow that all the art of rhetoric, besides order and clearness; all the artificial and figurative application of words eloquence hath invented, are for nothing else but to insinuate wrong ideas, move the passions, and thereby mislead the judgement; and so indeed are perfect cheats.[2]

Rhetoric, 'that powerful instrument of error and deceit', is for Locke a siren that lures the dedicated truth-seeker away from his or her appointed task. The discipline of philosophical prose, its sense of restraint with regard to language, is indexed to the requirements of truth. The virtues in this sort of writing are clarity and precision, the vices, passion and decoration. As Iris Murdoch puts it, 'when the philosopher is as it were in the front line in relation to his problem I think he speaks with a certain cold clear recognisable voice.'[3] The 'ideal language' is one that is wholly content-neutral, one that does not, by the way it puts things, introduce into the argument any unacknowledged bias. Rhetoric, on the other hand, is simply a vehicle for persuasion and entertainment, and acceptable in so far as it is understood only as such (Murdoch admits that good philosophical prose can include 'wit and occasional interludes').

What is particularly interesting is the way Locke seeks to represent 'style' as something feminine and 'content' as something masculine:

> Eloquence, like the fair sex, has too prevailing beauties in it to suffer itself ever to be spoken against. And it is in vain to find fault with those arts of deceiving, wherein men find pleasure to be deceived.[4]

Martha Nussbaum comments: 'Locke . . . writes that the rhetorical and emotive elements of style are rather like a woman: amusing and even delightful when kept in their place, dangerous and corrupting if permitted to take control.'[5] The contrast between the respective approaches to 'style' and 'rhetoric' in Locke and Nietzsche could not be more acutely expressed than in the juxtaposition of this passage with the following from Nietzsche:

> Supposing truth to be a woman – what then? Are there grounds for the suspicion that philosophers, insofar as they were dogmatists, have been very inexpert with women? The gruesome seriousness, the clumsy obtrusiveness with which they have tended to approach truth have been awkward and inappropriate ways of winning over a wench?[6]

The 'truth' Nietzsche suggests, does not give itself up to the prosaic advances of the 'ideal language'. The truth has to be wooed, seduced, teased out. The search for truth involves games-playing, persuasion, cycles of concealment and exposure, and, above all, passion. Rhetoric, far from being a hindrance to the pursuit of truth, is precisely the means by which the truth is apprehended. This approach doesn't necessarily indicate a more reconstructed approach to women; what it reveals is a wholly different approach to the significance of style. For Nietzsche a sensitivity to style and rhetoric is not *mere* decoration, it is not a second order concern, but at the very heart of intellectual inquiry. Philosophers, he claims, have tended to have no such sensitivity and consequently are always looking in the wrong place for 'truth'.

Nietzsche has consistently been the source of much philosophical frustration, for though many sense that he has an important philosophical contribution to make, they feel that the philosophical Nietzsche is hidden behind great swathes of rhetorical flamboyance and intellectual panache which serve only to mask the seriousness of his intent. A number of thinkers have therefore sought to 'translate' Nietzsche's work out of its original style and into one more suited to the philosophical task. Danto in 1965 writes of Nietzsche thus:

> Because we know a good deal more philosophy today, I believe it is exceedingly useful to see his analysis in terms of logical features which he was unable to make explicit, but toward which he was unmistakably groping. His language would have been less colorful had he known what he was trying to say, but then he would not have been the original thinker he was, working through a set of problems which had hardly ever been charted before. Small wonder his maps are illustrated, so to speak, with all sorts of monsters and fearful indications and boastful cartographical embellishments.[7]

On the back cover of *Nietzsche: A collection of critical essays* (ed. Soloman 1973) the collection is described thus: 'These essays strip away Nietzsche's flamboyant style, his tragic biography, his notorious influence, and reveal him purely as a philosopher.' Such things were written in the 1960s and early 1970s and the intellectual climate has since changed. These days it is generally recognised that it won't do to approach a thinker in this blatantly reductionist way, and it is, in no small part, the influence of Nietzsche that is responsible for helping to effect this sea-change in sensitivity. One of the consequences of the post-structuralist influence upon contemporary philosophy is that philosophers have become more aware that there is no such thing as an 'ideal language', no form of expression which is content-neutral. With this has come an increased sensitivity to the styles of writing particular thinkers adopt and the sense in which a writer reveals in his or her use of language what he or she takes rationality to be. This is more than simply a concern for the niceties of philosophical prose. For the method of one's approach to a particular topic significantly determines what sort of answer one is going to find, just as the sort of bait one uses affects the sort of thing one is going to catch in the trap. If you want to catch a rabbit you don't bait the trap with fish. Locke, in setting up his philosophical language as he does, indicates what sort of answer he is prepared to count as acceptable. Nietzsche, in using a very different style of language, is clearly after very different quarry.

Style of language therefore gives one an important clue as to the nature of what it is that interests a particular thinker. Moreover one's 'style', indicative as it is of a particular method of approach, carries with it a whole host of assumptions about the subject in question. The idea of re-potting Nietzsche into a philosophically acceptable 'style' fails to recognise that such a style is intrinsically linked to what it is that Nietzsche believes himself to be doing. The problem with 're-potting' is that it changes the assumptions loaded within the text and thus threatens to wholly misrepresent Nietzsche's priorities.

This re-potting has been particularly prevalent among a number of those who would seek to understand and explain Nietzsche's attack upon Christianity. All too often insufficient care is taken to understand what sort of problem Nietzsche takes the problem of God to be. Particularly among philosophers there has been an over-hastiness in assuming that the best way to understand Nietzsche's objections to Christianity has been to cast them as philosophy, as philosophical objections. But even to express things thus – Nietzsche's *objections* – begins a subtle slide towards a particular misrepresentation; for in the use of such language Nietzsche's anger and passion is slowly being drained away. Nietzsche does not object to Christianity with all the critical distance and balanced neutrality required by a forensic 'philosophical' approach; he doesn't seek to be unbiased, he doesn't seek to be unemotional, he doesn't seek to stand back and examine at a distance. 'I have absolutely no knowledge of atheism as an outcome of reasoning, still less as an event: with me it is obvious by instinct.'[8]

Nietzsche doesn't 'object' – he attacks. He doesn't seek a fair fight either: he is out to exterminate Christianity with all the passionate intensity of one who is still caught up within its workings.

The alacrity with which some interpreters seek to translate Nietzsche's attack upon Christianity into something 'philosophically' acceptable has distorted and flattened the vociferousness of his multi-dimensional campaign against Christianity – and that is to misunderstand precisely what this campaign is all about. One of the most significant and disastrous consequences of this move is the re-location of Nietzsche's thought within a particular, quite alien, theological paradigm which sets his ideas within the context of a set of problems that were not his own. The theological paradigm into which Nietzsche is commonly squeezed is that which understands the fundamental move in the theological enterprise to be the demonstration that God does or does not exist. This model conceives of theology as being essentially 'top-down': that the first question of theology has to be that of God's existence and all further theological issues are consequences of that first move and fall in line behind it. This, of course, is precisely the sort of assumption that Buckley is out to attack. Buckley quotes Etienne Gilson on Thomas Aquinas as illustration:

> It is natural that his first question should be about the existence of God. On this problem, however, a theologian cannot do much more than apply to the philosophers for philosophical information. The existence of God is a philosophical issue.[9]

The sense that Nietzsche, in attacking Christianity, begins with the 'conventional' question of God's existence is further supported by the prominence accorded Nietzsche's famous phrase 'the death of God'. Of course, 'God is dead' is not identical to the claim 'God does not exist', though if one is seeking to translate Nietzsche's work out of its original style and into the cold clear voice of philosophical prose it is easy to see how these things could be seen as amounting to the same thing. 'God is dead' is, on this way of looking at things, a theatrical and rhetorically arresting way of claiming that God does not exist. Richard Schacht, in his major study of Nietzsche, takes just this line:

> For Nietzsche, it would be difficult to overestimate the importance (both practical and philosophical) of the question of whether or not there is a God. As he observes, with regard to belief in God, so much 'was built upon this faith, propped up by it' that its abandonment has consequences beyond 'the multitude's capacity for comprehension' (GS 343). One could fairly characterise a good deal of his philosophising as an attempt to draw out these consequences, for a whole range of issues: to show what positions are thereby rendered as untenable, and to proceed to deal with these issues in a manner he takes to be indicated when both the very idea of God and the long 'shadow' cast by this idea over much of our ordinary and traditional thinking are banished.[10]

What is most surprising about this sort of interpretation is that Nietzsche explicitly denies it. Indeed, if one is to take Nietzsche at his word, it seems that he is relatively unconcerned with the question of God's existence. He writes: 'That we find no God – either in history or in nature or behind nature – is not what differentiates us.'[11]

And again:

> Hitherto one has always attacked Christianity not merely in a modest way but in the wrong way . . . The question of the mere 'truth' of Christianity – whether in regard to the existence of its God or to the legendary history of its origin . . . is quite beside the point.[12]

Schacht is aware of this sort of criticism and answers:

> It is suggested that passages of this sort show his actual concern to be with something quite different from the question of whether or not God exists – namely, with the problem of what is to be made of the kind of morality and scale of values associated with belief in the existence of such a God. While it is certainly true that Nietzsche was very much concerned with the latter issue, however, such a concern obviously does not preclude one's taking the question of the existence of God to be of great moment. Moreover, and more importantly, it should be observed that taking the position he does with respect to this morality and scale of values presupposes that one is prepared to answer this question in the negative.[13]

This last line is the give-away. Why must a concern for (or even attack upon) the kind of morality and scale of values associated with belief in the existence of God necessarily presuppose that one answers the question of God's existence in the negative? What, for instance, of Ivan Karamazov? What of Proudhon's 'God is evil'? It is perhaps unsurprising that as a philosopher Schacht is presuming that Nietzsche's approach to the question of God is, like that of Gilson's St. Thomas, a wholly philosophical affair.

One of the major problems with the general approach taken by Schacht, apart from Nietzsche's explicit denial of it, is that it finds it increasingly difficult to make sense of what Nietzsche means by his constant use of Christian imagery, ideas and concepts. What of his almost Biblical sense of gravitas? What of his use of a mock Gospel style for *Thus Spoke Zarathustra*? What of the self-confessed piety of his unbelief? Again and again, on almost every page, the direct influence of Christian language and patterns of thought is evident. Why did Nietzsche feel that he could never leave Christianity alone? If God is dead why go on about Him so much? Nietzsche clearly encourages his reader to puzzle over these complexities of which he is all too aware. For example, in *Thus Spoke Zarathustra*, Zarathustra meets in the woods an old pope who recognises within Zarathustra much of what motivated him before he also learned of God's death.

> 'What do I hear!' the old pope said at this point, pricking up his ears; 'O Zarathustra, you are more pious than you believe, with such an unbelief! Some god in you has converted you to your godlessness . . . Is it not your piety itself which no longer allows you to believe in a god? . . . In your neighbourhood, although you would be the most godless, I scent a stealthy odour of holiness and well-being that comes from long benedictions: it fills me with joy and sorrow.'[14]

Of course, the likes of Schacht do have responses to these puzzles. Nietzsche is tracking down and seeking to expose the 'shadows of God', which is why he continues to go on about Christianity. Others claim Nietzsche is being ironic in aping the Gospels. He is ridiculing religion. These explanations are all very well, but they are hardly exhaustive. One can, of course, attack and ridicule a religion while being unable to free oneself from it. Indeed, sometimes, the ferocity of the attack is a symptom of the hold it still has. In Nietzsche's case the 'odour of holiness' is unmistakable.

One of Schacht's mistakes is, I think, to assume that all atheists look the same; that a 'Catholic' atheist is the same as a 'Protestant' atheist. Atheism, however, is a more complex and variegated phenomenon. Nietzsche himself recognises that 'unbelief consequently signifies something altogether different in Catholic countries from what it does in Protestant'.[15] In order not to believe in God one has to have a particular conception of what it is that one doesn't believe in. The early Christians were accused of being atheists because they did not believe in the gods of Imperial Rome. It is therefore a much more subtle question to ask after Nietzsche's 'atheism'. (For instance, given that Nietzsche describes himself as a devotee of the god Dionysus, could it be that Nietzsche's atheism is analogous to that of the early Christian?) I will want to argue that Nietzsche's atheism is not *premised*, either intellectually or emotionally, upon a denial of the existence of God. This is not to say I believe Nietzsche did after all believe in God. Clearly he didn't. Nietzsche was unquestionably an atheist – my question is going to be: of what sort?

My answer to this will be, roughly speaking, that Nietzsche approaches 'the question of God' with the instincts of his Lutheran Pietistic upbringing. I will suggest that from this perspective the 'first question' of theology is not 'Does God exist?' but rather something like 'How are we saved?' Indeed I will hope to show that Nietzsche is obsessed with the question of salvation and much of his work is driven by an attempt to expose the pathologies of Christian soteriology and re-invent a very different soteriological scheme which, unlike its Christian parent, leads to genuine joy. One of the advantages of placing Nietzsche's concern with salvation centre-stage in his thought is that it goes some way to explain why Nietzsche continues to employ Christian ideas and images long after he has believed God to be dead. The death of God does not call to an end Nietzsche's concern with Christian theology because the death of God is, for Nietzsche, precisely that from which salvation is made possible. Salvation follows on from the death of God. Thus Nietzsche claims in one of the great crescendos of *Twilight of the Idols*: 'We deny God; in denying God we deny accountability: only by doing that do we redeem the world.'[16] And in seeking to describe the nature of this salvation Nietzsche reaches again and again for Christian imagery, as one might well do in seeking to articulate an account of salvation (albeit an 'atheistic' one).

The mistake made by Schacht is that he fails to appreciate the way in which Nietzsche's upbringing orientates him towards the question of God. Schacht is not unlike one of those of whom Nietzsche writes: 'they no longer have any idea what religions are supposed to be for and as it were merely register their existence in the world with a kind of dumb amazement.'[17] If I am right about the significance of Nietzsche's Pietist origins then there is another important reason why the cold clear voice of philosophical prose is categorically incapable of making sense of Nietzsche's work. In seeking to define the ideal philosophical language Locke had one particular enemy constantly in mind: 'enthusiasm'. It has been said that the only time Locke gets enthusiastic in his writing is when he is attacking religious enthusiasm. For Locke religious enthusiasts are lazy and deluded, they are tempted away from the rigours of the disciplined search for truth by the instant 'gains' of feeling and intuition. For Locke there is no peace to be had between the philosopher and the enthusiast. His philosophical language is, on one level, designed specifically to exclude the spurious arguments of enthusiasts. Nietzsche, as I read him, was an enthusiast, albeit an atheistic one. This is what has caused the puzzle among so many philosophers. For though many feel that his anti-Christian position, his 'atheism', has a part to play in the contemporary philosophical critique of Christianity, they are unable to appreciate that his 'enthusiastic' atheism plays by a quite different set of rules. Hence the complexity many have found in appropriating Nietzsche for the purposes of 'philosophical' atheism. For his part Nietzsche has little but scorn for those who seek to weigh up the question of God from the perspective of philosophical neutrality. The critical distance of the cold clear voice is a piece of arrogance which totally misunderstands and misplaces the nature of religious belief.

> The practical indifference to religious things in which he [the scholar] was born and raised is as a rule sublimated in him into a caution and cleanliness which avoids contact with religious people and things; . . . and how much naivety, venerable, child-like and boundlessly stupid naivety is there in the scholar's belief in his superiority, in the good conscience of his tolerance, in the simply unsuspecting certainty with which his instincts treat the religious man as inferior and a lower type which he has himself evolved above and beyond.[18]

Nietzsche was 'born and raised' in a quite different intellectual climate. 'One must have loved religion and art as mother and nurse', he claims, 'otherwise one cannot grow wise.'[19] Nietzsche was committed to his atheism with the passionate intensity of a religious belief.

The Christianity of Nietzsche's youth

> It was only out of the soil of the German Reformation that there could grow a Nietzsche.
>
> Dietrich Bonhoeffer[20]

Christianity was an ever-present reality in Nietzsche's childhood and early adult life. His father and both of his grandfathers were Lutheran clergymen. Indeed Nietzsche's cousin, Max Oehler, worked out that some twenty per cent of his ninety-eight known male ancestors were pastors. In his study of the *Young Nietzsche* Carl Pletsch comments:

> Thus, in the several generations immediately prior to Friedrich's birth, virtually all of his relatives occupied parsonages. This made Nietzsche an example of why the Lutheran pastorate was considered the genealogical source of Germany's intelligentsia. In fact, the ministry, or Pfarrerstand, was almost a caste. The best minds in Germany were selected from all classes by rigorous examination. Trained for the pastorate at the university, they became the educated elite of the country. And they tended to inter-marry, forming a sub-society within German society at large.[21]

Coming from this tight-knit Lutheran background the expectations upon Nietzsche were clear and firm. He would, like his father before him, become a Lutheran clergyman. Nietzsche himself acknowledged the great influence his father had upon him: 'In yet another point', he writes, 'I am merely my father once more and as it were a continuation of his life after an all too early death.'[22] In July 1849 Nietzsche's father died when Nietzsche was only five. The family had to move out from their parsonage in Röcken and take up residence with Nietzsche's father's family in Naumburg. Nietzsche had to grow up quickly, and in many ways, he sought to take up the role left by his father's death. He didn't get on well with children his own age and acted 'in many respects just like a miniature adult'.[23] His contemporaries nicknamed him the 'little pastor' and school reports speak of a pious and studious boy. At this time Nietzsche was known for his ability to recite passages from scripture and religious songs with great feeling. He was confirmed at seventeen, and despite growing uncertainties, enrolled to study theology at the University of Bonn where he was to win the university preaching prize. And although by 1864 the whole structure of Nietzsche's faith began to collapse, he came to recognise these early experiences as determining much of the shape of his later thought:

> I have tried to deny everything. Oh, it is easy to tear down, but to build up! And even tearing down seems easier than it is: these impressions of our childhood, the influences of our parents, our education determine us to our inmost depths, so that these deeply-rooted prejudices are not so easily weeded out by rational grounds or sheer will.[24]

Clearly, then, Christianity was deeply formative in Nietzsche's upbringing. But what sort of Christianity? What theological paradigm was at work in the Nietzsche household? What was being preached on Sundays? What did he learn about God at school? What were the theological issues of the day? In order to build up a picture of the theological influences at work in Nietzsche's intellectual formation I will concentrate on two areas. First of all I will look at Martin Luther and look in particular at a number of features of his work that shaped Nietzsche's intellectual world. I will argue that, in the broadest possible sense, Luther's theology of justification forms the basis of Nietzsche's theological paradigm.[25] That said, the sort of Lutheranism that Nietzsche himself encountered as a growing child and as a young man was really very different (in some cases almost the opposite) from what Luther himself believed. Secondly, therefore, I will look at what I take to be the importance of Pietism in the formation of Nietzsche's theological imagination. Of course, as a fairly widely read intellectual Nietzsche was open to other theological influences, and indeed in his later life he became more and more taken with Roman Catholic spirituality (though this may have as much to do with Nietzsche's love of all things Southern European, not least the climate, as much as any particular theological interest). Nonetheless I will argue that Luther and Pietism are the most active forces shaping Nietzsche's approach to and understanding of the question of God.

Nietzsche and Luther

Introducing a section on 'Nietzsche's Lutheranism' Duncan Large writes:

> Given the problems which Germany as a whole, and its theologians and historians in particular, have had with evaluating Luther's uncomfortable legacy over the years, it should come as no surprise that Nietzsche's image of Luther is conflicted and unstable, an uneasy mixture of identification and rejection which serves as a microcosm of the larger picture. With Luther being cited in such a plethora of cultural paternity suits, it is hardly surprising that Nietzsche's image of him should be marked by a combination of filial devotion and Oedipal revolt.[26]

Generally, of course, Luther so shaped the cultural landscape of subsequent generations that Nietzsche cannot but have been influenced by the theological revolution instigated by Luther. His translation of the Bible was the decisive move in establishing the East Central dialect of Early New High German as the basis of written German. In this sense Luther has a good claim on the title 'father of German literature'. And Nietzsche's adoption of a mock-Biblical style in *Thus Spoke Zarathustra* is clearly a testimony to Luther's influence. As Large points out in the lecture, in Nietzsche's writing 'the characteristic stamp of Luther's prose cadences and verse rhythms is discernable, the inimitable combination of down-to-earth directness with flights of the highest spirituality and lyricism.' In some degree, therefore, Nietzsche speaks the language of the German Reformation. It is the basis of his 'style'.

The key places of Nietzsche's upbringing – Röcken, Naumburg and Pforta – are in the very geographical centre of Lutheranism. As Large puts it, Nietzsche was brought up 'close by all the most important landmarks on what we would now call (and what east German travel agents doubtless do call) "The Lutheran Heritage Trail"'. Both geographically and theologically Nietzsche was raised in Luther country. Large's paper goes on to chart the changing estimation Nietzsche has of Luther throughout his life. He notes that early in his career, when Nietzsche was taken with ideas of German nationalism, to the extent of proudly acquiring the obligatory duelling scar, he thought very highly of Luther. In the early to mid 1870s Nietzsche produced a number of lists of 'German greats'. His list of heroes in 1872 was unchanged in 1875: Luther, Goethe, Schiller, Schopenhauer, Beethoven, Wagner. Always tempted to see historical figures as either heroes or villains, Nietzsche saw Luther, in this period at least, as a hero. Luther's transition from hero to villain comes about at the same time as Nietzsche's break with Wagner, and is, no doubt, connected with it. Nietzsche's fall out with Wagner prompted Nietzsche to re-think many of his intellectual affiliations. German nationalism is re-thought, so too Nietzsche's estimation of the Reformation (with which it is connected in his mind). From this point on Luther is increasingly subjected to the most ferocious of character assassinations. For the purposes of this argument, however, the changing estimation Nietzsche had of Luther is somewhat beside the point. What I want to suggest is that the way Luther conceives of theology, of what the theological task is all about and how it is to be conducted, has a general though pervasive influence upon Nietzsche's understanding of theology. Though there are a number of important qualifications, I want to suggest that the paradigm from which Nietzsche thinks the question of God is largely that which is bequeathed by Luther.

The theological revolution begun by Luther has, at its core, an attempt to found theology upon soteriology. With Luther, theology is re-invented as soteriology. Theology is not about abstract questions of God's existence or nature, it must have nothing to do with scholastic debates over the nature of divine 'substance', of what it means to call God the 'prime mover', of the nature of the soul as 'form', etc. – still less with how many angels can dance on a pin – theology is about human salvation.

The seed idea of the Reformation is generated through Luther's famous 'discovery' of the 'righteousness of God'. Luther initially conceived of salvation as being wrought on the basis of one's capacity for merit. He understood the 'righteousness of God' to refer to the fair and even-handed way God deals with human beings on the basis of their moral achievements; that God punishes sinners and exalts those who are just *quid pro quo*. Luther's anxieties about this theological construction were developed in response to his growing realisation that nothing he was capable of could possibly be enough to make him righteous in God's sight. Thus the phrase the 'righteousness of God' increasingly spoke to him of a God of condemnation, and one whom, he was later to admit, he had come to hate.[27] The constant cycle of failure and penance in which Luther felt himself inexorably caught was an experience of Hell itself (this the shadow side of the Pelagian's breezy moral optimism). Luther's theological breakthrough constituted a re-discovery (and a partial re-working[28]) of Augustine's understanding of human passivity in God's scheme of salvation. Only by acknowledging the failure of our own soteriological resources can we come to appreciate that God's righteousness is constituted by His saving of us, rather than our saving of ourselves. Only by admitting that we are unable to achieve anything at all without God's help, only by being stripped of all those moral and intellectual convictions which mask the extent of our alienation from God can we begin to be recipients of His grace:

> before man can be raised to the heights, he must be forced to descend to the depths; before he can be elevated by God, he must first humiliate himself; before he can be saved, he must first be damned; before he can live in the spirit, he must first be put to death in the flesh.[29]

It is within this context of the acknowledgment of human failure and of the consequent need for a self-emptying of all that sustains the delusions of human success, that Luther's conception of the theological enterprise is situated. Theology is exclusively characterised within the dimensions of human misery and God's exclusive power to save. The Scholastic approach to theology fails on a number of levels. First, in as much as it seeks to characterise the work of theology as disinterested speculation, it fails to capture the existential passion with which the theological enterprise is necessarily driven. But worse still, Scholasticism, in relying upon the power of human reason, cooperates with humanity's desire for self-glorification, thereby deflecting our attention away from the realisation of our utter dependency upon God. Trusting reason sustains a sense of human autonomy and fails to locate the business of theology as giving expression to human misery and divine justification. Hence the nineteenth of Luther's theses of the Heidelberg disputation:

> The man who looks upon the invisible things of God as they are perceived in created things does not deserve to be called a theologian.[30]

The understanding of God developed by those who proceed by way of a rational examination of the created order Luther calls the *Deus gloriosus*. The theology of 'glory' seeks a sense of God that will underpin and affirm human self-regard. It names a God in harmony with humanity and the created order, a God with whom human beings can feel at ease, a God determined by the dimensions of human conceivability. Thus, for Luther, it is not God at all (and all that is not of God is of the devil) but an expression of human arrogance. The correct way to begin theology is by humiliating all human efforts to articulate rationally the nature of God. God is to be apprehended not via rationality but through an appreciation of the nature of salvation. As he puts it in thesis 20:

> The man who perceives the visible rearward parts of God as seen in suffering and the cross does, however, deserve to be called a theologian.[31]

Those who take the question of God to be primarily a philosophical question as to God's existence are considered by Luther not only to be untheological, but to be muddling God up with the devil himself:

> reason is the Devil's whore, and can do nothing but shame and disgrace everything which God says and does.[32]

Luther is uncompromising in his rejection of philosophy as being of any help in seeking to understand who or what God is. On the contrary philosophy – i.e. any attempt to think the nature of God independent of the human need for salvation – is a perilous temptation of the whore reason.

In suggesting reason itself to be a whore Luther is pioneering a whole new area of what Ricoeur has come to call 'suspicion', Nietzsche, Marx and Freud being what he calls the 'masters of suspicion'. Luther's contribution to the historical development of 'suspicion' is enormous. Luther believed that his discovery of the 'righteousness of God', the true meaning of the Gospel message, had roused the devil into one last campaign against the truth. And the closer one comes to the truth the more active the devil becomes in seeking to conceal it. Luther had a strong and lively sense of the presence and activity of the devil, hence the need for suspicion. And one of the best tricks the devil has to play is to encourage the transformation of Gospel theology into Scholasticism. Heiko Oberman puts it like this:

> The Devil will readily help theologians to 'elevate' the zealous, fighting, wrathful loving god of Israel into the philosophical concept of an 'Omnipotent Being.' . . . Satan may be no doctor of theology but he is very well trained in philosophy and has had nearly six thousand years to practise his craft.[33]

Reason and philosophy are infected by the devil; they mislead and are to be handled with considerable suspicion. What is new and radical in Luther's approach is that he is suggesting rationality can be used in the service of some other agency to which it has become beholden. It is not that Scholastic rationality isn't rational enough or that the devil tricks one into making a 'false move', rather the whole rational enterprise, at least as it is conceived by philosophy, is a product of the devil and infected with satanic intention. In focusing attention upon the underlying and hidden motivations implicit within a certain structure of rationality Luther is developing ideas that prefigure Nietzsche's concern for genealogy and its capacity for unmasking hidden interests and motivations. Luther's whore reason is related to Nietzsche's 'supposing truth were a woman'. What Nietzsche hates, of course, is the sort of reason which prostitutes itself to the service of 'slave morality'; and here Nietzsche believes Luther to have succumbed to the beguiling advances of the whore reason.

All theology, rightly called, is, for Luther, *theologia crucis*. It begins with the experience of the cross and of all that confronts human hubris. Only that which enables human beings to face the extent of their complete dependence upon God will qualify as legitimate theology. The criterion of that legitimacy is the cross itself; that which, as Paul rightly notes in 1 Corinthians 1: 18 ff. cannot be grasped rationally.

> I certainly believe I owe it to the Lord to bark against philosophy and speak words of encouragement to holy scripture. For if perhaps another were to do this, who was not acquainted with philosophy from his own observation, he would not have the courage to do so, or would not have commanded belief. But I have worn myself out for years at this, and can see quite clearly from my own experience and from conversations with others that it is a vain and ruinous study. Therefore I admonish you all, so far as I am able, to be done with this form of study quickly, and to

make it your sole business not to allow these matters to carry any weight nor defend them, but rather to do as we do when we learn evil skills in order to render then harmless, and obtain knowledge of errors in order to overcome them. Let us do the same with philosophy, in order to reject it, or at least make ourselves familiar with the mode of speech of those with whom we have to deal. For it is time for us to devote ourselves to other studies, and to learn Jesus Christ and him crucified.[34]

On the cross God appears in the form of that which is not God, he appears *absconditas sub contrario*, in the form of His opposite. One of the consequences of this way of understanding how God chooses to reveal Himself is that it completely undermines any attempt to employ the principle of analogy, so favoured by the Scholastics, to underwrite a sense of the nature of God. In appearing as weak and inglorious, God thereby condemns all human conceptions of strength and majesty. Rowan Williams writes:

> So for all human beings God is to be met in all that 'contradicts' or opposes him, in sin, in hell, in pain and guilt and lonely despair; theology begins here, in the Godless world at its most extreme. Only here, in what negates and mocks all human conceptions of God, can God be himself. Paradoxically, the real and absolute transcendence of God can only be understood in circumstances and experiences where there are no signs of transcendence, no religious clues. It is, as Luther again insists in the 'proof' of thesis 20, useless to consider the transcendence of God, 'His glory and his majesty' independently of the human encounter with him in the godlessness of the cross.[35]

God is God supremely when God is reckoned most unGodlike. Could it be that somewhere in Nietzsche's theological imagination is the idea of out-bidding Luther? That God is most Godlike when he is dead. What is so extraordinary about this construction is that it manages, almost, to sound like a certain sort of theological orthodoxy. Could it be then that Nietzsche's 'the death of God' represents a post-Christian intensification of Luther's theology of the cross? The phrase the 'death of God', although popularised by Nietzsche, was not invented by him. Nietzsche probably borrowed it from Jean Paul. Hegel had used it previously and he had borrowed it from the lines of a chorale, 'O Sorrow, O Suffering', written around 1641 by the Lutheran, Johannes Rist:

> O great distress! God himself lies dead. On the cross he died, and by doing so he has won for us the realm of heaven.

In Lutheran circles the controversial words of this hymn were hotly debated. Could one say that 'God himself lies dead'? Some thought not and in later hymn-books the words are changed to 'The Lord is dead', or 'God's Son lies dead'.[36] Clearly at this stage the idea that God could be (have been) dead was a Christological question, and had no connotations of atheism. Indeed some of the early Church Fathers come very close to saying the same thing. For example, Tertullian comments: 'it is a part of the creed of Christians that God did die, and yet he is alive for evermore.'[37] Clearly then the genealogy of the 'God is dead' idea indicates that it is to be understood within the tradition of Christological dispute. Moreover, as the hymn goes on to make clear, the purpose of this death was soteriological: 'by doing so he has won for us the realm of heaven.' Nietzsche's use of the 'death of God' is governed by the same logic. Its purpose is essentially soteriological.

The parallels between Luther and Nietzsche ought not, however, to be overdrawn; over three centuries separate the death of Luther and the birth of Nietzsche. Luther is a key background figure; one whose general influence is ever present in German theology. Nonetheless, following Luther, many very different theologies have called themselves Lutheran, many of these bearing scant resemblance to the original thing. Therefore in order to appreciate the direct theological influences that the growing Nietzsche was subject to we have to look at a quite different theological phenomenon: Pietism.

Nietzsche and Pietism

In his major study of *German and Scandinavian Protestantism 1700–1918* Nicholas Hope comments 'By 1830, an awakened, Evangelical mood was visible in most German lands'. Early nineteenth-century Germany thus revisited theological ground that had developed with the Pietism of the eighteenth century, but this time with even greater fervour; 'eighteenth century popular piety pales in comparison' claims Hope.

> Lay preachers . . . artisans, or pious noble landowners preached the path to salvation . . . Together they prayed, sang hymns, and read passages of the Bible, or from devotional books, or collections of sermons. The New Testament message of sinful man's redemption through Christ's saving grace and converted and reborn hearts, was rediscovered in contrast to the modern preaching of moral progress based on mankind's natural moral predisposition.[38]

The story of this shift in theological vision, from the rationalism of the late eighteenth century to the revivalist Pietism of the early nineteenth, is reflected in the lives of Nietzsche's parents and grandparents. Nietzsche's father himself came from a family of theologians. His father and mother were very much of the Neologe rationalist school. Despite the considerable pressure they exerted, Nietzsche's father (whose relatively short life spanned the decisive revivalist years 1813–49) gradually shifted his allegiance away from rationalism and towards Pietism. His studies of the revivalist preacher Couard, whose sermons focused upon human sin and the need for redemption, made a significant impression upon him during his time at the University of Halle (Pietism's principal academic centre).[39] Though never able to become, as it were, a fully paid up member of the revivalist movement because of the powerful influence of a disapproving mother (who moved into the parsonage in Röcken after the death of her husband), Nietzsche's father became increasingly taken with the new theological mood. Martin Pernet in his essay 'Friedrich Nietzsche and Pietism' writes:

> Carl Ludwig's intensive reading of collections of revivalist sermons was not without its effect, and it was only because of the influence by Erdmuthe that he did not enter the revivalist movement lock, stock and barrel, given his clear residual affection for it. Even so, during the short time he was pastor at Röcken he continually sought links with this movement and must be reckoned as one of its sympathisers. After taking over his post in Röcken on 9 April 1842, he often went to prayer meetings and missionary events, gatherings which, of course, revivalism had brought into existence. He himself regularly held missionary prayer meetings. He continually praised his friend Schenk in contrast to the 'pious priests' and criticised the 'rationalists'. Likewise he made friends almost exclusively in revivalist circles, making an increasingly clear stand against rationalism.[40]

In contrast to Nietzsche's father, his mother encountered no such parental disapproval for her revivalism. On her theology Pernet comments:

> In line with her upbringing, Franziska preferred an emotional, sincere quiet piety to a dogmatic Christianity based on prescriptions. She was deeply influenced by the pietistic beliefs in her parental home, and nurtured both her own faith and that of her children, whose religious education had been left to her after the death of her husband.[41]

The case Pernet builds up for the influence of Pietism upon the young Nietzsche is broad and impressive. He examines the theological convictions of the leading families in Naumburg and notes the Pietistic influence upon Nietzsche exerted by the families of his two closest Naumburg friends, Wilhelm Pinder and Gustav Krug. Apart from his parents, however, the next most critical influence upon Nietzsche's developing theological consciousness came at school in the person of his theology teacher, Robert Buddensieg. Buddensieg was himself a convinced revivalist and the teacher whom Nietzsche most admired. Not only did Nietzsche attend his classes but he was prepared for confirmation by Buddensieg in 1861. A few months after his confirmation Buddensieg, who had become 'in a real sense his "spiritual father"', also died.

Pietism, therefore, clearly played a central role in shaping Nietzsche's understanding of the theological enterprise and of what he was to mean by

'God'. What then is Pietism? What specifically is Lutheran Pietism? And how does it understand the nature of the Christian life?

In his introduction to *Thus Spoke Zarathustra* R.J. Hollingdale seeks to draw out the parallels between some of the basic themes of the book and the theology of Lutheran Pietism which he notes formed the basis for Nietzsche's 'earliest ideas'. Hollingdale claims 'The teaching of Lutheran Pietism is before all that the events of life are divinely willed and that it is impiety to desire that things should be other than they are.'[42] This he takes to have formed the basis of Nietzsche's conception of *amor fati*.

> *Amor fati*: Lutheran acceptance of the events of life as divinely willed, with the consequent affirmation of life as such as divine, as a product of the divine will, and the implication that to hate life is blasphemous.

Hollingdale goes on to illustrate parallels between a number of the key ideas of *Thus Spoke Zarathustra* and Lutheranism. If *amor fati* is Nietzsche's equivalent to 'thy will be done', the eternal recurrence is 'the extremist formula of life affirmation, strongly influenced by Christian concepts of eternal life and the unalterable nature of God: what is, "is now and ever shall be, world without end".' Likewise the will to power: 'The corresponding Christian conception is that of unregenerate nature redeemed by the force of God's grace'. Nietzsche's injunction 'Live dangerously' has its equivalent in Christ's insistence that one must 'Take up one's Cross and follow me', and the 'Great noontide' is a development of the Christian idea of the second coming. Finally, in addressing the idea of the *Übermensch*, Hollingdale suggests:

> What the Christian says of God, Nietzsche says in very nearly the same words of the Superman, namely: Thine is the kingdom, and the power, and the glory, for ever and ever.

The problem with all of this is that Hollingdale spoils what is, I think, a genuine and important insight (that Nietzsche is deeply indebted to Lutheran Pietism) by seeking to draw out parallels that are far too specific. The idea that Nietzsche took certain Christian ideas and simply inverted them or re-employed them *prêt-à-porter* in the service of an altogether different philosophy is unconvincing. Furthermore in seeking to elicit the parallels on such a specific level Hollingdale fails to reflect upon the far more important paradigmatic continuity. The key thing, and Nietzsche says it himself, is to do with one's theological *instincts*, not the specifics of any particular line of theological argument that may result from the expression of such instincts. And this is why style is such an important consideration, for in Nietzsche's writing he reveals something of his instincts, the orientation of his approach to the question of God.

Pietism, likewise, is less about the specifics of one theological line; indeed Pietism sits fairly light to the finer details of theological debate (another reason why it is problematic to try to establish the sorts of links Hollingdale wants to). Rather Pietism is a much more diffuse phenomenon, characterised as much by its mood as by its 'enthusiasm' – by its instinct, so to speak. Pietism saw itself as indifferent to the details of theological orthodoxy or speculative dispute ('plain truth for plain people' as Wesley called it). Pietism called for a spiritual re-awakening, encouraging Christians to engage with Christ on a personal rather than an intellectual level. In this sense it did not see itself as pressing for a 'new theology' but rather sought to breathe emotional and spiritual life into existing theological constructions. It emphasised what evangelicals would now call a personal relationship with Christ as the basis of one's spiritual life. This intensity of theological mood is the most important thing Nietzsche shares with Pietism, and Hollingdale fails to mention this.

Nonetheless, though it is important to emphasise the indifference Pietism had for what it saw as the spiritually sterile world of academic theology, it would be mistaken to suggest that Pietism had no theological content or inheritance. Pietism was not simply a call to a certain devotional intensity, it also called for and resulted in renewed attention to Christian practice.

> There was, of course, a hearty active side to Pietism – its constant stress on neighbourly love and its denotation of 'neighbour' as 'any and every child of God, whomsoever and wheresoever'. Pietism stood for self-emptying philanthropy; pietists were conspicuous in their service to the deprived, neglected and suffering 'the stranger in distress, the widowed and the fatherless'. They were missionaries and peacemakers; they were in the forefront of prison reform; their denunciations of greed, waste, self-indulgence were a dike against the rampant epicureanism of their time.[43]

This emphasis on *praxis pietatis* had a powerful effect on Nietzsche's understanding of Christianity and even in the midst of one of his most emphatic denunciations of Christianity in *The Anti-Christ* he finds space for a caveat which seems to suggest a form of Christianity with which he is instinctively sympathetic:

> It is false to the point of absurdity to see in a 'belief' . . . the distinguishing characteristic of the Christian: only Christian practice, a life such as he who died on the Cross lived, is Christian . . . Even today such a life is possible, for certain men even necessary: genuine primitive Christianity will be possible at all times . . . Not a belief but a doing.[44]

It adds to my case that Nietzsche goes on from here to attack precisely the assumptions made by the theological paradigm I have associated with Schacht.

> States of consciousness, beliefs of any kind, holding something to be true for example – every psychologist knows this – are a matter of

complete indifference and of the fifth rank compared with the value of instincts . . . To reduce being a Christian, Christianness, to a holding something to be true, to a mere phenomenology of consciousness, means to negate Christianness.

In such observations Nietzsche reveals an understanding of Christianity that is learned not from books or from theorising; this is cradle Christianity and with it comes a very different take to that of the convert or the outside observer. Nietzsche appreciates that those who seek to quantify Christianity as simply a belief-system, as simply a set of propositions one affirms to be true, fail to recognise the way in which faith functions in the life of the believer. Nietzsche's childhood faith was not one that consisted in assent to a series of propositions. Childhood faith is something altogether more basic, it functions much more like 'trust' or 'dependence' and much less like intellectual assent. Bedtime prayers precede intellectual doubt, Church-going and *praxis pietatis* come first; Christian 'formation' is already well established long before Christianity is reflected upon and reduced to a series of propositions. Good evangelical that he was, Christianity was for Nietzsche not a philosophy but a relationship. Consider the tone and passion of this poem Nietzsche wrote in 1861 when he was seventeen entitled 'You Have Called – Lord, I Come':

You have called,
Lord, I rush
With circumspection
To the steps of your throne.
Glowing with love,
Your glance shines into
My heart so dearly,
So painfully:
Lord, I come

I was lost,
lurching drunken,
Sunken,
Tossed to hell and torment –
You stood from afar:
Your glance met me often
So ineffably,
So movingly: now I come gladly.

I feel a shudder
From the sin, the
Abyss of night
And dare not look backward.

I cannot leave you –
In the terrible nights
I look at you sadly
And must hold you.

You are so gentle,
Faithful and sincere,
Genuinely earnest,
Dear saviour image for sinners!
Quell my desire –
My feelings and thinking –
To immerse myself, to devote myself
To your love.[45]

There is no doubt that this is poetry deeply rooted in a Pietistic imagination. It is emotionally charged, unphilosophical, and it focuses upon the need and desire for salvation. Within the phenomenology of Pietist belief, God is met, first and foremost, as the one who saves.

> In this world, ruled by God with real sovereignty, man can always pray to God for help and relief in full confidence and can become certain of salvation and of the promise of forgiveness, which Jesus Christ had gained for those who follow him. At any rate, the consciousness of the interplay of sin and forgiveness and, connected with this, of reconciliation and Christology is essential to those who are 'awakened' or, as we would now put it, 'born again' . . . This was the type of pious attitude which the young Nietzsche encountered and learned to appreciate, one that is based not so much on reason but on an immediately experienced and felt conviction of being touched and affected deep in one's heart.[46]

From his university days onwards Nietzsche came to recognise in this 'theology' something pathological and repressive. It was the ideology of small-town piety and forever associated in his mind with the great burden of expectation heaped upon him following his father's death. On one level it is wholly unsurprising that Nietzsche saw his atheism as something liberating, redeeming even. For thus he broke free of the claustrophobia of expectation. Atheism meant the chance to define an identity for himself rather than seeking always to be a copy of his father, as, it seemed, his mother and sister and grandmother all wanted. But just as Nietzsche's atheism represented a tremendous emancipation, the absence of God, just like the absence of his father (both now dead), continued to manifest themselves in Nietzsche's life. Nietzsche's association of Christianity and guilt, for instance, has a complicated connection with his taking leave of God. The powerful effect that the absence of God has upon Nietzsche is, in part, what the famous 'madman' passage in *The Gay Science*, 125 is all about. The madman, the proclaimer of

God's death, seems to be the only one distressed by the thought of impending emptiness. Those to whom the madman gives his message couldn't care less: they never really believed in God anyway and can't see what all the fuss is about. Here two fundamentally different forms of 'atheism' are being contrasted. And there is no mutual understanding between the two; those standing around in the market place ridicule the intensity of the madman's proclamation. They do not appreciate the full force of the madman's torment: given that God is dead, who will save us now?

Nietzsche continues to be conflicted about Godlessness throughout his life. It is this conflict that gives his work so much of its energy and it is this conflict that perpetuates the God question throughout the different stages of his thought. In a section of *The Gay Science* entitled 'How we, too, are still pious' Nietzsche confesses: 'We godless anti-metaphysicians still take our fire, too, from the flame lit by a faith that is two thousand years old.'[47] Those closest to Nietzsche recognised the fundamentally religious nature of his intellectual drive. Lou Salomé writes:

> Not until the beginnings of Nietzsche's late philosophy does it become fully clear to what degree it is the fundamental religious drive which governs Nietzsche's nature and outlook . . . And just for this reason do we encounter in these late works such a passionate struggle with religion, with belief in God and the neediness-for-redemption, i.e. because he was so dangerously drawn to them himself.[48]

3   Facing the truth, outfacing the horror

It was as though a veil had been rent. I saw on that ivory face the expression of somber pride, of ruthless power, of craven terror – of an intense and hopeless despair. Did he live his life again in every detail of desire, temptation, and surrender during that supreme moment of complete knowledge? He cried out in a whisper at some image, at some vision – he cried out twice, a cry that was no more than a breath – 'The horror! The horror!'

Joseph Conrad, *Heart of Darkness*

Identifying a basic soteriological model

It is notable that many of the stories which attempt to articulate the nature of human salvation (be they religious, political, psychoanalytic, philosophical, etc.) share a similar shape. They begin by suggesting that humanity (or in some cases an individual person) has become alienated or estranged from something of fundamental importance and then proceed to describe the means by which that alienation is overcome. Christianity speaks of our estrangement from God (an estrangement linked to human disobedience) and then proceeds to offer Christ as the means by which we can once again become one with Him. This basic soteriological pattern is not limited in use to, nor indeed was it invented by, Christianity. It is at least as old as Plato[1] and as contemporary as the current concern for the environment. These stories, and they are deeply woven into the pattern of European thought, present salvation as 'becoming one with', as 'being at one with' something that has been lost, stolen, defaced or forgotten – hence at-one-ment.

Another common feature of this basic soteriological pattern, so common as to be virtually invisible, is that the saved person is the person who becomes 'one' with the truth; that is, 'ultimate' truth. Of course, what distinguishes the great variety of soteriological perspectives is that they differ as to their respective understandings of the nature of this truth (or set of truths). It may be, for example, that the 'ultimate' (saving) truth is a truth about oneself that has become obscured, as in psychoanalysis. For others this truth may have to do with political or economic social organisation. For some it is the truth that human beings are part of the natural order. So fundamental is the belief that truth lies at the very centre of human need that few have ever felt the need to question it. Thus the most basic of all soteriological lemmas: the truth will set you free. But, as Nietzsche himself has made us aware, so called 'truths' such as these do not and have not dropped directly from the heavens, but have been constructed and re-worked over time. In order to situate Nietzsche's own reflections upon salvation it is therefore important that, albeit briefly, we offer some historical perspectives upon the relationship between truth and salvation. And, as so often with things Nietzschean, the best place to begin telling the story is with the Greeks.

Greek tragedy shows human lives at the mercy of forces over which we have little or no control. Such is the vulnerability of human beings before the might of fortune that we are powerless to resist its potential for ruining even the most considered and honourable of our attempts to secure a space for human flourishing. To use an image from Pindar: like a young plant human growth is contingent upon circumstances conducive to its nurture. We are exposed to the elements. Our dependence upon those circumstances which sustain our happiness and moral integrity is such that we are forced to recognise the fragility of human efforts to maintain them. Human beings are ruined not just by being corrupt or stupid, but also by the gratuity of circumstance, by being at the wrong place at the wrong time, by bad luck. Thus it is that Martha Nussbaum takes what she calls 'the fragility of goodness' to be an overriding theme of much classical Greek philosophy.

According to Nussbaum the underlying motivation for Plato's philosophical project is to achieve release from the contingencies of fortune. He seeks to articulate a sense of human value immune from the vagaries of change and chance, something self-sufficient and abiding, secure unto itself. That is: goodness without fragility. The appeal of this project to the Athenian world is evident. Plato is offering nothing less than salvation from the devastation inflicted upon social life by the ravages of war and plague. Plato's is an attempt to offer a locus for moral and spiritual value which is not undone by the way of the world, but can be reliably sustained independent of those forces that threaten to crush it.

The basis for that locus, Plato argues, is in security of reason and in the successful eradication of all that is subject to the fleetingness of our desires. Crucial to Plato's strategy are a series of distinctions, soul/body, material/ immaterial, changing/eternal, appearance/reality which are intended to define a space (soul, immaterial, eternal, reality) in which all that is worthwhile about being human can be insulated from the ravages of fortune. Our emotional life, for instance, is deemed subject to external manipulation and thus dependent upon fortune for its success. Moreover our emotions, being subject to change, compromise the pristine self-mastery that can be secured by rationality. Plato's answer to the problem posed by tragedy is to set up, and rigorously maintain, a series of exclusions which defend human value. But in doing so, of course, they redefine it. As Charles Taylor reflects: 'Plato's work should be seen as an important contribution to a long-developing process whereby an ethic of reason and reflection gains dominance over one of action and glory.'[2] An ethic of action and glory is, of course, precariously balanced upon the knife-edge of fortune. (It could be fairly said that it is here, and not, as Heidegger insists, in the realm of metaphysics, that Nietzsche is seeking to invert Plato. Nietzsche clearly wants to return us to an ethic of action and glory.)

Plato's philosophy is, however, more than a redefinition of ethics; for what it constitutes, above all, is a redefinition of reality. In attempting to situate the locus of moral and spiritual value in a realm unaffected by the shifting favours of moral luck, Plato is faced with the criticism that he achieves release from the effects of fortune only to the extent that he withdraws from reality. Nietzsche, in particular, will indict Plato's rational asceticism, and its Christianised cousins, with the charge of cowardice. Platonic (and Christian) other-worldliness is a reflection of his failure to face with courage the way of the world. Plato, however, would deny the charge of withdrawal. On the contrary, reality is that which is perceived only by virtue of releasing human perceptions from the constraints of appearance. Real reality (*to ontos on*), as it were, is constituted by changelessness and order – the world of appearance, by change and chaos. Thus the appearance of things, characterised by change, is a deceit, and real reality is apprehended only in as much as one is able to see beyond it. For Plato, rational asceticism is not a withdrawal from reality, but the basis for its genuine recognition.

Undergirding Plato's response to the moral threat of radical transience is therefore a complex metaphysics in which reality is taken to exist in the realm of changelessness and order. (Hence Nietzsche's insistence that, with Plato and those who came to be strongly influenced by him, moral cowardice becomes inscribed into the very basis of our world-view.) Plato's theory of Forms is a sustained attempt to describe the nature of that reality. It is through his theory of Forms that a mechanism is described whereby the protected self can be aligned to reality without being exposed to fortune. The development of the Forms idea is generated by the assumption that reality is unchanging. It appears to Plato that we are unable to answer effectively the question as to the nature of, for instance, justice, unless there is some sense of justice that exists independently of the fluctuations in human usage and conventions. So too we are unable to identify what it is about a table that makes it a table unless we propose that there is some perfect Form of a table which, by being a (more or less imperfect) copy of a table actually is a table. The key idea here is that of participation. The table is a table in virtue of participating in the Form of tableness. Goodness is good in virtue of participating in the Form of the Good, which is for Plato the ultimate and absolute in the hierarchy of Forms.

A number of scholars have noted that this idea of participation pre-figures the Christian idea that salvation consists in a mystical union with the divine. Plato describes the soul's journey of ascent towards full participation with the ultimate of Forms in explicitly spiritualised terms. Not that his commitment to rationality is compromised, but rather that he perceives rationality to have a crucially mystical dimension. Plato's use of reason is not therefore akin to the cold empiricism of the Positivists, but is the expression of a contemplative ideal that, in its most advanced stages, translates itself into ecstatic encounter. Bernard McGinn puts it thus:

> the seeing that is involved in Plato's contemplation is not a defining, but is based on 'an immediate encounter . . . of a mystical order' in which both knowledge and love play complementary roles in attaining an intuitive contact with the presence of true being. While beatitude for Plato is essentially a cognitive state, because the Good that is grasped in the act of contemplation is identified with the beautiful that is the goal of Eros, contemplation also produces loving joy in the soul.[3]

E.R. Dodds, in similar fashion, comments:

> The supreme act of cognition will thus not be strictly cognitive at all, but will consist in the momentary actualisation of a potential unity between the Absolute in man and the Absolute outside man.[4]

The final destination of the soul's journey of ascetic contemplation is to achieve identity with the ultimate Form of things, by which all things are what they are. Herein lies salvation:

> to take flight from this world to the other, and that means becoming like the divine so far as we can, and that again is to become righteous with the help of wisdom.[5]

Plato's philosophy, in its various forms, had a pervasive influence throughout the formative years of Christian doctrinal development. Even those theologians (and one thinks particularly of Tertullian) who sought to reject philosophy as a threat to the integrity of the Biblical message were more shaped by Plato than they could see, or were prepared to acknowledge. For, like Plato, the Church Fathers tended to understand salvation as being achieved through some sort of deification, either as becoming God (*theosis*) or, at least, as becoming like God (*homoiosis theoi*). To be saved was to participate in the divine life. On this level there was a common acknowledgment that Platonic soteriology and the soteriology of the Bible held an important affinity. For even the Hebrew Scriptures emphasised the centrality of coming into the presence of God, whether mediated through temple worship, or, as in apocalyptic literature, through bodily ascent (1 Enoch 14) or, more commonly, through dreams and visions. And while such scriptures continue to maintain a strong sense of a threshold between humanity and God – in particular one notes the warning not to look upon God's face (Exodus 33: 20) – the Hebrew Scriptures nonetheless offer albeit qualified support for the idea of salvation as *theosis*. The New Testament, on the other hand, is thick with passages which suggest such an understanding. Above all one thinks of the participatory language in John's Gospel and of passages such as 1 Corinthians 13: 12 which were to exert such a considerable influence upon the theology of Augustine. Consider, for instance, 2 Peter 1: 3–4:

> His divine power has granted to us all things that pertain to life and godliness, through the knowledge of him who called us to his own glory and excellence, by which he has granted to us his precious and very great promises, that through these you may escape from the corruption that is in the world because of passion, and become partakers of divine nature.

What Platonism provided for many of the Fathers was a compelling explanation as to the philosophical mechanics of this participation. Thus it is that Nietzsche thinks of Christianity as Platonism for the people.

The influence of Schopenhauer's metaphysics of salvation upon *The Birth of Tragedy*

In the rest of this chapter I will show how this model of soteriology had a powerful and decisive effect on Nietzsche's early thinking, and in particular upon the construction of *The Birth of Tragedy*. I don't mean that Nietzsche adopts unquestioningly this particular soteriological paradigm; rather, that much of Nietzsche's early, and indeed subsequent thought can be understood as various reactions to, rebellions against, and sophistications of this particular model. Indeed, I believe that the trajectory of much of Nietzsche's thinking can be plotted against the background of theosis-type soteriology. And the crucial link between Nietzsche and theosis-type soteriology is Arthur Schopenhauer.

Nietzsche's early thinking is dominated by Schopenhauer. Nietzsche first read Schopenhauer as a university student and immediately became infatuated with his ideas. It was largely because of Schopenhauer that Nietzsche's academic career turned away from philology and towards philosophy. Schopenhauer, as he was later to claim, was his philosophical 'educator'. Indeed such was the extent of Schopenhauer's influence, both intellectually and emotionally, that many of Nietzsche's friendships at this time, most notably with Wagner, though with others also, were built upon a common estimation of Schopenhauer. And though increasingly from around 1876 onwards Nietzsche rejected Schopenhauer's philosophy, and regretted (and to some extent attempted to deny) the influence Schopenhauer had exerted on his thinking, it is clear that at the time of writing *The Birth of Tragedy* Nietzsche's thought was crucially shaped by that of his philosophical mentor.

Schopenhauer's starting point is the belief that human life is essentially characterised by suffering and pain:

> If we were to conduct the most hardened and callous optimist through hospitals, infirmaries, operating theatres, through prisons, torture chambers, and slave-hovels, over battlefields and to places of execution; if we were to open to him all the dark abodes of misery, where it shuns the gaze of cold curiosity, and finally were to allow him to glance into the dungeon of Ugolino where prisoners starved to death, he too would certainly see in the end what kind to world is this *meilleur des mondes possibles*. For whence did Dante get this material for his hell, if not from this actual world of ours?[6]

The pervasiveness and extent of human misery is not a contingent feature of some unfortunate lives, but rather, is nothing less than the truth of existence itself.

> If the immediate and direct purpose of our life is not suffering then our existence is the most ill-adapted to its purpose in the world: for it is absurd to suppose that the endless affliction of which the world is everywhere full, and which arises out of the need and distress pertaining essentially to life, should be purposeless and purely accidental.[7]

Why then is human existence so utterly wretched? It is notable that Schopenhauer's answer is exactly the same as Plato's: because of time and becoming. Schopenhauer comments: 'Time is that by virtue of which everything becomes nothingness in our hands and loses real value.'[8] Human beings live in a perpetual state of unrest, they strive to achieve but in achieving they do not find satisfaction but yet still more to strive after. The anticipated satisfaction of achieving the object of one's desires is simply an illusion, for the result of having achieved one's desires is boredom. Human beings are therefore trapped in an inexorable cycle of desire and disappointment.

> In such a world, where no stability of any kind, no enduring state is possible, where everything is involved with restless change and confusion and keeps itself on its tightrope only by continually striding forward – in such a world, happiness is not so much as to be thought of. It cannot dwell where nothing occurs but Plato's 'continual becoming and never being'.[9]

Schopenhauer's attempt to describe the means by which human beings can free themselves from the ravages of time is thoroughly dependent upon Kant. At the centre of Kant's revolution in philosophy was the argument that human beings do not have direct experience of the world as it is, but rather, that such experience as they do have has been mediated through a number of basic concepts, including that of time. Time, space and causality are the means by which we experience reality, but are not themselves a feature of that reality which lies beyond our capacity to make sense of it. Time, space and causality are mediating concepts that allow us to make sense of the world, they are preconditions of the possibility of experience, but not characteristics of the world as it is, in itself. Kant's metaphysics is thus structured around the distinction between the phenomenal world and the noumenal. The phenomenal world is the world as it is experienced, the world as it appears through the mediation of these basic concepts. Of the noumenal world, the world as it is, in itself, little can be sensibly said, for, by definition, we cannot experience anything other than by experiencing it; there is no such thing as unmediated experience. As Schopenhauer himself remarks, for Kant the noumenal is some mysterious X about which little can be said.

Schopenhauer however sought to say more of the noumenal than Kant. Unlike a number of post-Kantians, in particular Fichte, who sought to cut out the noumenal as inconsistent with the basic principles of Kantian logic, Schopenhauer was more loyal to Kant and retained a sense that there remains an objective reality to the world that exists beyond our capacity to experience it. The existence of the noumenal, though unable to be demonstrated directly, is evidenced through the principle of sufficient reason which insists that the phenomenal world requires an explanation that only the postulation of a noumenal world can provide.[10] Whereas, for Kant, the noumenal was simply a limiting concept that stood for the boundaries of that which it is possible to conceive, Schopenhauer sought to demonstrate that the essential nature of the noumenal is 'will', a unified and omnipresent force that animates all things. Of significance here is the fact that Schopenhauer insists that the noumenal is undifferentiated, that it is essentially one. Thus Schopenhauer refers to the ultimate metaphysical reality not only as 'will', but also as 'the primordial unity'.

The basic blocks of Schopenhauerian soteriology are now in place. The vanity of human lives, the pervasiveness of suffering and pain, are a feature of the temporality of human existence. Time, however, is not objectively real but transcendentally ideal, it is a feature of the phenomenal world, of the world as it is experienced, but not of the noumenal world, of the world as it is in itself. So too human existence has a phenomenal aspect, a life lived in time, and a noumenal sub-structure, that is, 'our intrinsic and essential being' that is non-temporal. Death, Schopenhauer insists, is merely the destruction of our phenomenal selves, whereas our essential being is indestructible. Death is simply, as it were, a return to the noumenal oneness that underlies and pervades our phenomenal existence. Like those homely funeral orations, Schopenhauer sees death as the return of an individual drop of water to the vast and undifferentiated sea of being, or rather 'will'.

All this means, to be sure, that life can be regarded as a dream and death as the awakening from it; but it must be remembered that the personality, the individual, belongs to the dreaming and not to the awakened consciousness, which is why death appears to the individual as annihilation. In any event, death is not, from this point of view, to be considered a transition to a state completely foreign to us, but rather a return to one originally our own from which life has been only a brief absence.[11]

Individuation, the *principium individuationis*, is constitutive of the phenomenal life and not of the noumenal, where, of course, it is incompatible with undifferentiated one-ness. One can partially pre-figure the union with the noumenal in the phenomenal world by seeking to step outside the endless cycle of desiring, and by developing a radical indifference to the seductions of worldly ambition. That is, salvation can be anticipated by the practice of asceticism. Thus it is that Schopenhauer comes to value the tradition of Christian asceticism as having discovered an important truth about the nature of the world and the means by which its horrors can be defeated.

Another means by which salvation can be glimpsed is through aesthetic contemplation. Again following Kant, Schopenhauer believed genuine aesthetic contemplation to be characterised by 'disinterestedness'. The appreciation of works of art or of the beautiful is wholly non-functional; that is, aesthetic contemplation cannot be pressed into the service of human desire. When we experience a thing aesthetically we are drawn out of ourselves. Schopenhauer writes that 'the person who is involved in this sort of perception is no longer an individual, for in such perception the individual has lost himself; he is pure will-less, painless, timeless subject of knowledge.'[12] Iris Murdoch illustrates this experience thus:

> I am looking out of my window in an anxious and resentful state of mind, oblivious of my surroundings, brooding perhaps on some damage done to my prestige. Then suddenly I observe a hovering kestrel. In a moment everything is altered. The brooding self with its hurt vanity has disappeared. There is nothing now but the kestrel.[13]

Schopenhauer notes that in such an act of aesthetic contemplation time stands still and that the particular is invested with the significance of the universal. We are, albeit temporarily, released from desperate circumstances of individuation and temporality, and offered a sense of being one with the ultimate nature of things. It is interesting to note that art, for Schopenhauer, performs the same function as asceticism. It is significant that Schopenhauer, like Nietzsche, valued music above all other art-forms. Its particular value for Schopenhauer was that in being wholly non-representational it did not depend upon the phenomenal world for its subject matter. Music potentially affords a direct articulation of the noumenal.

The aim of Schopenhauer's philosophy therefore is, as Magee puts it (and here its dependence upon our basic soteriological model is clearly illustrated): 'to grasp the ephemeral and illusory nature, and hence the essential nothingness, of the phenomenal world, and to free the self from its bondage, and the will from its service, and to gain some apprehension of the noumenal (which in many cases they call "God").' Though Schopenhauer rejected Christianity and the idea of a personal God, his thought is nonetheless framed around the basic soteriological model that we have traced back, through Christianity, to Plato. Indeed Schopenhauer was himself aware of the proximity of his project to a number of religious and philosophical systems that sought to articulate the means by which human beings can be saved, and acknowledged that his particular philosophy was not unique in being able to point humanity towards the means by which that salvation is achieved:

> that great fundamental truth contained in Christianity as well as in Brahminism and Buddhism, the need for salvation from an existence given up to suffering and death, and its attainability through the denial of the will, hence by a decided opposition to nature, is beyond all comparison the most important truth there can be.[14]

What these various approaches share is a sense of the noumenal;

> that it is not knowable; that it is one and undifferentiated, and yet exists in and through all apparently separate things; that it lies outside space and time, and yet that the human individual is, or can be, 'at one' with it in some ultimate way; that when this state is achieved of a oneness with the noumenal unobscured with the phenomenal, the boundaries of the self disappear altogether; and that this unqualified union with the noumenal is the most desirable of all conditions, notwithstanding the fact that it involves the dissolution of the self.[15]

Turning now to *The Birth of Tragedy* it becomes apparent that Nietzsche has borrowed many of the ideas and strategies that are used by Schopenhauer. From the outset Nietzsche's use and positive evaluation of Schopenhauer is clearly evident. In complete contrast to Nietzsche's later works in which Schopenhauer is rejected, *The Birth of Tragedy* begins by articulating, albeit in a particularly stylised form, a version of Schopenhauer's appearance/reality distinction. Apollo is the divinity of appearances; so Nietzsche explains 'we might apply to Apollo the words of Schopenhauer when he speaks of man wrapped in the veil of māyā'[16] and that 'we might call Apollo himself the glorious divine image of the *principium individuationis*'[17] i.e. that principle of individuation that is characteristic of phenomenal existence. Dionysus, on the other hand, represents the ability to puncture mere appearance and to lead one into communion with ultimate reality. Paul de Man therefore comments:

There is little difficulty in matching the two mythological poles, Dionysus and Apollo, with the categories of appearance [i.e. 'phenomena'] and its antithesis [the 'noumenal'] . . . From its first characterisation as dream, Apollo exists entirely within the world of appearances. The dream . . . is mere surface. This state of illusion happens to coincide with what is usually called 'reality' in everyday speech, the empirical reality in which we live . . . All appearance, as the concept implies, is appearance of something that, in the last analysis, no longer seems to be but actually is. This something can only be Dionysus . . . the origin of things. As such, the Dionysian condition is an insight into things as they are . . . The Apollonian appearance is the metaphorical statement of this truth.[18]

Thus de Man rightly concludes that Nietzsche 'uses and remains faithful to the Kantian element in Schopenhauer's terminology and this allegiance is itself epistemologically founded'.

Dionysus and redemption

One would expect, therefore, that if Nietzsche is to follow Schopenhauer, Dionysus (the one who is able to puncture appearance and seek and find the ultimate nature of things – which is the basis of salvation) would become the linchpin of Nietzsche's attempt to articulate the possibilities of human salvation. And, at least in the early stages of *The Birth of Tragedy*, this expectation is met:

Under the charm of the Dionysian not only is the union between man and man reaffirmed, but the nature which has become alienated, hostile, or subjugated, celebrates once more her reconciliation with her lost son, man. Freely, earth proffers her gifts, and peacefully the beasts of prey of the rocks and desert approach. The chariot of Dionysus is covered with flowers and garlands; panthers and tigers walk under its yoke . . . Now the slave is a free man, now all the rigid, hostile barriers that necessity, caprice, or 'impudent convention' have fixed between man and man are broken. Now, with the gospel of universal harmony, each one feels himself not only united, reconciled and fused with his neighbor, but as one with him, as if the veil of māyā had been torn aside and were now merely fluttering in tatters before the mysterious primordial unity.[19]

On the evidence of this passage alone the considerable influence of Schopen-hauerian soteriology is clearly present. But why does Nietzsche employ the figure of Dionysus as the central character in this soteriological drama?

Dionysus was one of the most popular of the Greek deities. The festivals at which he was celebrated were characterised by drinking, frenzied dancing and collective hysteria. In Dionysus the irrational was celebrated and enacted. The aim of these powerful rituals was to achieve a state of such complete intoxication, bordering on temporary insanity, that one is freed from the dominion of the everyday. As E.R. Dodds puts it:

> The joys of Dionysus had an extremely wide range, from the simple pleasures of the country bumpkin, dancing a jig on greased wineskins, to the . . . ecstatic bacchanal. At both levels, and at all the levels be-tween, he is Lusios, 'the Liberator' – the god who by very simple means or by other means not so simple, enables you for a short time to stop being yourself. That was, I think, the main secret of his appeal to the Archaic age: not only that because life in that age was a thing to escape from, but more specifically because the individual, as the modern world knows him, began to emerge for the first time from the old solidarity of the family, and found the unfamiliar burden of individual responsibility hard to bear. Dionysus could lift him from it.[20]

Nietzsche's invocation of Dionysus is, on one level, an echo of Schopenhauer's desire to liberate the individual from individuation. Thus Nietzsche writes of 'the blissful ecstasy that wells from the innermost depths of man, indeed of nature, at this collapse of the *principium individuationis*'. In the midst of Dionysian frenzy the participants experience an 'intoxicated reality, which likewise does not heed the single unit, but even seeks to destroy the indi-vidual and redeem him through a mystic feeling of oneness'. In the early stages of *The Birth of Tragedy* Nietzsche sets out on a project that is explicitly soteriological. Moreover, it shares both with Plato and with Christianity a soteriological model that equates salvation with 'becoming one with' ultimate reality. 'In spite of pity and fear, we are happy living beings, not as individuals, but as the one living being, with whose creative joy we are united.'

One interesting connection worth pointing out is the similarity of Nietzsche's description of salvation with what is commonly said in dance-culture about the experience of raves and of taking the drug 'ecstasy' (indeed Nietzsche speaks of the Dionysian worshippers as being 'enchanted, in ecstasy'). Raves are the contemporary equivalent of Dionysian festivals. Indeed Nietzsche himself anticipates something of this by making similar connections between drugs and dance; he notes, for instance, that commonly such dancers are 'under the influence of the narcotic draught'.[21] Raves are not simply hedonistic experiences, though they, along with the Dionysian, are that too, but those who go to them frequently speak of a shedding of social inhibitions and the experience of being united with each other in love. The seething mass of bodies that crowd the dance floor becomes as one in its slavish acquiescence to the repetitive and insistent beat. In raves individuation is temporarily suspended and one's sense of identity becomes so bound up with the corporate experience that some speak of being at one with, indeed even in love with, the mass.

Another interesting contemporary phenomenon that has its similarities with Dionysian frenzy is to be found in certain Christian charismatic worship-experiences, in particular with the so-called 'Toronto Blessing' where worshippers, claiming to be under the influence (intoxication) of the Holy Spirit, are known to collapse with laughter, make animal noises, and give themselves up to uncontrollable impulses. With this in mind consider the following passage:

> In song and dance man expresses himself as a member of a higher community; he has forgotten how to walk and speak and is on the way toward flying into the air, dancing. His very gestures express enchantment. Just as the animals now talk, and the earth yields milk and honey, supernatural sounds emanate from him too: he feels himself a god, he himself now walks about enchanted in ecstasy, like the gods he saw walking in his dreams.[22]

One of the central arguments of Dodds' seminal study *The Greeks and the Irrational* is that in Hellenistic culture there continued a widespread association of madness with divine intervention. Epileptics, for instance, were regarded as having some sort of divine gift (as well as curse) that gave them the capacity to communicate with the gods. Similarly the festivals of Dionysus were thought of as enabling participants to grasp an order of things inaccessible through our 'ordinary' experiences (so too the 'Toronto Blessing'). To translate this into Schopenhauerian idiom: madness represents the capacity to transcend the limits of Kant's forms of intuition, that is, the forms in which reality exists for us as appearance, and offers a direct, exceptional and unmediated awareness of the noumenal; it is the privileged inner eye of intuition.

Nietzsche is of course aware that in invoking Dionysus he is invoking a figure of religious significance. Indeed far from seeking to mask the theological import of Dionysus he draws the reader's attention to it. If we return to the above passage 'Under the charm of the Dionysian' etc. (BT 1) we are aware of a passage thick with imagery that has been taken from Biblical texts. In speaking of a reconciliation between humanity and nature Nietzsche reaches for a double-entendre; the phrase *'der verlorene Sohn'* that has been translated above as 'the lost son' can also be translated as 'the prodigal son'. One is also reminded of Isaiah's description of the coming of the Messiah in Isaiah 11: 6 ff. 'The wolf shall dwell with the lamb, and the leopard shall lie down with the kid, etc.' The slave becoming a free man is also, and just as clearly, a reference to the Biblical notion of redemption. Nietzsche was far too well versed in the Scriptures for these to be anything other than intentional. Nor can these be dismissed as mere irony. *The Birth of Tragedy* is Nietzsche's least ironic work. Only later does he develop irony as a significant aspect of his rhetorical technique. The whole passage, far from distancing Dionysus from the Crucified, actually encourages the comparison. Dionysus appears in just the way the Christian imagination has come to picture Christ's triumphant second coming. In borrowing Christian imagery Nietzsche is underlining his soteriological intentions. Silk and Stern suggest that at the end of this passage they 'fully expect to find: There is neither Jew nor Greek, there is neither bond nor free, there is neither male nor female: for ye are all one in Christ Jesus.'[23]

Although he seeks to persuade his readers to the contrary, Nietzsche did not, in fact, 're-discover' Dionysus. Though he speaks of himself as being 'the first to take seriously the marvellous phenomenon which bears the name Dionysus' the truth is quite the contrary, for the figure and religious significance of Dionysus had become a recurring theme throughout a considerable amount of Romantic literature that Nietzsche knew well. As Max Baeumer has convincingly demonstrated:

> Winckelmann, Hamaan and Herder had already discovered, comprehended, and formulated the concept of the Dionysian long before him. Novalis and Hölderlin united it with Christian elements in the form of poetic inspiration; Henrich Heine and Robert Hamerling, a much read novelist in Nietzsche's time, anticipated his famous antithesis 'Dionysus vs. the Crucified One'; and in the research of the German Romantics in the areas of mythology and classical antiquity the antithesis Apollonian–Dionysian had been employed for decades.[24]

This uniting of Dionysus 'with Christian elements' was just one aspect of a general attempt by a number of German Romantics to engineer some form of exchange between Christianity and Classical religion. Of particular significance in the formation of Nietzsche's early thought are the writings of Hölderlin who attempted to cross-breed the deities of ancient Greece with overtly Christian imagery. In Hölderlin's hymn *The Only One* Dionysus is called the brother of Christ. This uniting is, for Hölderlin, significantly captured in the Eucharist – for not only is the Eucharist a means of remembering Christ and an anticipation of his return, it is also a celebration of the wine-god Dionysus. In Hölderlin's poem *Bread and Wine* the symbol of wine attempts to combine both a sense of Dionysian intoxication and a sense of Christian sacrament. At school Nietzsche spoke of Hölderlin as 'my favorite poet' (alongside Heine, Jean Paul, Hoffman, Shelley, Shakespeare and Byron), and much to the displeasure of his teachers who considered Hölderlin an unsuitable subject for study, Nietzsche wrote an extended essay extolling the virtues of Hölderlin's poetry.

Dionysus' appearance in *The Birth of Tragedy* has considerable parallels in Romantic literature which corroborate its soteriological intentions. Novalis, for instance, celebrates the return of the wine-god as a saviour figure who comes to unify human beings with nature. Again Christian imagery is extensively employed. He speaks of one:

> consumed as bread and wine, embraced as a loved one, breathed as air, comprehended as word and song, and finally received, amid the greatest sufferings of love, as death into the innermost part of the failing body.[25]

That Nietzsche was thoroughly indebted to the Romantics is widely accepted. In his early work Nietzsche's use of such characteristically Romantic themes as the exultation of art and the quest for an organic reconciliation between human beings and nature confirms his place within the Romantic tradition, a tradition that continued to be fascinated with reformulating Christianity. Indeed the Romanticism of *The Birth of Tragedy* is openly acknowledged when Nietzsche, returning to consider this work in 1886 (writing a new introduction to the second addition entitled 'Attempt at Self-Criticism') comments 'But my dear sir, what in the world is romantic if your book isn't?' He continues:

> Isn't this [*The Birth of Tragedy*] the typical creed of the romantic of 1830, masked by the pessimism of 1850? Even the usual romantic finale is sounded – break, breakdown, return and collapse before an old faith, before the old God.[26]

What Nietzsche finds so disturbing about the Romanticism of *The Birth of Tragedy* is that he comes to recognise Romanticism as little more than thinly veiled Christianity. 'In sum', he concludes, 'as romantics end, as *Christians*'. This connection was clarified in Nietzsche's mind by Wagner's supposed 'conversion' to Christianity. Wagner's music, Nietzsche claims in 1888, is 'underhand Christianity'.[27] In fact Wagner's Christianity was arguably never much more than a loyalty to Schopenhauer's instance that Christianity, along with other world religions, embodied profound metaphysical and soteriological truths. Nonetheless Wagner's very public embrace of 'Christianity' revealed to Nietzsche the extent to which his own early work, so considerably influenced by Wagner, was itself of a piece with the Christian faith he had come to despise.

The Birth of Tragedy was clearly written in a climate in which the boundaries of the Christian faith were considerably blurred. Nietzsche's employment of Christian imagery is, however, more than mere eclecticism; the language of Christianity is clearly a language that comes readily to hand if one is concerned with describing the possibilities of human salvation. 'He can avoid a discussion of Christianity' comment Silk and Stern 'but he cannot avoid expounding the Dionysiac, and there an invocation of the religion of his youth is always likely to appear.'[28]

Facing the truth

> To what extent Schopenhauer's nihilism still follows from the same ideal that created Christian theism. – One felt so certain about the highest desiderata, the highest values, the highest perfection that the philosophers assumed this as an absolute certainty, as if it were a priori: 'God' at the apex as a given truth. 'To become as God', 'to be absorbed into

God' – for thousands of years these were the most naïve and convincing desiderata.[29]

Above all, however, the most significant feature of the Dionysian instinct is that it offers an apprehension of the truth of things. As we have already noted, 'truth' is the central pivot in the various accounts of human salvation. Those who already know something of Nietzsche will be aware, however, that he comes to develop a complex and ambivalent attitude towards truth. In a quite extraordinary way, Nietzsche calls the very value of truth into question, and explores the possibility that, in some way, lies and untruth might be more valuable, even more true, than truth itself. In order to recognise what is afoot here it is important to recognise that Nietzsche's later comments upon truth are premised upon an investigation of the value of truth that has its origins in a tension clearly evident as early as *The Birth of Tragedy*.

Although one has to be aware that Nietzsche uses the word true in a number of different ways without necessarily signalling to the reader the sense in which he is using it, for the most part he is not interested in what one might call philosophical truth. Nietzsche is not particularly interested in providing an account of the sort of thing truth is, or a philosophical theory as to the nature of truth. Any approach that seeks to position Nietzsche's writings on truth into an analytic tradition is always going to run up against this indifference. At the very least Nietzsche's rhetoric – that truths are lies, for instance – should signal that there is a world of difference between what Nietzsche is up to and the measured philosophical debate to which Nietzsche's relationship is, at the very best, oblique. It is significant that when he speaks of the truth in *The Birth of Tragedy* it is commonly not as something that is known or deduced, but rather as something seen, or faced, or recognised. The Dionysian is one who has 'once looked truly into the essence of things'; who has gazed into the abyss and experienced naked reality. Later he writes of the 'frank, undissembling gaze of truth'.[30] The sense of truth Nietzsche is employing here, that of 'facing the truth', is therefore not one which necessarily requires great intelligence or skilled use of logic, but rather one which requires most of all honesty (to acknowledge the truth) and courage (to face up to the truth). Thus it is that, for Nietzsche, honesty and courage become the *primary* virtues.

What is this truth that is experienced within Dionysian ecstasy and which Nietzsche calls us to face? It is the truth that, at base, the world is cruel, painful and destructive and that human life is without given purpose or design. Nietzsche quotes Sophocles' story of Silenus in *Oedipus at Colonus* as an illustration:

There is an ancient story that King Midas hunted in the forest a long time for the wise Silenus, the companion of Dionysus, without capturing him. When Silenus at last fell into his hands, the king asked what was best and most desirable of all things for man. Fixed and immovable the demigod said not a word, till at last, urged by the king, he gave a shrill laugh and broke out into these words: 'Oh, wretched ephemeral race, children of chance and misery, why do you compel me to tell you what it would be expedient for you not to hear? What is best of all is utterly beyond your reach: not to be born, not to be, to be nothing. But the second best for you is – to die soon.'[31]

As a companion of Dionysus, Silenus has looked into the nature of things and recognised its terrifying reality. It would be hard to overstate the significance of this recognition for understanding the nature and purpose of Nietzsche's thought. For in identifying the truth as wretched Nietzsche has dislodged the key-stone that kept upright the whole architecture of Western soteriology. It is this observation that sets Nietzsche about the task of re-inventing salvation.

For Schopenhauer a unification with the ultimate truth is, as Magee puts it, 'the most desirable of all conditions'. His whole philosophy of appearance and reality, his sense of the importance of rational asceticism, is premised upon the understanding that the truth of things, a truth that hides behind the veil of appearances, is intrinsically valuable. Without this his whole philosophy comes to nothing. To some extent Silenus concurs with Schopenhauer: both recognise the earthly, that is phenomenal, existence of humanity to be characterised by suffering and pain, and both conceive of death as offering a means of escape. But the crucial difference between them is that Schopenhauer regards the alternative to phenomenal existence, though it necessitates a dissolution of the self, as being something better, as being valuable in itself. For Silenus, however, death is valuable only to the extent that it is a way of not being subject to the horror of the world; it offers nothing valuable as an alternative. Silenus' wisdom: to be nothing is better than to be. For Silenus there is no ultimate truth that offers salvation. The 'ultimate truth' is horror too. 'Conscious of the truth he has once seen, man now sees everywhere only the horror or absurdity of existence.'[32]

One of the consequences of this conclusion is that it leads to an enormous dissonance within the structure of *The Birth of Tragedy*. For while Nietzsche borrows significantly from Schopenhauer, what he borrows is a philosophical structure whose purpose is to lead one to a truth that Nietzsche rejects. That is, the origins of Nietzsche's eventual and explicit rejection of Schopenhauer are already at work within a book that is in many other ways so thoroughly Schopenhauerian. Again in his later 'Attempt at Self-Criticism' Nietzsche reflects upon the dissonance of *The Birth of Tragedy* thus:

How I regret in those days I still lacked the courage (or immodesty?) to permit myself in every way an individual language of my own for such individual views or hazards – and that instead I tried laboriously by means of Schopenhauerian and Kantian formulas strange and new valuations which were basically at odds with Kant's and Schopenhauer's spirit and taste! . . . I observed and spoiled Dionysian premonitions with Schopenhauerian formulations.[33]

Whether or not Nietzsche managed to resolve this dissonance within his later work is itself questionable. Could it be, for instance, that Dionysus vs. the Crucified, as a summation of Nietzsche's work, is not a reference to Nietzsche's challenge and opposition to Christianity, but rather a reference to the tension that exists within his work? An internal grappling with influences that he was unable to reconcile?

Throughout Nietzsche's work he sought ways of expressing Dionysian premonitions alongside strategies developed so as not to allow them to destroy him. His understanding of the death of God, as well as being an occasion for celebration (and we shall look at why later on) is also an aspect of Silenian wisdom in that it reveals the terrifying absurdity and purpose-lessness of human life. The madman who announces the death of God is hardly edified by his demise, rather he is terrified by the emptiness: 'Do we not feel the breath of empty space? Has it not become colder? Is not night continually closing in on us?' 'How shall we comfort ourselves?' he continues (GS 125). Whither salvation?

The engine that drives Nietzsche's exploration of the soteriological is fuelled by his desperate desire to overcome the crippling recognition that human life is cruel and absurd. Like the Psalmist, Nietzsche seeks redemp-tion from the pit. And while Nietzsche changes his understanding of the means by which that redemption is achieved, his sense of that from which one stands in need of saving remains largely consistent. The reality of the world and human life is emphatically horrific. The Dionysian instinct which discloses the true nature of reality does not therefore constitute a means of salvation, but rather expresses our very need for it.

Nietzsche's soteriology is thus, in part, about facing the truth. But Nietzsche differs from Platonic and Christian conceptions of salvation in that he thinks that the truth as disclosed by Silenus, far from offering the basis for salvation, is actually that from which we need saving. This is Nietzsche's problem. For if, generally speaking, the truth is considered as the basis for human flourishing, then the purpose of one's soteriology will be to describe how it is that human beings are able to realise, or become one with, this truth, or set of truths. That, of course, involves a multitude of complex philosophical problems – the avoidance of error, the possibilities of deceit, etc. The overall pattern, however, is a straightforward one; that of 'being one with' the truth. Nietzsche's attempt to construct a soteriology, however, cannot adopt this model, for the truth, as Silenus reveals it, is precisely the problem not the solution. 'In this sense the Dionysian man resembles Hamlet: both have looked truly into the essence of things, they have gained knowledge.'[34]

But the knowledge they gain is not knowledge capable of redeeming them, quite the reverse, it is 'an insight into the horrible truth', a truth that lures them to nausea, to inertia, and potentially to destruction.

Nietzsche's search for a convincing soteriology is transformed by his not sharing the common understanding that truth is conducive to, indeed, in some cases constitutive of, human salvation – at least, truth and salvation are not seen as mutually supportive in any straightforward way. For Nietzsche 'the truth' and the demands of soteriology are in conflict. And it is precisely because of this conflict that Nietzsche is led to question the value of truth itself.

> What really is it in us that wants 'the truth'? – We did indeed pause for a long time before the question of the origin of this will – until finally we came to a complete halt before an even more fundamental question. We asked after the value of this will. Granted we want truth: why not rather untruth? And uncertainty? Even ignorance?[35]

'It seems to us', he continues 'that this problem has never before been posed.' Of course, there is no reason to pose such a question if the truth is that which saves. But if the truth is that which damns, then a wedge is driven between truth and salvation and the question of their respective value is thus raised. Prima facie the choice seems to be this: either fully face the truth and be damned, or live in various degrees of illusion and be saved:

> The falseness of a judgement is to us not necessarily an objection to a judgement: it is here that our new language perhaps sounds strangest. The question is to what extent it is life-advancing, life-preserving, species preserving, perhaps even species breeding; and our fundamental tendency is to assert that their falsest judgements (to which synthetic judgements a priori belong) are the most indispensable to us. . . . [To] renounce false judgements would be to renounce life.[36]

In questioning the value of truth Nietzsche is seeking to challenge one of philosophy's sacred cows; though it is important to note that elsewhere he remarks that he calls truth into question 'experimentally'. His interrogation of truth operates, on one level, to disclose the affinity of philosophical conceptions of the purpose and value of truth and the Christian approach to salvation. The two have developed an unhealthy symbiosis, each offering the other protection of an otherwise exposed flank (the one deflects the question of the truth of (ultimate) value, the other deflects the question of the (ultimate) value of truth). Hence, for instance, Augustine's claim that 'where I found truth, there I found my God, for God is the Truth itself'.[37] Conjoined in mutual support each has a vested interest in maintaining the good health of the other. In order to raise the question of salvation in the way Nietzsche thinks it must be raised, this unholy alliance has to be broken.

What is most revealing is the way in which Nietzsche sets about dismantling this alliance. The common atheistic approach would be to attack the claim that the ultimate value, i.e. God, is true. On this line the claims of religion are subjected to concerted philosophical scrutiny thereby revealing them not to be true at all. Nietzsche's line of attack, however, is to challenge the other pole of the alliance and question the ultimate value of truth. This line is potentially just as devastating to religion, but is equally, and by the same token, just as potentially devastating to the interests of traditional philosophy; for, if successful, it undermines the very means by which the philosophical atheist seeks to challenge religion. What it also reveals is that Nietzsche's principal interest is not, so to speak, with the question of truth (at least not truth *per se*) but with the question of salvation: his challenge to the assumption of truth's ultimate value is that the truth is condemning and absurd, and therefore cannot be that upon which human salvation is premised.

The Egyptianism of salvation

Nietzsche recognises, however, that the alliance between truth and salvation is far more than a marriage of convenience. For the Platonist and the Christian both share a common enemy: change. Plato, as we have already noted, conceived of salvation as the release from the contingencies of fortune, from the constant process of becoming and change that is ever pregnant with the possibility of human downfall. To that extent Plato and Christianity concur with Silenus and Dionysus that the world, at least the world as it seems, is inscribed with horror and meaninglessness. (It is arguable that a sense of the world as being painful and absurd is a necessary condition of soteriology, for without that, or something closely equivalent, there would be nothing for salvation to save us from; soteriology would have no point or purpose.) And just as constant change undermines the realisation of human salvation, so too it undermines any appeal to truth for, quite simply, the truth cannot change. Clearly, for Plato, if the truth changed then it wouldn't have been the truth in the first place. Hence the possibility of truth and the possibility of human salvation are both bound up with the attempt to articulate the nature of a somewhere not subject to becoming. Hence heaven, hence metaphysics, hence the notion of 'real' reality existing beyond contingency and change.

For Nietzsche, however, this vision of another world is clearly one more ruse to avoid the full extent of Silenus' wisdom. This means, another strategy to avoid facing the truth. Here it is easy to become confused, for Nietzsche is charging Plato's conception of the truth with a profound avoidance of truth. Nietzsche and Plato concur on one point: that the world is characterised by becoming and change. There are two possibilities that follow from this insight. Either, like Plato, one remains committed to the idea that the truth is changeless and thus one seeks another basis upon which truth is grounded (i.e. the Forms), or, like Nietzsche, one accepts that the truth is itself fluid and subject to the same forces of change that affect everything else – hence Dionysian wisdom.

In one of his sermons St. Augustine addresses the criticism that his sense of heaven leaves human beings hopelessly inactive. 'What will I do?' his imaginary interlocutor asks 'There will be no work for our limbs; what, then, will I do?' Augustine's response is that to be in the presence of God is surely sufficient for anyone. 'Is this not activity; to stand, to see, to love, to praise?' Clearly however, whatever else it may be, this is not a very active sort of activity. Why, one must ask, is Augustine hesitant to introduce into heaven anything more active than standing, seeing, loving and praising? As we have already noted, Augustine equates God with absolute truth. And like absolute truth, God is impassible. He is not subject to change and thus is outside time itself. In a passage where Augustine criticises those who have 'not learnt to understand you' he continues:

> Try as they may to savour the taste of eternity, their thoughts still twist and turn upon the ebb and flow of things in past and future time. But if only their minds could be seized and held steady, they would be still for a while, for that short moment, they would glimpse the splendor of eternity which is for ever still. They would contrast it with time, which is never still, and see that it is not comparable. . . . But in eternity nothing moves into the past: all is present.[38]

For Augustine heaven is timeless and without change, so if there is going to be any sort of activity in heaven, it has to be a sort of activity that does not require the doing of anything! For Plato, like Augustine, the ultimate state of salvation is that of contemplation. Again, a completely inactive form of 'activity'. Indeed only by ridding human life of anything that might conceivably be related to change can Plato protect human life from its dependence upon *fortuna*.[39] This, though, creates an enormous problem, for anything that is wholly without the capacity to change cannot convincingly be portrayed as being in any way alive. At best these conceptions of salvation hold within them a sense that the best form of life is like eternity in a flotation tank, and, at worst, indistinguishable from death itself. Consider all the vocabulary we use to describe the nature of life, not just human life, but life in general. We speak of life as being dynamic, as vital. Above all we would want to point to life's capacity for growth, to its coming into being and passing away. Life, that is, necessarily involves change. And anything that does not change at all is dead.

For Nietzsche, the Platonic/Christian celebration of a world beyond time and change is the ultimate expression of nihilism, of the divinisation of death and nothingness. The problem of the whole trajectory of Plato's soteriology is that, in seeking to liberate us from a world of change, chance and becoming, it is actually severing human life from that which makes it what it is. Plato's soteriology is metaphysical suicide. So too that of Christianity. It is not a means of overcoming nihilism, but its ultimate expression. Nietzsche insists:

> God degenerated into the contradiction of life, instead of being its transfiguration and eternal Yes! In God a declaration of hostility towards life, nature, the will to life! . . . In God nothingness deified, the will to nothingness sanctified.[40]

For Nietzsche one of the principal tributaries of this wholly misconceived soteriology is Plato's idea of truth. That is, of truth being wholly static. And this sense of truth underwrites not only Christian soteriology but also the whole tradition of Western philosophical thought.

> You ask me of the idiosyncrasies of philosophers? . . . There is their lack of historical sense, their hatred of even the idea of becoming, their Egyptianism. They think they are doing a thing a favour when they dehistorisize it, *sub specie aeterni* – when they make a mummy of it. All philosophers have handled for millennia are conceptual mummies; nothing actual has escaped their hands alive. They kill, they stuff, when they worship, these conceptual idolaters – they become a mortal danger to everything they worship. Death, change, age, as well as procreation and growth, are for them objections – refutations even. What is does not become and what becomes, is not.[41]

Although Nietzsche is writing of philosophers, much of what he claims here applies also to Christian conceptions of salvation. In the unchanging suspension of the Augustinian God-head the human is drained of life and mummified. According to Nietzsche the only philosopher whose basic ontology does not insidiously celebrate death is Heraclitus who takes as his starting point the conviction that all things exist in a state of flux. Similarly Nietzsche thinks it is crucial to recognise that becoming is the only basis upon which life itself can be premised. But that, of course, is the very thing that Platonic and Christian conceptions of salvation are designed to free us from.

One contemporary writer who develops a similar line to that of Nietzsche is Martha Nussbaum. Nussbaum claims that a conception of 'heaven' that has no place for becoming or risk, and that is set up so as to offer human beings maximal safety from the contingencies of fortune, is actually one in which all that we would want to celebrate in human life would necessarily atrophy. The very protection it affords is wholly unconducive to human flourishing. In establishing this claim Nussbaum focuses on the idea of love and of the possibilities of its survival in such a heavenly realm.

> Take, first, the love of spouse and family. Here we have to note, first of all, that the gods have none of the motives we have for caring about their children and for preserving the structures of family life as a context

for nurture and education for children. They lack our anxious relation to our own future, our desire to extend ourselves through progeny; they lack too, the more altruistic motives, the desire to nourish and protect that which is weak and fragile, the desire to contribute to the future of the world. Divine children are not really children; divine parents are not, therefore, really parents. Next, we notice, as well, that their limits with respect to risk limit, as well, their ability to care for one another in anything like a human way. There is no room for taking risks or making sacrifices for the person one loves; no room for loyalty so strong that it confronts death itself. In consequence of these and other lightness, there is a kind of playfulness and lack of depth about the loves of the gods – and one finds in fact that it looks perfectly rational for a human being to prefer the human bond, with its deeper and stronger intensities.[42]

Nussbaum is, of course, writing of the Hellenic deities, and of the weight-lessness and insubstantiality of their form of 'existence' as compared to ours. It is little wonder, she muses, that such gods often fall in love with human beings rather than their own kind. What would it be for the gods to be in love with each other? What could be meant by love here? In the Platonic/ Christian 'heaven' one could say that love is characterised by mutual con-templation, like lovers staring dreamily into each other's eyes. Indeed the Christian tradition has within it a number of intimations that the contem-plation of God has an erotic aspect. And yet, while Augustine is prepared to admit that our heavenly bodies will retain genitals, there will be nothing for them to do. Why not? Because sex is an activity, and moreover, one that implies the whole pattern of birth, life and death that is misplaced in heaven. But this is surely just another indication that contemplative love is wholly robbed of any context in which it can be meaningfully characterised as love at all. 'It comes as no surprise', Nussbaum adds, 'that Dionysus, the erotic divinity par excellence, is the only divinity who dies, the divinity whose rhythms of birth, growth, death, rebirth inhabit the context of nature and have a close relation to human time.'[43]

Nietzsche's great genius is to recognise that much that has gone into the construction of Western metaphysics is dictated by the demands of a mis-conceived soteriology of safety. Given that the world as it 'appears' is unable to offer such safety, another world, the 'real' one, is postulated. The whole idea that the world as it appears to us is *merely* appearance, and that there is another world that, for some, can be perceived beyond appearance, and where the conditions are conducive to our salvation, is that which cements Christianity and metaphysics in mutual dependence. This 'other world' over-comes the problems of becoming at the expense of life itself. The price of safety is death. For Nietzsche, if humanity is to be redeemed, if it is to find some way of transfiguring the wisdom of Silenus, this has to be achieved within the context of a world that constantly changes, that is, the one Plato and Christianity have insisted is merely the 'apparent' world.

Salvation as art

We possess art lest we perish of the truth.[44]

Despite Nietzsche's enormous hostility to the Christian account of salvation it is important to recognise the extent to which his own position is related to, and clearly comes out of, the Christian tradition. In a sense Nietzsche's invocation of Silenian wisdom continues that estimation of the world and human life that is clearly evident in the likes of St. Augustine and Luther. In what we might call the Augustinian tradition, the overwhelming need for salvation is generated by a negative assessment of the world. At least, that is how it is often depicted. Nietzsche, of course, makes a good deal of this, indicting Christians with the charge of being world-denying life-haters. But is Nietzsche himself any better? At least the Christian tradition does have about it the very strong insistence that God made the world and so, ultimately, the world is good (Genesis 1: 31: 'and God saw all that he had made, and it was very good'). This is one of the most important features of Augustine's work which differentiates it from that of the Manichees. The 'negative' assessment of the world made by Christianity can only ever be provisional. With Silenus, however, this assessment becomes total and final. A combination of a hyper-Augustinian sensibility with a denial of God's existence leads Nietzsche into a position where he looks to be more world-denying and life-hating than the most extreme Christian ascetic.

Salvation from this most terrifying version of nihilism comes, for Nietzsche, in the shape of art. This, then, his first experiment in redemption:

> In this sense the Dionysian man resembles Hamlet: both have once looked truly into the essence of things, they have gained knowledge, and nausea inhibits action; for their action could not change anything in the eternal nature of things; they feel it ridiculous or humiliating that they should be asked to set right a world that is out of joint . . . true knowledge, an insight into the horrible truth, outweighs any motive for action, both in Hamlet and in Dionysian man . . . Here when the danger to his will is greatest, art approaches as a saving sorceress, expert in healing. She alone knows how to turn these nauseous thoughts about the horror and absurdity of existence into notions with which one can live.[45]

If the reality of human life is existentially unbearable, 'salvation' has, at the very least, to enable one to live in the world in such a way that one is not destroyed by it. Nietzsche's sense of how this is possible develops over time. Nonetheless, throughout his career (with the possible exception of the so-called 'positivist' period around 1877 in which he wrote *Human All Too Human*) he associates salvation with art. As he famously opines in *The Birth of Tragedy*, life is only justifiable as an aesthetic phenomenon. However, although Nietzsche sticks to this basic principle, his understanding of the way in which art saves undergoes a number of revisions. His first line on this is that art saves by, as it were, stylising life. Life is reproduced by art in a manner in which the 'beauty' of its representation overshadows – or rather, transfigures – the horror of its content. We are able to live with a stylised representation of Silenian wisdom, if not with the real thing. Just as if we want to look directly at the sun we have to do so through some sort of darkened glass, so too, if we want to look directly at Silenian wisdom, we have to do so through the transfiguring, beautifying, stylising lens of art.

Earlier in this chapter I suggested that, in as much as the Apollo/Dionysus typology was a continuation of Schopenhauer's appearance/reality distinction, we would expect Dionysus to be the agent of salvation in Nietzsche's scheme. The traditional understanding of salvation, if I can call it that, is that we are saved from appearance by establishing contact with (ultimate) reality. And this is, basically speaking, how it works with Schopenhauer. Of course, this approach only makes sense on the assumption that the truth saves, and this is precisely what Nietzsche denies. Thus Nietzsche's soteriological scheme is inverted, and Apollo becomes the saving agency. Salvation is enacted through appearance. Form saves us from content. One thinks of Baudelaire's appreciation of the dandy. Though the dandy may be terribly ill and deeply miserable, nonetheless he will dress up in his finest apparel and by so doing reinterpret his unhappiness as gaiety. On this model the true image of the *Übermensch* is Oscar Wilde, carefully ironing his shirts and writing poems about the horror of Reading gaol.

As discussed in the previous chapter (when considering the question of style), to insist upon a strong sense of distinction between appearance and reality or form and content, is generally speaking no longer a popular option in contemporary thought. Scholars tend to be deeply suspicious of these supposedly foundational binary oppositions; 'the medium is the message' and so forth. One of the reasons Nietzsche is so seminal a thinker is that one can see in his work, perhaps for the first time, the collapse of faith in these distinctions. His famous chapter 'How the "Real World" at last Became a Myth'[46] presents a 'history of an error'; a compact and schematic genealogy of the appearance/reality distinction. That chapter is divided into six sections, the first three representing the various layers of construction (Platonic, Christian, and Kantian) that the appearance/reality distinction has undergone. For Plato, the real world is the world reflected by wisdom and virtue. The Christian contribution is to defer this 'real world' into the hereafter, it becomes a world 'unattainable for the moment, but promised to the wise, the pious, the virtuous man'. Kant philosophises this distinction, and by so doing further distances us from 'reality'; the 'real world' becomes a thing-in-itself, something 'unattainable, undemonstrable', an idea grown 'pale, northerly, Königsbergian'. For Nietzsche the sum total of this history has been both to amplify the need for redemption and yet to make it increasingly impossible.

The real world – unattainable? Unattained, at any rate. And if unattained also unknown. Consequently no consolation, no redemption, no duty: how could one have a duty to something unknown?[47]

The real world has therefore become 'an idea no longer of any use'; an idea no longer capable of expressing the location or provenance of salvation. Hence Nietzsche's advice, 'Let us abolish it!':

We have abolished the real world: what world is left? the apparent world perhaps? . . . but no! with the real world we have also abolished the apparent world![48]

Following Nietzsche's deconstruction of the distinction between appearance and reality, the typology Apollo/Dionysus becomes more and more obsolete. Nietzsche's response is to drop Apollo, and in Nietzsche's later work Apollo hardly gets a mention. Instead a different conception of the saving potential of art develops.

Already, in the course of *The Birth of Tragedy*, the conventional distinction between appearance and reality has undergone considerable revision. For what Nietzsche's first stab at working out an aesthetic soteriology involved was swapping round the values attached to the opposing poles appearance/reality. Furthermore, given Nietzsche's increasing sense that appearance has about it more reality than reality itself, it becomes increasingly difficult to distinguish what he actually means by appearance and reality.

One is an artist at the cost of regarding that which all non-artists call 'form' as content, as 'the matter itself'. To be sure, then one belongs to a topsy-turvy world; for henceforth content becomes something merely formal – our life included.[49]

This topsy-turvyness is a result of dealing with the fall-out from Nietzsche's ground-breaking denial of the distinction between appearance and reality.

The new world into which we are thrown by the break up of these distinctions is one in which art still has a central role to play in articulating human salvation. What has disappeared, however, is the idea that art has to be in some sense mimetic. Art does not save us from a terrifying reality by a benign mimesis of that reality. Art no longer feels it has to imitate, however indirectly, a reality external to it; what it can do now is create for itself alternative worlds, alternative realities, alternative valuations unrestricted by a sense of 'the real world'. Just as, in the visual arts, art becomes non-representational, encouraging the viewer to value the art-work not as a more or less accurate copy of reality, but as something else entirely, as creating a new world for itself. This is the new model upon which Nietzsche seeks to articulate human salvation, the next instalment of his developing soteriology. We are saved from the horrific reality of Silenian wisdom by re-inventing ourselves, as one might 'invent' or create a painting or a work of literature. We are not to feel constrained by reality, we must re-invent ourselves. Just as, in the Christian scheme, we are created and affirmed by God, for Nietzsche we have to give birth to ourselves – to act out the whole process of redemption within ourselves.[50] This is highly sophisticated do-it-yourself salvation. Thiele puts it thus:

> In the absence of God, the redemption of life rests with man; he must behold himself as a work of art, as his own creation. He must become both the playwright and spectator of the ongoing drama of his will in the world.[51]

One can see how this fits in with Nietzsche's increasingly unconventional remarks upon truth.

> 'Truth' is . . . not something out there, that might be found or discovered – but something that must be created and that gives its name to a process, or rather a will to overcome that has in itself no end – introducing truth as a *processus in infinitum*, an active determining – not a becoming conscious of something that is in itself something firm and determined.[52]

As Alexander Nehemas has pointed out in his important and influential *Nietzsche: Life as Literature*, it would be premature to conclude from the above passage that truth is always 'made' as opposed to 'found'. Nehemas' line is that truth, for Nietzsche, is as it were both made and found; a combination which can be seen in the formation of works of art, particularly literature.

> Making and finding, creating and discovering, imposing laws and being constrained by them are involved in a complicated, almost compromising relationship. Our creations eventually become our truths and our truths circumscribe our creations.[53]

Nehemas' favourite example is the construction of Proust's *The Remembrance of Things Past*. Proust's narrator believes that 'in fashioning a work of art we are by no means free, that we do not choose how we shall make it but that it pre-exists and therefore we are obliged, since it is both necessary and hidden, to do what we should have to do if it were a law of nature, that is to say discover it'. One has to create in order to discover – and discover in order to create. So it is that Nehemas explains Nietzsche's otherwise puzzling formulation: 'Become who you are!'

> One thing is needful. – To 'give style' to one's character – a great and rare art! It is practiced by those who survey all the strengths and weak-

nesses of their nature and fit them into an artistic plan until every one of them appears as art and reason and even weaknesses delight the eye.[54]

Nietzsche is performing a complex balancing operation here and it is important to be aware of what is going on. As I have already suggested Nietzsche is not interested in providing a theoretical account of what it means to speak of something as 'truth'.[55] So what then of all this complexity with regard to truth being made or found? The complexity is generated, I suggest, by Nietzsche's concern to articulate a sense of human salvation that does not capitulate to Silenian wisdom, which would be the consequence of the truth being something found, nor one which spins off into fantasy and denial, which would be the result of pretending Silenian wisdom not to exist and believing one could simply construct – create – alternative truths, alternative realities, which are more palatable or edifying. This is the double-bind of Nietzsche's approach to salvation. His answer to it is to seek to maintain a balance between truth as discovered and truth as created. He seeks to steer what I believe to be, ultimately, an impossible path between the Scylla of nihilism (Silenian wisdom) and the Charybdis of fantasy. This, in part, is why Nietzsche is so elusive, so difficult to pin down, in his remarks upon truth. Any settled position on the nature of truth would clearly look like a capitulation either to nihilism or to fantasy. We see this more clearly in his first 'mimetic' aesthetic soteriology. Art lets us live with Silenian wisdom by transforming it into something more stylised and (subsequently) less horrific. It can't totally blot out Silenus' truth (for that would equal fantasy) nor can it face it unadorned (without succumbing to despair). Thus Nietzsche has to perform a philosophical dance of the seven veils – a dance which is not resolved in the progression to a post-mimetic aesthetic soteriology, but simply made more complex, more interesting, more elusive. The attempt to both acknowledge and avoid Silenian wisdom has Nietzsche forever on the hop, which, despite all the fancy footwork, is exactly where we suspected Nietzsche might end up as a hyper-Augustinian in a God-less universe.

4   Redeeming redemption

And one day Zarathustra made a sign to his disciples and spoke these words to them: here are priests: and although they are my enemies, pass them by quietly and with sleeping swords! . . . But my blood is related to theirs and I want to know my blood honoured even in theirs . . . I suffer and have suffered with them: they seem to me prisoners and marked men. He who they call Redeemer has cast them into bondage – Into the bondage of false values and false scriptures! Ah, that someone would redeem them from their Redeemer!

Nietzsche, *Thus Spoke Zarathustra*[1]

The nihilism of salvation

There is, of course, an obvious objection to the claim the Nietzsche's work ought to be read primarily as soteriology, for isn't it precisely the very desire for redemption that Nietzsche is out to eliminate? And isn't Nietzsche's reputation for unflinching honesty founded upon his refusal to betray human life for dreams of another world? His message is surely that we must give up all hopes of being saved and that we must find the courage to live life as it is. Salvation, on the other hand, is the attempt to imagine that there is some other form of life for us to have, a life free from the restrictions of embodiment, a life without pain, without growing old and without death. These, however, are profoundly damaging fantasies, for they are prompted and sustained by the thought that our bodily humanity is something second best, something positively shameful. Salvation necessarily disparages the world in which we live and encourages a sense of human worthlessness in order to make a case for itself:

[Christianity] crushed and shattered man completely and buried him as though in mud: into a feeling of total depravity then it suddenly shone a beam of divine mercy, so that, surprised and stupefied by this act of grace, man gave vent to a cry of rapture and for a moment believed he bore all heaven within him.[2]

This, then, is the nihilism of Christian soteriology: at the heart of the Christian world-view is a powerful counter-factual that asserts life is meaningful if and only if there exists some non-worldly realm that invests human lives with significance. That is simply to say, without God life is meaningless. And the more Christianity is able to demonstrate the meaninglessness and worthlessness of human life the more it is able to promote God as the one who saves. The disparagement of the merely human is thus the flip side of Christian evangelism. Christianity has spread a disease of self-hate simply in order to sell itself as the cure.

With the death of God (a historical happening for which Nietzsche claims no credit) these patterns of *ressentiment* and self-hate are exposed. No longer masked by a belief that, as St. Paul puts it, 'the sufferings of the present are not worth comparing with the glory that is to be revealed to us' (Romans 8: 18), European humanity now faces its own hopelessness (a hopelessness created by centuries of Christian evangelism) unglossed by promises of future glory. Nietzsche, however, saw this 'death of God' as an opportunity to address whether human life actually required redemption, whether human life could stand alone unsupported by false intrusions of the divine. To what extent can human life be affirmed in itself, as simply human-all-too-human? Nietzsche recognised that his window of opportunity was brief. The vacuum created by the death of God would give rise to prophets of new salvations (nationalism? capitalism?) which, once established, would again mask the nihilism underlying European culture. In such circumstances *ressentiment* would simply re-group. Self-hatred, Nietzsche recognised, was capable of an almost infinite capacity for re-invention.

It is here that we can see most clearly that Nietzsche's target is not God *per se* but rather patterns of thought inscribed into European culture by Christian soteriology. For a culture that retains a basic belief in the necessity of some saving agency external to human life, the loss of belief in God prompts one of two responses: either it responds in despair at the meaninglessness of life, or it simply replaces the God idea with another agency, another false idol, which, though it may not look anything much like God, performs the same role. Thus post-Christian cultures which have not dug out the roots of their Christian past and which consequently inherit the 'Christian' counter-factual will simply replace 'God' with another, less theological sounding centre, which is just as damaging as the God idea. The 'death of God' is not enough. Nietzsche's message is not just that there is no God, but that the very idea that human life requires some source of meaning external to itself is both false and ultimately degrading. His is not an alternative soteriology, but a denial that salvation is either possible or necessary. In this spirit Nietzsche writes: 'The last thing I should promise would be to "improve" mankind. No new idols are erected by me; let the old ones learn what feet of clay mean.'[3]

This, at least, is the dominant view of Nietzsche's attitude towards salvation. The fly in the ointment for this interpretation is the *Übermensch*:

But some time, in a stronger age than this mouldy self-doubting present day, he will have to come to us, the redeeming man of great love and contempt, the creative spirit who is pushed out of any position 'outside' or 'beyond' by his surging strength again and again, whose solitude will be misunderstood by the people as though it were a flight from reality –: whereas it is just his way of being immersed in reality so that from it, when he emerges into the light again, he can return with the redemption of this reality: redeem it from the curse which its ideal has placed upon it up till now. This man of the future will redeem us not just from the ideal held up till now, but also from the things which will have to arise from it, from the great nausea, the will to nothingness, from nihilism, that stroke of midday and of great decision which makes the will free again, which gives earth its purpose and man his hope again, this Antichrist and anti-nihilist, this conqueror of God and of nothingness – he must come one day.[4]

How is it possible to square a passage such as this with the idea that Nietzsche's fundamental insight is that those who speak of salvation are being disloyal to their humanity? This is a problem which has exercised a number of Nietzsche scholars who, by and large, have been enthusiastic students of his attack upon soteriology. For Keith Ansell-Pearson 'Nietzsche's yearning for a new humanity can itself be seen as an expression of the nihilistic condition he wishes us to overcome. It reveals a dissatisfaction with the present, with "man", expressing the same kind of negative attitudes, such as revenge and resentment towards life as it is, which characterises the ascetic ideal.'[5] Daniel Conway claims that in this passage Nietzsche is 'betraying a nihilistic commitment to the deficiency of the human condition',[6] and, in the same vein, Maudemarie Clarke condemns the *Übermensch* as an expression of Nietzsche's desire to revenge himself against life.[7] Thus it has become common practice to try to push aside Nietzsche's anticipation of the 'redeeming man' and passages like it. Conway thinks we should not take passages such as this all that seriously. At best this is Nietzsche being ironic, ridiculing our neediness-for-redemption, at worst Nietzsche is simply repeating the mistake that elsewhere he does so much to expose.

But is there really a contradiction between loyalty to one's humanity and the desire for salvation? It depends, of course, on what one means by salvation. For part of the problem with the dominant view that Nietzsche rejects all and every expression of salvation is that it presumes a very restricted model of what constitutes salvation. It is, for instance, potentially misleading to refer to Christian soteriology when there are among Christian thinkers a whole range of different and competing accounts of what salvation involves.[8] There is no doubt that Nietzsche is unreservedly hostile to any conception of salvation that means trading in our humanity for a stake in the hereafter: 'do not believe those who speak to you of super-terrestrial hopes!' he insists.[9] But not all attempts to speak of human salvation invoke the super-terrestrial or seek to break through the constituent boundaries of our humanity. For instance, the paradigm conception of salvation within the Jewish scriptures is the Exodus, an act of liberation from captivity which seeks to express the full worth of the human-all-too-human – a worth that is denied by slavery and is re-established in and through human freedom. Likewise salvation language is used to speak of Jesus healing those who are sick. These are not models of salvation that point us away from human life but, on the contrary, suggest that salvation is to be had by becoming ever more fully human.

Karl Barth, in particular, has insisted that it is a dangerous temptation to regard the limits of our humanity, our finitude, as some sort of lack waiting to be overcome or as something from which we require saving: 'We must divest ourselves of the idea that limitation implies something derogatory or even a kind of curse or affliction' he insists.[10] It is in this same spirit that Barth attacks Fichte for conceiving of the human self as completely without restriction:

> The man of Fichte is from the very first capable of infinite expansion.
> ... Only one thing is lacking to this man: the very thing that he must
> lack because of this infinite abundance. He is poor – inconsolably poor –
> only at the point which constitutes his remarkable wealth. He has no
> limits, he thus lacks the very thing which is proclaimed in the title of
> Fichte's work: a determination.[11]

For Barth, human salvation is not to be had by breaking through the limits of our humanity, instead it is realised in becoming ever more fully human, which for Barth means, ever more fully Christ-like. Christ is the paradigm human: 'Dieser Mensch ist *der* Mensch.' Any salvation that seeks to divest the human being of his or her humanity is, in fact, a denial of the full humanity of Christ. That is to say, for Barth *ressentiment* begins with docetism.

At the very least then, it is not altogether clear that all conceptions of salvation necessarily involve the sort of disloyalty or *ressentiment* with which the notion of the *Übermensch* has also been charged. And the case against the claim that Nietzsche continues to think in terms of redemption is not completed simply by noting his uncompromising this-worldliness. What is needed in order to think further through this problem is a more sophisticated map of the soteriological possibilities.

Internal and external transcendence

Barth's attack upon Fichte has a great deal in common with Nussbaum's description of the weightlessness of the Greek gods touched upon in the previous chapter. Both suggest that the very unlimitedness of their respective subjects is a fundamental poverty: to lack limits is to lack definition, that is, to lack any shape at all; thus it is to be nothing. The price of hubris is non-existence.

For Nussbaum, this means that we should reject the aspiration to become something other than human, even *Über*-human, and give ourselves over, without regret and without remainder, to the human-all-too-human. The hero of this rejection is, for Nussbaum, Odysseus. Odysseus has become shipwrecked on an island ruled over by the goddess Calypso who falls in love with him and, in an attempt to keep him, offers him immortality and eternal youth. If he stays with her on the island he will not be subject to the 'limitations' characteristic of human existence. Odysseus rejects her offer:

> Goddess and queen, do not make this a cause of anger with me. I know the truth of everything that you say. I know that my wise Penelope, when a man looks at her, is far beneath you in form and stature; she is mortal, you are immortal and unageing. Yet, notwithstanding, my desire and longing day by day is still to reach my own home and to see the day of my return. And if this or that divinity should shatter my craft on the wine-dark ocean, I will bear it and keep a brave heart within me. Often enough before this time have war and wave oppressed and plagued me; let new tribulations join the old.[12]

In choosing the riskiness of the 'wine-dark ocean', in choosing the certainty of eventual death over Calypso's world of calm and beauty, 'beyond the reach of death', Odysseus is exhibiting an extraordinary 'loyalty to the earth'. Much of Nussbaum's work can be said to be an attempt to explain why Odysseus has made the right choice.

On one level her point is a logical one. For, as she rightly points out, certain activities only make sense relative to the 'limits' of human forms of life. How would it be possible for the gods to have an athletic contest, for instance, when there are no limitations on their activity? What could such a contest mean, what would it look like when they could transport themselves from one point to another instantaneously and without effort? Indeed the very unlimitedness of these gods means that they are not able to do certain sorts of things that require limit. So too, as we have seen, the gods are unable to love. They are incapable of heroism (not being subject to risk, etc.). No wonder Calypso falls in love with Odysseus: in comparison to his, her own world is cold and lifeless. Like the Augustinian God-head, her world is without life. Calypso's offer is one of disguised death.

But Nussbaum's attack upon the desire to be super-human is not simply a logical one. For, like Nietzsche, Nussbaum believes that the desire to transcend the supposed frailties of the human-all-too-human, a desire nurtured particularly by Christianity, leads to a certain sort of self-hate. Nussbaum is at her most vociferously anti-Christian in her reading of Beckett's *Molloy* trilogy.[13] 'We could summarise the emotion story that is Molloy's life by saying that it is the story of original sin, of the fear of God's judgement, and

of the vain longing for salvation.' Nussbaum continues: *Molloy* is concerned
with 'the particular and highly specific learned tonality that makes the
Christian world of these people a world of highly concrete and distinct form
and feeling, in which the ubiquity of guilt and an anal form of disgust (and
humor) colour every emotion and perception.'[14] The flip side of the Christian
doctrine of salvation is that the world and human life are shit. Molloy speaks
of his mother: 'her who brought me into the world, through the hole in her
arse if my memory is correct. First taste of the shit.'[15] This is Beckett's take
on original sin. For Augustine, sin is transmitted through the sexual act;
Beckett translates this into the idiom of 'shit' and finds that from this shit
there is no escape, no salvation. Indeed, for Nussbaum's Beckett, salvation
and shit each give rise to the other. Nussbaum elaborates Beckett thus:

> So the basic fact in this world, the fact that structures all of its geog-
> raphy, is the fact of the filthiness of conception, the fact that the pregnant
> married woman is by her act wrapped in shit, and the new baby, even
> before it acts and feels, is born into the world through the shit. His
> entire life is lived from then on in shameful proximity to vagina, anus
> and balls. Inasmuch as the child is a child born of a woman, he is
> covered in her filth. Inasmuch as he is a man who feels sexual desire (a
> resident of Bally), he compounds the transgression. His desire is filthy
> because of the original filth and also because it is a desire for the mother,
> who is already seen as covered, herself, in filth. The journey back to the
> mother's room or womb, which might in one way be a project of atone-
> ment, an attempt to cancel the sin of his birth by returning to a fetal
> condition, is, in the light of the sexual desire that motivates it, a guilty
> desire for filthy penetration and a compounding of original guilt ('that
> this atonement was itself a sin, calling for more atonement, and so
> on').[16]

This vision of human life trapped within self-disgust is, for Nussbaum, a
consequence of Christian stories of salvation. The importance of Beckett's
text is that in revealing the connections between shame, self-disgust and the
teaching of redemption he opens up 'a clearing beyond disgust and guilt',
'an acceptance of nature and body that does not ask them to be redeemed by
any beyond'. 'We can be redeemed only by ending the demand for redemption, by ceasing to use the concepts of redemption' she insists. As Stanley
Cavell puts it in an influential reading of Beckett's *Endgame*:

> The greatest endgame is Eschatology, the idea that the last things of
> earth will have an order and a justification, a sense. That is what we
> hoped for, against hope, that is what salvation would look like. Now we
> are to know that salvation lies in reversing the story, in ending the story
> of the end, dismantling Eschatology, ending this world of order in order
> to reverse the curse of the world laid on it in its Judeo-Christian end.

Only a life without hope, meaning, justification, waiting, solution – as we have been shaped by these things – is free from the curse of God.[17]

But, for Nussbaum at least, this is not the end of the story. In the course of a spirited exchange with Charles Taylor, himself a Roman Catholic, Nussbaum concedes that there are indeed forms of transcendence which she admires and wishes to affirm. Nussbaum's heroes, novelists such as Henry James and Marcel Proust, offer versions of what she calls internal transcendence or 'transcending by descent, delving more deeply into one's self and one's humanity, and becoming deeper and more spacious as a result'. And though it goes against many of her instincts – being counted, as Kerr puts it, among those who share the 'Nietzschean hatred of religion'[18] – Nussbaum is nonetheless prepared to see the possibility that Christianity exhibits some aspects of this sort of transcendence: 'For Christianity seems to grant that in order to imagine a god who is truly superior, truly worthy of worship, truly and fully just, we must imagine a god who is human as well as divine, a god who has actually lived out the non-transcendent life and understands it in the only way it can be understood, by suffering and death. If this is what Taylor means when he says that Christianity has turned us back to our own world with new attention and concern, I believe that he is undoubtedly pointing to something important.'[19]

As a young man, and while still a Christian, Nietzsche sought ways of expressing Christian versions of internal transcendence. Nietzsche recognised that the Christian story of salvation could be put in such a way that it did not involve disloyalty to the earth.

That God became man only indicates that man should not search for his blissfulness in infinity, but establish his heaven on earth; the delusion of an extraterrestrial world had brought man's spirituality to a false position regarding this earthly world.[20]

This indicates that Nietzsche recognised that the desire for redemption does not necessarily capitulate to disloyalty to the earth, a point which he is trying to make once more in his anticipation of the *Übermensch* 'whose solitude will be misunderstood as though it were a flight from reality: whereas it is just his way of being immersed in reality so that from it . . . he can return with the redemption of this reality'. Dieser *Übermensch* ist *der* Mensch, to rephrase Barth.

But although the distinction between internal and external transcendence can open up a way of understanding the redemptive activity of the *Übermensch* that does not necessarily contradict Nietzsche's emphasis on remaining true to the earth, this distinction is not an absolute one, and there are degrees of danger. Nussbaum again: 'When does the aspiration to internal transcendence become the aspiration to depart from human life altogether? There is, and should be, no clear answer to this question. Its answer can only be given in and by human history itself, as human beings look at the limits as their own struggles have constituted them.'[21] That is, the dangers of exceeding the legitimate remit of internal transcendence are not laid down in advance – what of the advances in medical science? what of genetic engineering? (note especially that Nietzsche speaks of the *Übermensch* as having to be 'bred') – but are negotiated along an invisible boundary described by 'the claims of excellence, which lead us to push outward, and the necessity of the human context, which pushes us back in'. The athlete who seeks to run ever faster or to throw the discus ever further, is seeking to push outwards the 'limits' of the human, which is clearly a perfectly acceptable form of internal transcendence. But what of performance enhancing drugs? Is that internal or external transcendence? Does the desire to re-form one's body with drugs in such as way that it bears increasingly less and less resemblance to your body or mine constitute a legitimate desire to push out the boundaries of human possibility, or does it encapsulate a dissatisfaction with the human, a sense that to be *simply* human is not enough? The answer is not clear. And nor is it entirely clear with Nietzsche's *Übermensch*. But the danger signs are there, sure enough: 'I teach you the *Übermensch*. Man is something that should be overcome.' And, even more seriously perhaps: 'What is the ape to man? A laughing stock or a painful embarrassment. And man shall be just that for the *Übermensch*.'[22]

Before we conclude too soon that passages such as these are decisive we must position Nietzsche's salvation language within the context of his attack upon Christianity and, more specifically, within the context of his sense that Christianity is an illness from which Western humanity is suffering. Nietzsche's story of the development of Christian soteriology is a story of the development and spread of a particularly pernicious disease. The *Übermensch* is also, as Nietzsche describes him, the 'one of great health' which suggests, of course, internal transcendence. From this perspective Nietzsche is not seeking to redeem us from our humanity, he is seeking to restore our full humanity by redeeming us from the Christian illness. In order to examine more closely the nature of this disease it is time now to turn our attention to Nietzsche's genealogy of Christianity.

Nietzsche's story of Judeo-Christianity

Given what Nietzsche comes to say about Christian belief and the use made of God by the Christian Church, it is surprising to find that he thinks of the 'original' sense of God as something worthy of admiration.

> Originally, above all in the period of the Kingdom, Israel stood in a correct, that is to say natural relationship to all things. Their Yahweh was the expression of their consciousness of power, of their delight in themselves, their hopes of themselves: in him they anticipated victory and salvation, with him they trusted that nature would provide what

the people needed – above all rain. Yahweh is the God of Israel and consequently the God of justice: the logic of every nation that is in power and has a good conscience about it. These two aspects of a nation's self-affirmation find expression in festival worship: it is grateful for the destiny that has raised it on high.[23]

In this 'original' sense God was a focus for a people supremely at ease with itself, a means by which, through the enactment of worship, society was able to offer thanksgiving for its own prosperity. In this context life is affirmed and celebrated. The emphasis for Nietzsche is on the very 'naturalness' of this state of affairs. This is pre-lapsarian religiosity. The problem, however, is that this confident self-affirmation is tied to the fragility of good fortune. The fall from this state of 'healthy' spirituality begins with the Exile, following which a number of crucial theological questions are raised for the first time. How could a God who was the expression of a nation's self-confidence survive the deportation and enslavement of His people? How was it possible for a people in exile to make sense of a God who was so closely associated with the flourishing of their own land? God had to be re-imagined. As Nietzsche suggests 'One altered the conception of him: at this price one retained him.'[24] It is a commonplace for Biblical scholars to note that the dramatic experience of exile radically transformed the theology of the ancient Israelites. For Nietzsche this means that God comes to be defined by enslaved people who seek to express through the notion of God a sense of somewhere or somewhen in which things are better than in reality. God becomes the product of the hopeful imaginings of an enslaved people.

Furthermore God becomes a vehicle for imagined revenge against the slave-masters. Consider, for example, Psalm 137. It begins with the cry of an enslaved and tormented people:

By the waters of Babylon, there we sat down and wept, when we remembered Zion. On the willows there we hung up our lyres. For there our captors required of us songs, and our tormentors, mirth, saying 'Sing us one of the songs of Zion'.

Such circumstances are a breeding-ground for fantasies of violence. Thus the psalmist concludes his lament: 'Happy shall he be who takes your little ones and dashes them against the rock!' Of course, by definition an enslaved people are unable to inflict their desire for violent revenge upon their oppressors. And it is precisely because of this powerlessness that their hatred grows to excessive proportions.

As we know, priests make the most evil enemies – but why? Because they are the most powerless. Out of this powerlessness, their hate swells into something huge and uncanny to a most intellectual and poisonous level.[25]

How then does this hatred express itself given the physical inability of the powerless to inflict violence upon their captors? It becomes sublimated into the divine. God becomes an instrument of revenge – or rather, a vehicle for the fantasies of imagined revenge.

One of the consequences of this transformation of the idea of God is that the former association of God with human flourishing and prosperity comes to be reversed.

> It was the Jews who, rejecting the aristocratic value equation (good = noble = powerful = beautiful = happy = blessed) ventured, with awe inspiring consistency, to bring about a reversal and held it in the teeth of their unfathomable hatred (the hatred of the powerless), saying 'Only those who suffer are good; only the poor, the powerless, the lowly are good; the suffering, the deprived, the sick, the ugly, are the only pious people, the only ones saved, salvation is for them alone, whereas you rich, the noble and powerful, you eternally wicked, cruel, lustful, insatiate, godless, you will be eternally wretched, cursed and damned.[26]

Hence *ressentiment* comes to be built into the very fabric of salvation. Salvation becomes an instrument of violence and revenge. Supporting these conclusions Nietzsche points his reader towards the glee with which certain Christian theologians have described the sufferings of hell. He notes Aquinas' claim that 'The blessed in the heavenly kingdom will see the torment of the damned so that they may even more thoroughly enjoy their own blessedness.'[27] Similar sentiments are expressed by Tertullian:

> What ample breadth of sights there will be then! At which shall one gaze in wonder? At which shall I laugh? At which rejoice? At which exult, when I see so many kings who were proclaimed to have been taken up into heaven, groaning in the deepest darkness. And when I see those governors, persecutors of the Lord's name, melting in the flames more savage than those with which they insolently raged against Christians! . . . I believe that they [these sights] are more pleasing than the circus or both of the enclosures, or than any race track.[28]

Nietzsche concludes that Christianity is inherently vicious; that above the gate of paradise should be written the words 'Eternal hate created me as well'. Indeed it is the terrible genius of Christianity to proclaim and celebrate as love what is basically the product of hate.

One of Nietzsche's most penetrating suggestions is that the hate that is produced by *ressentiment* comes to have a life of its own that is independent of the circumstances of its birth. While incubated by persecution *ressentiment* (partly because it has been so successfully incorporated into the theological imagination and partly because it is a temptation to which human beings readily succumb) is able to mutate so as to adapt to, and successfully operate

in, different circumstances. Consequently *ressentiment* has many manifestations and goes by a number of different disguises. One such mutation
Nietzsche is keen to illuminate is that which commonly occurs in periods of
peace and prosperity. Hatred requires something to hate if it is to survive.
But if we have no enemies who is there left to hate? What happens when
Christianity becomes not the religion of the down-trodden but that of the
establishment, that of the comfortable bourgeoisie? Nietzsche's response is
that without an enemy to hate we come to hate ourselves.

> Lacking external enemies and obstacles, and forced into the oppressive
> narrowness of conformity and custom, man impatiently ripped himself
> apart, persecuted himself, gnawed at himself, gave himself no peace and
> abused himself, this animal who battered himself raw on the bars of his
> cage and who is supposed to be 'tamed'; man full of emptiness and torn
> apart for homesickness for the desert, has to create from within himself
> an adventure, a torture-chamber, an unsafe and hazardous wilderness –
> this fool, this prisoner consumed with longing and despair, became the
> inventor of the 'bad conscience'. With it, however, the worst and most
> insidious illness was introduced, one from which man has not yet recov-
> ered, man's sickness of man, of himself.[29]

This, then, is the sickness Nietzsche wants to treat. Having demonstrated
the ways in which *ressentiment* takes root Nietzsche proceeds to argue that far
from being opposed by the religious establishment, *ressentiment* is harnessed
by it as a source of power. In order to cement their control over this source
of power the 'priests' develop a theology of guilt, sin, and eventually of
forgiveness, which allows them to be the mediators of a complex mechanism
of reward and punishment. The prophets, for instance, respond to the experience of exile by proclaiming that the suffering experienced by Israel represents a punishment for past sins. To claim a special contact with God is to
claim the right to condemn and the authority to be obeyed. Thus Nietzsche
suggests 'By allowing God to judge they themselves judge; by glorifying
God they glorify themselves.'[30] Elsewhere he comments: 'Supreme Law: "God
forgives him who repents" – in plain language: who submits to the priests.'[31]

The suffering established by the internalisation of *ressentiment* provides the
priest and the spiritual guru with his or her *raison d'être*. Without careful
maintenance of that suffering the priest is out of business.

> He brings ointments and balms with him, of course, but first he has to
> wound so that he can be the doctor; and whilst he soothes the pain
> caused by the wound, he poisons the wound at the same time.[32]

Nietzsche's attack upon Christianity is based upon the observation that
Christian salvation, far from being a legitimate means of saving human
beings, actually constitutes much of – and certainly reinforces – their bondage.

Christian soteriology is salvation which damns. It is a charter for cruelty and the degradation of both self and others. And though it offers empowerment to those who are weak and vulnerable it does so in such a way as to secure their dependence and weakness rather than overcome it. It makes a virtue of weakness and vulnerability so as to enslave people into a power structure that is engineered by a religious establishment obsessed with its own control. And just as it amplifies the vulnerability of the vulnerable, by the same token it seeks to weaken those who are not so vulnerable so as to establish appropriate conditions for the dependency of all. 'Christianity desires to dominate beasts of prey; its means of doing so is to make them sick – weakening is the Christian recipe for taming, for "civilization".'[33] Christianity is thus a protection racket of metaphysical proportions. It offers security as the price for acquiescence, and establishes a system of punishment and reward to police the acquiescence of those who submit to its domain.

> What does 'moral world order' mean? That there exists once and for all a will of God as to what man is to do and what he is not to do; the value of a nation, of an individual is to be measured by how much or how little obedience is accorded the will of God; the ruling power of the will of God, expressed as punishment or reward according to the degree of obedience, is demonstrated in the destiny of the nation, of an individual. – The reality displaced by this pitiable lie is: a parasitic kind of human being which prospers only at the expense of every healthy form of life, the priest abuses the name of God: he calls the state of society in which the priest determines the value of things 'the kingdom of God'; he calls the means by which such a state is achieved or perpetuated 'the will of God'; with cold blooded cynicism he assesses nations, epochs, individuals according to whether they were conducive to the rule of priests or whether they resisted it.[34]

Christian theology is simply a product of the Church and a means of its manipulation; a thought-police charged with sustaining human reliance. And this policing is nowhere more effective than when it speaks of redemption: 'the concepts "beyond", "Last Judgement", "immortality of the soul", and "soul" itself are instruments of torture, systems of cruelties by virtue of which the priest becomes master.' An omnipotent, omniscient and omnipresent God 'to whom all hearts are open and from whom no secrets are hid', but who is Himself shrouded in darkness, is the ultimate weapon in maintaining obedience; the dark centre of the panopticon.

What is perhaps surprising about Nietzsche's 'story' is the place he gives to Jesus. Jesus, according to Nietzsche, challenged priestly authority and sought to rid religious observance of *ressentiment*. Jesus attacked the 'Jewish Church' as a corrupt and self-serving organisation whose theology was designed to enhance its own power (a view remarkably similar to Nietzsche's own). His was a 'no uttered towards everything that was priest and theologian'. The message Jesus proclaimed was that the kingdom of heaven was not a distant possibility but a present reality. For Nietzsche Jesus held a fully realised eschatology.

> What are the 'glad tidings'? True life, eternal life is found – it is not promised, it is here, it is within you: as a life lived in love, in love without deduction or exclusion, without distance. Everyone is a child of God – Jesus definitely claims nothing for himself alone – as a child of God everyone is equal to everyone else.[35]

No longer are the conditions for entry to this Kingdom determined by the priestly caste.

> In the entire psychology of the 'Gospel' the concept guilt and punishment is lacking; likewise the concept reward. 'Sin' and any kind of distancing relationship between God and man, is abolished – precisely this is the 'glad tidings'. Blessedness is not promised, it is not tied to any conditions: it is the only reality – the rest is signs for speaking of it.[36]

Nietzsche believed that Jesus threatened to put the priests out of business – 'He no longer required any formulas, any rites for communicating with God' – and that is why they murdered him. But they did worse than crucify him, they inverted his message. The Church came to be formed 'out of the antithesis of the Gospel'.

The architect of this reversal, indeed the founder of Christianity itself was Paul. Whereas Nietzsche is keen to find in Jesus a kindred spirit, Paul represents all that Nietzsche despises in Christianity. With Paul *ressentiment* once again came to dominate the construction of the theological landscape; Paul was 'a genius of hatred'.

> His requirement was power; with Paul the priest again sought power – he could employ only those concepts, teachings, symbols, with which one tyrannises over masses, forms herds . . . The invention of Paul, his means for establishing a priestly tyranny, for forming herds: the belief in immortality – that is to say the doctrine of judgment.[37]

Paul redefined the life and death of Jesus in such a way as to bring about maximum human subservience. The cross became a symbol not of liberation, but of guilt and shame. Whereas Jesus sought to free his disciples from their dependence upon the intricacies of 'religion', Paul's genius was to twist this teaching in such a way that Jesus' followers were encouraged to bow down before Jesus himself, thus perpetuating the very bowing down that Jesus sought to eliminate.

The enraged reverence of those utterly unhinged souls could no longer endure the evangelic equal right of everyone to be a child of God which Jesus had taught, and their revenge consisted in exalting Jesus in an extravagant fashion, in severing him from themselves: just as the same Jews in an extravagant fashion, in revenge on themselves, had previously separated their God from themselves and raised him on high.[38]

In Nietzsche's history Jesus sought a return to that 'original' and 'natural' relationship between God and humanity. For Jesus worship was, once again, an expression of thankfulness and abundance of life. Through Paul worship becomes 'we-are-not-worthy' obsequiousness. Once again the priest is able to hijack a healthy spirituality in his own lust for power.

Suffering and the ascetic ideal

A community infused with *ressentiment* is dangerously unstable; nurtured by hate it remains in constant danger of ripping itself apart. 'For every sufferer instinctively looks for a cause of his distress, more exactly, for a culprit.'[39] And if there is no obvious candidate outside that society then the sufferer looks for one closer to home.

> The sufferers, one and all, are frighteningly willing and inventive in their pretexts for painful emotions; they even enjoy being mistrustful and dwelling on wrongs and imagined slights: they rummage through the bowels of their past and present for obscure, questionable stories which will allow them to wallow in tortured suspicion, and intoxicate them with their own poisonous wickedness – they rip open the oldest wounds and make themselves bleed to death from scars long-since healed, they make evil-doers out of friend, wife, child, and anyone else near them.[40]

A society thus constituted requires a careful and comprehensive political management if it is not to disintegrate completely. The trick achieved by the priest, Nietzsche suggests, is to re-focus *ressentiment* in such a way that society no longer presents a threat to itself.

> Actually he defends his sick herd well enough, this strange shepherd, – he even defends it against itself and against the wickedness, deceit, malice, and everything else characteristic of those who are diseased and sick, all of which smolders in the heart itself, he carries out a clever, hard and secret struggle against anarchy and the ever-present threat of internal disintegration of the herd, where that most dangerous and explosive of blasting materials, *ressentiment*, continually piles up. His particular trick is to detonate this explosive material without blowing up either the herd or the shepherd.[41]

Thus the priest is the 'direction changer of *ressentiment*', channelling blame away from those around and back onto the sufferer himself. The priest concurs with the sufferer (of whom he is one) about the need to blame but, with the construction of the notion of 'sin', points the blame back at the sufferer. In this way the priest 'solves' a number of different problems at the same time.

Politically, of course, to convince others that they are responsible for their own suffering is to find a way of preserving society. And this enables the Church to make itself indispensable to the authorities, thus securing its own power. But, more fundamentally, Christianity recommends itself by providing an answer to the question of why we suffer. This, for Nietzsche, is crucial in understanding the attraction of Christianity. Suffering *per se* is not itself the principal cause of humanity's greatest distress, but rather the idea that suffering is pointless, that it is gratuitous and meaningless. Without meaning suffering pushes human beings towards suicide. But if that suffering could be shown to have a purpose, to play a part in a wider scheme of things, then the threat of suicide is abated and human beings can be persuaded to celebrate their own pain as a necessary pathway to salvation. Indeed it doesn't even really matter what sort of meaning is attached to suffering, or what part it plays in the wider scheme, just as long as it points beyond the pain. Just as long as the pain is imagined as having a point, then it is bearable.

But being so keen to hear the message that suffering is purposeful we have failed to notice the consequences of accepting the Christian answer, for what that answer brings with it is an intensification of pain, a new sort of suffering, more damaging than the first, a 'deeper, more internal, more poisonous suffering'. This internal pain has a range of expressions, though its most common are self-loathing and self-flagellation. Being responsible for our own suffering we become our own torturers. We have accepted the logic of Eliphaz, Bildad and Zophar; we are responsible for our own suffering and we must repent 'in dust and ashes'. We must deny ourselves sex, food, even happiness, in the desperate desire to create the conditions for our redemption. And Christian imagery, not least that of Christ's crucifixion, serves to strengthen the link between suffering and redemption. Read from the perspective of the ascetic ideal the cross speaks of the necessity and desirability of torture, that Christ's pain (and therefore our own) is something to be admired. The price paid for accepting the Christian meaning to suffering turns out to be self-flagellation, and such is our desperate desire for 'meaning' that we prefer a religion of self-hate to no religion at all.

In one sense, then, the ascetic ideal is a response to the problems posed by *ressentiment* and a means by which human beings are able to live with the pain of existence (in this way, Nietzsche admits, the ascetic ideal is a means for the 'preservation of life') but by seeking the answer in self-denial the ascetic ideal transforms *ressentiment* into something wholly hostile to life. This is what Nietzsche means when he speaks of the doctor being at the same time also the poisoner.

Avoiding pain

A preliminary conclusion to the question of Nietzsche's use of soteriological imagery can now be advanced. Salvation, for Nietzsche, is about healing (and as such can be counted, it seems, as a form of 'internal transcendence'). Humanity suffers from a disease brought about by a misplaced attempt to ameliorate suffering with the imagined comforts of Christian redemption. But the Christian 'doctor' hooked his patient on the medicine and secured his authority by controlling its supply. And just as it is for the junkie, the pain of addiction comes to be far worse than the pain from which the narcotic promised initial release; the logic of which is to initiate and sustain a vicious circle of dependence in which more 'medicine' is required to deal with the ever increasing pain that is produced by it. This is the sort of circle in which Nietzsche believes human beings have become trapped. The death of God is the beginning of cold-turkey. 'Has it not become colder?' the madman asks. 'Is not night continually closing in on us?'

Nietzsche knew a great deal about the experience of living in constant pain and was severely ill most of his life. As a boy he was 'constantly troubled by shifting headaches' as his school report puts it. From childhood onwards Nietzsche would spend long periods of time, sometimes days, incapacitated by migraines. Of his sight he noted: 'Condition of the eyes, sometimes approaching dangerously close to blindness.'[42] He also had considerable stomach problems which explains his obsession with food and diet. Some have diagnosed his condition as syphilis caught from visiting prostitutes while a student and made worse by diphtheria and dysentery contracted during his time as a medical orderly in the Franco-Prussian war. Others have claimed that he suffered from an inherited brain disorder of the sort that killed his father. Whatever it was, the symptoms were, at times, almost unbearable and it is clear that from about 1875 onwards Nietzsche was little more than an invalid. And though for the most part Nietzsche seeks to present himself as an 'affirmer', as one who says 'yes' to life, there are times, particularly in his letters to friends, when he reveals an altogether different side of his character. He writes to Malwida von Meysenburg:

> My life's terrible and unremitting martyrdom makes me thirst for the end, and there have been some signs that the stroke that will liberate me is not too distant.[43]

In the next year he wrote to his friend Overbeck:

> Pain is vanquishing my life and my will. What months, what a summer I have had! My physical agonies were as many and varied as the changes in the sky . . . Five times I have called for Doctor Death, and yesterday I hoped it was the end – but in vain.[44]

During these 'sleepless, tormented nights' Nietzsche contemplated suicide. In a telling aphorism in *Beyond Good and Evil* he comments: 'The thought of suicide is a powerful solace: by means of it one gets through many a bad night.'[45] From 1883 Nietzsche was regularly depressed. He was forever falling out with his friends, and subsequently became increasingly isolated and lonely. His love-life was a disaster. In a letter to Erwin Rohde he wrote 'I have now forty-three years behind me and I am just as alone as I was when a child.'[46] Alone, sick, unloved and unsung – Nietzsche knew the temptations of *ressentiment*.

Arthur Danto develops an interpretation of Nietzsche's attack upon Christianity (and its 'spiritual' relatives) that claims Nietzsche's aim in writing a book such as *On the Genealogy of Morals* – 'a medical book: etiological, diagnostic, therapeutic, prognostic'[47] – is to release the patient from the grip of unnecessary suffering. In forwarding this analysis Danto makes what has come to be an oft-cited distinction between extensional and intensional suffering. Asking 'what sort of disease' the book was designed to deal with, Danto continues:

> I think the answer must lie in a distinction between what I shall term extensional and intensional suffering, where the latter consists in an interpretation of the former. As I see Nietzsche's thesis, it is this: the main suffering human beings have throughout history been subject to is due to certain interpretative responses to the fact of extensional suffering. It is not clear that Nietzsche thinks he can deal with extensional suffering. But he can deal with intensional suffering, thus helping reduce, often to a significant factor, the total suffering of the world.[48]

The example Danto gives to illustrate this liberation from unnecessary suffering is something of a give-away. Impotence, he claims, causes a great deal of pain for men and those sexually involved with them; 'it can lead, it does lead, to suicide, depression, despair and divorce'. In itself, however, the inability to get an erection is hardly all that serious, and compared to all sorts of other medical problems 'a flaccid penis seems pretty minor'. The problem, Danto seems to be saying, the unnecessary suffering generated by impotence, is a consequence of a particular evaluation of sexual activity. If we were able to rid ourselves of this particular evaluation then a flaccid penis would be simply that; it would generate no intensional suffering. Danto thinks this is a 'good example of moralised physiology' of the sort attacked by Nietzsche. If only we could view suffering as a brute fact, and not place it within some interpretative matrix (such as Christianity) which serves only to make things worse. Conway sums up what follows from Danto's argument:

> Although Nietzsche can do little to reduce the level of extensional suffering in the world, and in no events exhibits any inclination to do

so, he can perhaps eliminate some degree of intensional suffering by providing an alternative, non-moral interpretation of extensional suffering. Drawing on Danto's distinction we characterise the goal of Nietzsche's critical philosophy as the elimination of surplus suffering engendered by Western morality.[49]

This then is 'salvation': to accept the total meaninglessness of life. Danto speaks of 'what is essentially the most liberating thought imaginable, that life is without meaning'. Only thus is 'unnecessary' suffering expunged.

But isn't this simply a clever way of rephrasing the defeatist advice: if you don't care about anything you cannot get hurt? For it is presumably the case that the impotent man is able to rid his life of intensional suffering by ceasing to care about sexual activity. That is, he can avoid unnecessary pain by refusing to value sex. But why stop there? Why not refuse to value other people, why not refuse to value relationships or families or community, etc.? By so doing you will open yourself to less intensional suffering. Indeed it doesn't even matter what one chooses to count as valuable: to value something at all, whatever it is, opens one up to intensional suffering.

Danto's position is odd for a number of reasons. It is surely extremely odd to characterise Nietzsche as a liberal humanitarian (almost a utilitarian!) concerned, above all, with limiting the amount of pain and suffering in the world. Odd, not least because it is precisely this instinct that Nietzsche believes responsible for *ressentiment*. What is wrong with Christianity, as far as Nietzsche is concerned, is that it is created out of a failure to stand ground in the face of suffering. Religion that is pathological (and, for Nietzsche, not all religion is pathological – he, for instance, proclaims himself as a follower of the god Dionysus) is so precisely because it has sought to re-define itself so as to compensate its adherents for their sufferings. If only the original folk-religion, as Nietzsche imagined it, could have remained unaffected by the experience of exile. But it capitulated to those who sought solace and escape from the pain of captivity. This capitulation marked the beginning of the end, for it is precisely the desire to minimise suffering at all costs, to make the minimisation of suffering a fundamental dimension of one's life policy, that leads to pathological religion. And just as it can lead to pathological religion, it can lead to pathological humanism just the same. Of course, part of Nietzsche's critique of this desire to escape suffering at all costs is to argue that Christianity is unsuccessful in lessening suffering and that, in terms of suffering, it actually makes things worse rather than better (and I think the same is true of Danto's policy as well). But this is an *ad hominem* point contra Christianity. The main problem is that Christian values are created by cowardice and that they inscribe cowardice and fearfulness into the very heart of our world view.

The higher man is distinguished from the lower by his fearlessness and his readiness to challenge misfortune: it is a sign of degeneration when eudaemonistic valuations begin to prevail (– physiological fatigue, feebleness of will –). Christianity, with its perspective 'blessedness,' is a mode of thought typical of a suffering and feeble species of man. Abundant strength wants to create, suffer, go under.[50]

If the fear of suffering is so great that the avoidance of it becomes a defining part of one's evaluative scheme, then that scheme is infected with cowardice. Indeed this is the very nature of *ressentiment*. Going back to the case of the impotent man; his 'decision' to cease to care about sexual activity (and how can you just decide something like that?) is a re-evaluation of the world motivated by the desire to avoid suffering at all costs. And, just as it is with the religious equivalent of this policy, we suspect that this person is storing up for himself a great deal more suffering than he supposedly avoids by (somehow) declaring sex to be unimportant. In this instance a Christian writer such as Simone Weil is much closer to Nietzsche when she writes: 'We should seek neither to escape suffering nor to suffer less, but to remain untainted by suffering.'[51]

The key passage that demonstrates that Nietzsche and Danto are, in fact, on opposite sides of the argument is GM III: 17. Nietzsche and Christianity (and Danto) begin with the recognition of human sickness and see their fundamental task as bound up with responding to that sickness. The difference, as Nietzsche sees it, between his approach and the Christian approach, is that Christianity is concerned simply with the reduction of pain and not with seeking to address the fundamental causes of human pain.

> It is only suffering itself, the discomfort of the sufferer, that he combats, not its cause, not the actual state of being ill – this must constitute our fundamental objection to priestly medication.[52]

As we shall see, Nietzsche is not recommending tackling the cause of the illness so as to eliminate the pain all the more effectively. Indeed Nietzsche's conception of health is not of a pain-free state – on the contrary, he sees pain as a necessary constituent of great health. Rather it is the Christian policy that seeks anesthesia. And not just Christianity, so too Buddhism: both are fundamentally about blocking out pain and persuading people that the absence of pain is the same as salvation. Thus Nietzsche speaks disparagingly of 'the supreme state, that of salvation itself' as being a 'state of total hypnosis and tranquility'. And, linking the desire for this condition with the world-weariness of the sick he comments: 'The hypnotic feeling of nothingness, the tranquility of the deepest sleep, in short the absence of suffering – this may be counted as the highest good, the value of values, by the suffering and by those who are deeply depressed.' Those who are after genuine health must seek beyond the promises of anesthesia which weaken the spirit and eventually turn people into cabbages. This, then, is yet another proof of Christian 'Egyptianism'.

Indeed not only does Nietzsche believe pain to have a important part to play, at times he suggests that sickness itself is a necessary prerequisite of health. Traditionally health is defined negatively as the absence of sickness: you are healthy if nothing is wrong with you. Health, thus understood, is a neutral condition, some sort of golden mean achieved by moderation and the avoidance of excess. The position Nietzsche comes to in reflecting extensively on the nature of health is that health is demonstrated in the way one deals with one's own sickness, and not in the absence of sickness. Health is a quality of the way in which one is able to transcend the experience of suffering and pain.[53] Sickness itself is, or at least can be, a stimulant to 'great health'. Writing in the preface to the second edition of *The Gay Science*, Nietzsche reflects back upon a period of severe sickness that preceded the writing of the book:

> You see I do not want to take leave ungratefully from that time of severe sickness whose profits I have not yet exhausted even today. I am very conscious of the advantages that my fickle health gives me over more robust squares . . . Life – that means for us constantly transforming all that we are into light and flame – also everything that wounds us; we simply can do no other. And as for sickness: are we not almost tempted to ask whether we could get along without it.[54]

Genealogy, sickness and health

As Nietzsche himself became ever more ill, so his interest in questions of health and sickness became ever more obsessive (see, for example, the opening passages of *Ecce Homo*). Malcolm Pasley has gone so far as to claim:

> After 1875 . . . matters of health and sickness become themselves a main object of his reflections, and medical or pseudo-medical categories come to furnish the very framework of his thinking. Indeed by the final stage, by 1888, one can almost say that there are no other topics, that the question of health has swallowed up everything else.[55]

One question immediately suggests itself: does Nietzsche simply replace criteria such as 'good' or 'true' – concepts which have been traditionally used to discriminate between various 'perspectives' – with a semi-moralised notion of health? That is, is 'health' the foundational value against which differing approaches to the world are judged and evaluated?

Here again, Nussbaum makes a useful guide. In her interesting book *The Therapy of Desire*, Nussbaum describes the centrality of what she calls 'therapeutic arguments' in the philosophy of a number of different schools of Hellenistic philosophy.[56] Her thesis is simple: many ancient philosophers saw the purpose of philosophical activity as being to promote 'health'; philosophy, many of the Greeks believed, was healing by argument. Hence Epicurus:

Empty is that philosopher's argument by which no human suffering is therapeutically treated. For just as there is no use in a medical art that does not cast out the sicknesses of bodies, so too there is no use in philosophy, unless it casts out the suffering of the soul.[57]

It makes a good deal of sense to see Nietzsche's development of genealogy being inspired, to some degree, by the medical analogy popular among the ancients. For here is a way of discussing value, a way of discriminating between various positions which does not appeal to notions of good and evil, and which seeks neither praise nor blame. By the time of writing *The Twilight of the Idols* in 1888 Nietzsche has come to a settled position on the function of what he calls 'symptomatology'.

Judgments of value, concerning life, for or against it, can in the end never be true, they have value only as symptoms, they are worthy of consideration only as symptoms, in themselves such judgments are stupidities.[58]

It could be argued, therefore, that the genealogical technique developed by Nietzsche is the philosophical equivalent of seeking to uncover one's medical history. His diagnosis of the state of European cultural health is based upon a keen eye for symptoms of decay and an awareness of the hereditary weaknesses to which that culture is prone.

Nietzsche's fascination with health and sickness was not unique among thinkers of the nineteenth century. Developments in scientific medicine, in bacteriology, the fascination with eugenics, the building of hundreds of hospitals (by the end of the nineteenth century Germany had more hospitals than any other country in the world), the increasing professionalisation of medicine all contributed to establishing issues of medicine and health at the very top of the cultural agenda. To many it seemed that the same ideas Darwin had applied with such success to biology could well be applied, and with equal success, to society in general. Paul Weindling, in his major study of late nineteenth- and early twentieth-century German attitudes to sickness and health, describes this use, reminding us of the ancient appeal to the 'social organism' and 'body politic':

Scientifically educated experts acquired a directing role as prescribers of social policies and personal lifestyle. The scientific creeds of Social Darwinism and eugenics offered general models for constructing an ordered and developing society. As such, science and medicine provided an alternative to party politics, by forming a basis for collectivist social policies to remedy social ills . . . The concept of a fit and healthy social organism provided a means for realising renewed stability, social integration and national power.[59]

Thus biology is given a significant moral and political charge. But unlike the progressivist message of the social Darwinists, Nietzsche's approach is to be counted among those who drew very different conclusions from this new thinking. For although Nietzsche's genealogical technique can be seen as applying the perspective of heredity to philosophical discourse, his conclusion was not that society was strengthening but rather that it was weakening. *On the Genealogy of Morals* is Nietzsche's attempt to prove the survival of the weakest, not the survival of the fittest. Again, elsewhere he writes:

> Anti-Darwin. – What surprises me most when I survey the broad destinies of man is that I always see before me the opposite of what Darwin and his school see or want to see today: selection in favour of the stronger, better-constituted, and the progress of the species. Precisely the opposite is palpable: the elimination of the lucky strokes, the uselessness of the more highly developed types, the inevitable domination of the average, even sub-average types . . . Strange though it may sound, one has always to defend the strong against the weak; the fortunate against the unfortunate, the healthy against those who are degenerating and afflicted with hereditary taints.[60]

Again, in forwarding this analysis Nietzsche was not alone. A great deal of middle to late nineteenth-century literature was obsessed with proving and investigating degeneracy. Nietzsche's *On the Genealogy of Morals* can be categorised alongside the likes of Morel's *Treatise*, Lombroso's *Criminal Man*, Maudsley's *Body and Will*, Lankester's *Degeneration*, Krafft-Ebing's *Psychopathia Sexualis* and Nordeau's *Degeneration*, all of which were concerned to demonstrate the workings of cultural degeneracy.[61]

Degeneracy, for Nietzsche, is a consequence of what he calls anti-natural morality. The values of the healthy arise out of the natural world and are bent upon the affirmation of life. Like the spirituality of the 'original' religious instinct described in *The Anti-Christ* the healthy are at one with their environment and with the biological and physiological constitution of the human. Physicality is not seen as a lack but as something to be celebrated. Thus physical strength is prized and valued, whereas for degenerate anti-natural morality physical strength is demeaned. Anti-natural morality is the morality of those who seek to redefine value in such a way that value promotes the cause of the weak and fearful; these are the enemies of health for they inscribe within our systems of evaluation a promotion of anti-naturalism. Nietzsche sums up all this thinking in an important aphorism in *Twilight of the Idols*:

> I formulate a principle. All naturalism in morality, that is all healthy morality, is dominated by an instinct of life – some commandment of life is fulfilled through a certain canon of 'shall' and 'shall not', some

hindrance and hostile element on life's road is thereby removed. Anti-natural morality . . . turns on the contrary precisely against the instincts of life . . . Life is at an end where the 'kingdom of God' begins.[62]

The extraordinary thing about passages such as this is that they give the impression that concepts such as 'life' or 'nature' function for Nietzsche as points of moral reference. Commentators who are committed to the perspectivist Nietzsche find this privileging of the healthy or natural perspective an uncomfortable blemish on Nietzsche's otherwise impeccable relativism instigated by his attack upon 'truth'. For surely this appeal to the natural considerably damages Nietzsche's standing as the godfather of post-modernity?[63]

What then is the nature of the natural? What is this 'life' against which our moral values must be aligned? Before the fall Adam and Eve wandered in the garden of Eden, living off the garden, at one with their own naked humanity and at one with the abundance of life with which they were surrounded. Christian soteriology has been continually influenced by the idea that salvation is constituted by a return to the condition enjoyed by Adam and Eve – a return to how things were before the fall, a return to nature. So does Nietzsche see nature in anything like this way? No, for as we have already seen in reflecting upon his commitment to Silenian wisdom, Nietzsche conceives of reality as something hostile and exploitative. And likewise with 'nature' and 'life':

> Everywhere people are now raving, even under scientific disguises, about coming conditions of society in which 'the exploitative aspect' will be removed – which sounds to me as if they promised to invent a way of life that would dispense with all organic functions. 'Exploitation' does not belong to a corrupt or imperfect and primitive society, it belongs to the essence of what lives, as a basic organic function; it is a consequence of the will to power, which is after all the will of life.[64]

Likewise in *On the Genealogy of Morals* he comments: 'life operates essentially, that is in its basic functions, through injury, assault, exploitation, destruction and simply cannot be thought of at all without this character.'[65] This, then, is the principal reason why giving the avoidance of pain a determining function in one's life-policy is, for Nietzsche, always going to lead to anti-naturalism and life-denial. For life is painful and the only way to get rid of pain is to get rid of life: hence salvation as anesthesia. The fundamental reality of human existence is conflictual and mutually antagonistic. Life is the will-to-power and nothing else besides.

It is because of this that a number of scholars have argued that Nietzsche's fundamental ontology, his appeal to 'life', supports and justifies a politics of violent exploitation that prefigures and, to some degree, prepares the way for, the political rhetoric of Nazism. Thus, for instance, Warren claims:

Nietzsche explicitly claims that political exploitation can be deduced as necessary to any society from the fact that life is essentially the will to power . . . there is no mistaking Nietzsche's point: exploitation of one person by another is ontologically rooted in life as such. Exploitative social relations can be removed from society only at the expense of 'life'. Since 'life' is at the source of value, it follows that political exploitation is both natural and even desirable.[66]

Likewise John Milbank accuses Nietzsche of succumbing to a myth of 'ontological violence'.[67] Wayne Klein has sought to exonerate Nietzsche from this charge by arguing that Warren presumes Nietzsche to be advocating a naive version of ethical naturalism, as if Nietzsche was simply advocating reading off values from a bloody and hostile nature, thus generating a bloody and hostile ethics. Klein, more comfortable with the anti-metaphysical Nietzsche for whom no perspective is privileged, points out that there is some evidence (though not all that much, it has to be said) that Nietzsche thinks of nature as itself something constructed. That is: nature is not altogether 'natural'.[68] So, for instance, Nietzsche distances himself from Rousseau's understanding of a 'return to nature': 'Rousseau . . . preached a "return to nature" – to what did he actually want to go back? I speak of a return to nature although it is not actually a "return back", but an "advance towards".'[69] And again: 'Not "return to nature" for there has never been a natural humanity.'[70] Nature, then, is not an objective given to which the healthy are rightly aligned. Rather it is, somehow, a product of the quest for health as much as a point of departure.

But exonerating Nietzsche from the charge of promoting a conflictual and antagonistic ontology is not secured by questioning the reliability of the ascription 'metaphysical' or 'ontological'. For even if those who believe in Nietzsche the post-modernist are right and there is no fundamental metaphysical base to Nietzsche's ethical sensibility, it remains the case that he promotes a *mythology* of conflict and antagonism which he prefers to one of peace. Milbank, for instance, does not seek to challenge Nietzsche by claiming a metaphysical foundation for his position, 'but one can try to put forward an alternative mythos, equally unfounded, but nonetheless embodying an "ontology of peace", which conceives of differences as analogically related, rather than equivocally at variance'.[71] Accusing Nietzschean post-modernism of the very crime that it has levelled with such alacrity at all else, namely succumbing to the false logic of the dialectic, Milbank offers his own Christian *mythos* on (the post-modernist) Nietzsche's own terms:

Yet does one need to interpret every disturbance, every event, as an event of war? Only, I would argue, if one has transcendentally understood all differences as negatively related, if, in other words, one has allowed a dialectical element to intrude into one's differential philosophy . . . To argue that the natural act might be the Christian, (supernatural) charitable act, and not the will-to-power, is therefore to argue that such an 'analogical relation' is as possible a transcendental conception as the positing of an *a priori* warfare. And what is more, the former conception permits a *purer* 'positivism', a purer philosophy of difference, still less contaminated by dialectics.[72]

For Nietzsche the problem with the Christian account of salvation is that it represents a retreat from the dynamic and the vital. This may be so, but to acknowledge that many of Nietzsche's attacks upon Christianity are successful is one thing; to agree with his alternative scheme quite another. The way Nietzsche presents his genealogy one could be forgiven for presuming there are only two 'lifestyle choices'. One can become a Christian ascetic, morbid and life-denying, or one can be a hero – a Polish cavalry officer, a Homeric nobleman, a Julius Caesar-type, a Napoleon-type, take your pick. And, as Milbank puts it, 'Nietzsche is not able to demonstrate that such a taste is more primordially lodged in human existence than the despised desires for security, consolation, mutuality, pleasure and contentment.'[73] And though Nietzsche is able to illustrate that such values are never wholly innocent, he is manifestly unwilling to turn the powerful lens of his suspicion upon his own chosen values. How would they fare under such scrutiny? Isn't *ressentiment* to be found here too?

There is a children's TV programme called *Mr. Benn* in which a bored accountant-type visits a magical costume shop. Having tried on whatever exotic costume takes his fancy Mr. Benn goes through a magical door and proceeds to have an adventure as the character whose costume he has chosen – pirate, soldier, explorer, etc. We don't know much else about Mr. Benn's life other than what we find out through his visits to the costume shop. But he does go to the shop a great deal, and it seems fair enough to say that these fantasy adventures, these little holidays, dominate his life. How indeed could the ordinary pleasures of life like a nice walk or a meal with loved ones compare with navigating the Yangtse or fighting off hordes of Zulus at Rorke's Drift? But couldn't we speak of a *ressentiment* against life here as well – not, admittedly *ressentiment* against 'life' as Nietzsche understands it, but *ressentiment* against 'ordinary' life, a disparagement of the familiar and the everyday?

Of course, some may argue that holding up the everyday and the ordinary in this way can become a pretext for repression and a failure of ambition. Why can't one go off and navigate the Yangtse? Moreover, one of the things that has been learned from the post-modernist Nietzsche is that these ordinary and familiar realities – ordinary life – are themselves constructed. Our way of life is not privileged over others or justified by metaphysical foundations. Human life is much more plastic than we have been led to believe; the moral of which is that, given sufficient strength and ingenuity, you can re-invent yourself as you wish.

The problem with this line is that it has come to blur the distinction between fantasy and 'reality', and though we might have learned to put 'reality' in brackets, acknowledging its partial (or even total) human constructedness,[74] such a recognition ought not to obviate the important difference between what is fantasy and what is not. The problem with Nietzsche-the-post-modernist (that is, the Nietzsche who champions the idea that truth is made and not found) is that he has erased the doorway in the shopkeeper's magic shop. *But Nietzsche was not a Polish cavalry officer.* And philosophy, particularly philosophy that tackles important subjects such as warfare and human suffering, should not be conducted in fancy dress.

Nietzsche's imagination forged numerous identities for him to try on. Nietzsche returned throughout his writings to what he called 'the problem of the actor'. In the latter stages of his life he began to sign himself in letters to friends 'Dionysus' and 'Christ' and 'The Crucified'. And although these 'delusions' are taken as symptoms of what was to cause his subsequent mental collapse, Nietzsche had for a long time experimented with fantasy identities; indeed he was to say of his 'dissembling' and his 'ability to transform himself' that it constituted 'a flaw in his character'.[75] A social misfit, Nietzsche drew comfort from the idea that he was a great warrior spirit. And, from this perspective, his attack upon peace, his attack upon mutuality and caring for the weak, can be interpreted as revenge against that world in which he could not find a place.[76] However, the real problem with Nietzsche's dispensation to fantasy is not that it reveals him as a sad and sorry misfit, but rather, that a number of his most important philosophical discussions are distorted by their proximity to his fantasy life and are thereby rendered extremely shallow. Nowhere is this more true than in Nietzsche's depiction of pain and suffering.

For despite all his dazzling rhetoric about the abyss and so on, the suffering Nietzsche speaks of is highly selective and celebrates a particular aesthetic of pain rather than pain itself. Nussbaum, for instance, accuses Nietzsche of having a specifically bourgeois conception of pain (a suggestion that would have been deeply threatening for Nietzsche):

> We might say, simplifying things a bit, that there are two sorts of vulnerability: what we might call bourgeois vulnerability – for example, the pains of solitude, loneliness, bad reputation, some ill health, pains that are painful enough but still compatible with thinking and doing philosophy – and what we might call basic vulnerability, which is the deprivation of resources so central to human functioning that thought and character are themselves impaired and not developed. Nietzsche focuses on the first sort of vulnerability, holds that it is not so bad; it may even be good for the philosopher. The second sort, I claim, he merely neglects.[77]

Nussbaum argues that, for all Nietzsche's posturing about the needs and importance of the body and the physical, he fails to notice the obvious; basic bodily needs, and the pains associated with such needs not being met. What does Nietzsche have to say about hunger? about being cold? about homelessness? about earning a living or bringing up a family? 'Who provides basic welfare support for Zarathustra? What are the "higher men" doing all the day long? The reader does not know and the author does not seem to care.'[78] All of this, one might say, develops out of a *ressentiment* against 'ordinary' life. Nussbaum concludes:

> Nietzsche is really, all along, despite all his famous unhappiness, too much like the 'famous wise men': an armchair philosopher of human riskiness, living with no manual labour and three meals a day, without inner understanding of the ways in which contingency matters for virtue.[79]

Like Mr. Benn's adventures, Nietzsche's philosophy is philosophy gone on holiday (to echo Wittgenstein). The 'armchair philosopher of human riskiness' is too content to develop a soteriology to suit the virtual reality of his fantasy life.

In a postscript to his exploration of Nietzsche's understanding of the bio-positive nature of illness David Farrell Krell, himself a Nietzsche enthusiast, speculates that since the outbreak of AIDS Nietzsche's celebration of illness as the engine of great health looks like the sentimental (fantasy) imaginings of one for whom the destructive power of illness was never fully appreciated. 'We never dreamt that when Nietzsche's Zarathustra said "The human being is something that must be overcome" a highly mobile virus was preparing to undertake this task quite literally, as though it missed the metaphor.' He concludes:

> The death of God never troubled us, because we believed that God died so that Eros might live. Now that Eros is in its final throes, not merely poisoned by the culture of Christendom but in our secular and infectious age administered the lethal dose, one wonders what could possibly keep Thanatos at bay a while longer, what could possibly prolong the detour that is leading us to endless stasis by one more turn, one more round.[80]

If there is anything that can reinstate the distinction between fantasy and reality it is this. Naming a suffering such as AIDS provides a 'reality check' on Nietzsche's soteriological aspirations. For the idea of the *Übermensch*-as-redeemer may seem plausible from within the fantasy world of Nietzsche's adventures, but would one trust the *Übermensch* to shoulder the horrors of AIDS? Or is Nietzsche simply trying on costumes in the shopkeeper's magic shop? Isn't Zarathustra himself simply yet another costume? In just the same way one really wonders: isn't Nietzsche's preference for a *mythos* of war rather than a *mythos* of peace only possible for one who has not fully experienced the horrors of the battlefield, let alone those of mustard gas, carpet bombing or nuclear weapons?[81] And though, calling to mind his time as a medical orderly, he certainly came closer to war (for three weeks in 1870) than I ever have,[82] I suspect that Nietzsche's celebration of war and conflict was shaped far more by his adolescent fencing games conducted while a member of the student fraternity Franconia.[83] Consider the story of how he acquired his duelling scar. Having met a boy from a rival fraternity in the town square 'We had a very animated conversation about all things, artistic and literary, and when we were saying goodbye, I asked him in the politest way to duel with me.' The fight was described thus:

> They locked swords, and the glinting blades danced around their unprotected heads. It scarcely lasted three minutes, and Nietzsche's opponent managed to cut a low carte at the bridge of his nose, hitting the exact spot where his spectacles, pressing down too heavily, had left a red mark. Blood trickled to the ground, and the experts agreed that past events had been satisfactorily expiated. I packed my well-bandaged friend into a carriage, took him home to bed, assiduously comforted him, forbade him visits and alcohol. Within two or three days our hero had fully recovered, except for a small slanting scar across the bridge of his nose, which remained there throughout his life and did not look at all bad on him.[84]

5 Parables of innocence and judgement

The Pilgrim way has led to the Abyss.
Was it to meet such grinning evidence
We left our richly adorned ignorance?
Was the triumphant answer to be this?
The Pilgrim Way has led to the Abyss.

We who must die demand a miracle.
How could the eternal do a temporal act.
The Infinite become a finite fact?
Nothing can save us that is possible:
We who must die demand a miracle.
W.H. Auden, For the Time Being[1]

Born again

Nietzsche's keen attentiveness to the historical trajectory of thought – his awareness, for instance, that Christian theology is narrated via a succession of historical landmarks (creation, fall, crucifixion, resurrection, second coming) – provides him with the clue to Christianity's undoing. For not only does Nietzsche appreciate that the careful unpicking of Christian history is far more threatening to the life-blood of the Christian faith than a challenge to its philosophical credibility, he also has a clearer sense of what it takes to reverse the process of spiritual catastrophe that he believes Christianity has brought about. The Ariadne's thread, laid down by his genealogical analysis, has to be retraced and a new humanity born by undergoing, in reverse, the pattern of the Christian story. Thus Nietzsche re-narrates Christian salvation-history, re-interpreting what Christians have called 'redemption' as, in fact, the fall, and positing a 'new creation' as leading to redemption. That is, Nietzsche does not seek to neutralise history of its spiritual charge, rather he seeks to change the poles of that charge and twist Christian history into a new shape.

It is important to note that in describing this redemption from redemption Nietzsche returns to strongly Christian imagery. For instance, in keeping with his evangelical past, Nietzsche associates even his own positive account of redemption with being 'born again'. Just as with St. Paul there is the old man, cast in the mould of Adam, and the new man, who is able to break free from the domain of Adam by realigning himself with Christ, so too in Nietzsche there is unredeemed humanity, cast according to the dimensions of the Christian-moral ideal, and the new man, the *Übermensch*, who invents his or her own values and ideals. On both accounts the transition from one realm to the other is described in much the same way: the self constituted under the first regime must be broken in order for the liberated self to emerge. (Stanley Cavell makes one of his characteristically perceptive comments when he writes: 'Christianity appears in Nietzsche not so much as the reverse of the truth as the truth in foul disguise'.)[2] Being born again requires a dying to self. For example, Nietzsche writes:

> You must be ready to burn yourself in your own flame: how could you become new, if you had not first become ashes? . . . I love him who wants to create beyond himself and thus perishes.[3]

As it is with a certain sort of Christian account of redemption, the metamorphosis of the self required by Nietzsche involves a descent into darkness and despair. Luther in particular emphasises the necessity of falling before the foot of the cross in utter hopelessness as a precondition of receiving the gratuity of God's grace. Only when one has descended into the bottom of the pit will one emerge redeemed. Alister McGrath describes it thus:

> [B]efore man can be raised to the heights, he must be forced to descend to the depths; before he can be elevated by God, he must first humiliate himself, before he can be saved he must first be damned, before he can live in the spirit he must first be put to death in the flesh.[4]

Nietzsche seeks salvation in an inverted version of Lutheranism; that is, by urging his readers to undergo, in reverse, that process by which humanity came to hate itself in the first place. On Luther's model, God stands forever over against human flourishing. Luther himself puts it starkly: 'Whoever humiliates himself in the eyes of the world is totally exalted in the eyes of God.'[5] Nietzsche believes this to be the voice of authentic Christianity. To love God is to hate oneself. And, given there is no God, human beings are left marooned, nursing a deeply ingrained self-hate from which there is no escape. No escape, that is, unless one is prepared to undergo a similar process once again, a process, however, that is even more terrifying than its Lutheran counterpart, for through it one has to give up the comfort of divine acceptance and wager that one has the capacity to give meaning to one's own existence unaided by some external agency. It is, as it were, a process in which one has to give up something for nothing. There are no advance guarantees that such a transformation will lead to any increase in happiness or that through it one will necessarily achieve greatness. There is an event horizon to Nietzsche's abyss and no way of prejudging the consequences of one's journey into its unknown. Indeed, Nietzsche warns, the likelihood is that one will not be able to stand the tremendous weight of responsibility required for a successful transformation and that most people will end up destroyed by the process. ('Enter through the narrow gate. For wide is the gate and broad is the road that leads to destruction, and many enter through it. But small is the gate and narrow the road that leads to life, and only a few find it.' Matthew 7: 13–14) The potential benefit of this transformation, however, is that if you survive it you will be released from the clutches of self-hatred and that you will be able to love yourself and wholeheartedly to affirm your own being.

Nietzsche's allegorical rendering of this inverted re-birth is presented early on in *Thus Spoke Zarathustra* in a chapter entitled 'Of the Three Meta-morphoses'. There can be no doubt that this is a central chapter of *Thus Spoke Zarathustra*; indeed John Clayton has gone so far as to claim that 'in this single parable the whole of Nietzsche's message is contained'.[6] The parable tells the story of a series of transformations – from camel to lion to child. The camel is a symbol of humanity laden down with the guilt that has been foisted upon it by the Christian-moral interpretation of life. In becoming a lion, that is, in becoming an autonomous individual capable of pride and self-respect, one has to take on, and by a supreme act of will, overcome those moral imperatives – the 'Thou shalts', as Nietzsche calls them – which have proved so burdensome to the camel. The lion is, of course, essentially a figure of strength and power. And this is what many imagine Nietzsche takes the *Übermensch* to be; a blond beast, like a lion, who overcomes Chris-tianity by some heroic and magnificent show of strength. And yet, however much Nietzsche may indeed celebrate the great warrior virtues of strength and courage, the lion is not the *Übermensch*, indeed the lion has to become something quite other than a lion if the process of spiritual transformation is to be completed. The task of the lion is to prepare the ground, to overcome the weight of guilt. But simply clearing the ground of spiritual traps is not sufficient to secure that great triumph of the spirit Nietzsche anticipates. Echoing St. Paul's description of being-in-Christ as being a new creation Nietzsche claims that the lion is incapable of achieving re-creation because as a warrior the lion is essentially uncreative.

> To create new values – even the lion is incapable of that: but to create itself freedom for a new creation – that the might of the lion can do.[7]

The lion is simply the nihilistic vanguard in the creation of a new humanity. In order to complete the process of spiritual transformation the lion must turn itself into a child.

> But tell me, my brother, what can the child do that even the lion cannot? Why must the preying lion still become a child? The child is

innocence and forgetfulness, a new beginning, a sport, a self-propelling wheel, a first motion, a sacred Yes. Yes, a sacred Yes is needed, my brothers, for the sport of creation.[8]

Again Nietzsche shadows the Bible, this time repeating that sentiment expressed in Matthew 18: 3: 'unless you change and become like little children, you will never enter the kingdom of heaven'. So the *Übermensch* is not a lion at all, nor some mighty warrior, but an innocent child playfully re-creating herself and her surroundings untroubled by, indeed unconscious of, her spiritual status.

The Biblical parallels are once again instructive and once explored reveal that more is at work in Nietzsche's text than simply Biblical pastiche. The story of Genesis speaks of the fall as being a fall from innocence, from unselfconscious nakedness. Having eaten from the tree of the knowledge of good and evil Adam and Eve come to recognise themselves as shameful. Through this original act of disobedience, an act through which human beings come by the knowledge of good and evil, self-conscious guilt is rooted in the human soul. It is remarkable how closely Nietzsche sticks to the logic of this story in seeking to redeem humanity from the guilt and shame he too sees as humanity's principal affliction. What is required is for human beings to go beyond good and evil once again, to lose that sense of self-conscious guilt effected by the knowledge of good and evil, and return to pre-lapsarian innocence. In this respect Adam and Eve prior to the fall are decidedly *übermenschlich*. Erich Heller puts it particularly well:

> in the language of Genesis: The curse fell upon him with his eating from the Tree of Knowledge, the curse was believed, by St. Matthew and the other evangelists of salvation, to be removable only through faith that is the child's. Without this faith there is only the affliction of self-consciousness, the grown man's shame and embarrassment at being his naked separate self, the particular punishment within the universal punishment that is the Fall. Yet as long as God was, there was the hope of redemption. It was only when the malady came which, in Nietzsche's diagnosis, originated in the death of God, that human minds applied themselves to the huge task of designing a historical future as paradise regained: this would come about with the overcoming of self-consciousness and with the recovery, or with the new creation, of innocence and naïve spontaneity.[9]

Nietzsche's invocation of the child is, however, a symptom of his failure to escape from the spiritual circumstances he has diagnosed. For though it is relatively easy to make sense of the process by which the camel is transformed into the lion – that is by a stupendous effort of the will – it is enormously difficult to see how the lion could become a child. How can a warrior, marked with the scars of his victory, ever reclaim that innocence in which the terrors of battle are forgotten and through which the unself-conscious enjoyment of play is made possible? How can the lion forget his lion-ness? Nietzsche all but admits that he cannot by claiming the child to be a 'new beginning'. The practitioners of deconstruction, who see Nietzsche as their ideological forebear, have taught us to be suspicious of the idea of wholly 'new beginnings', of *tabulae rasae* and the like. And yet here is Nietzsche premising his whole vision of salvation upon the new beginning of childhood. Nietzsche, it seems, takes the 'born again' metaphor more literally than was intended.[10] Michael Tanner writes:

> That phrase 'a new beginning' is dangerous. For it is usually Nietzsche's distinction as a connoisseur of decadence to realise that among our options is not that of wiping the slate clean. We need to have a self to overcome, and that self will be the result of the whole Western tradition, which it will somehow manage to 'aufheben', a word that Nietzsche has no fondness for, because of its virtual Hegelian copyright, and which means simultaneously 'to obliterate', 'to preserve' and 'to lift up'. Isn't that just what the Übermensch is called upon to do, or if we drop him, what we, advancing from our present state, must do if we are to be 'redeemed'?[11]

Nietzsche's recourse to the image of the child suggests a point of fundamental weakness in his overall salvation story. One can, of course, see why Nietzsche wants to promote the child, and not the lion, as the epitome of spiritual achievement. For the problem of the lion is that, though he may have come to triumph over the burden of guilt, his victory will remain incomplete in so far as he bears the wounds of battle, which, as wounds, will always be potentially the source of further infections, further *ressentiment*. The lion is a victim of the struggle, a war veteran unable to readjust to the circumstances of peace. The child is an image of *ressentiment* overcome. A new-born unaffected by, because uninvolved with, those battles which have made her innocence possible. One can understand the theory, but not how that theory can be implemented. It is like saying the prostitute can only be redeemed by virginity. One can see what that might mean metaphorically but not how it is possible in practice.

In this respect, Christianity operates a far more realistic sense of what it is to be redeemed. For the Christian, redemption is made possible by repentance and forgiveness. And while Nietzsche castigates this model as the very engine of *ressentiment* (asking one to view one's past as sinful), the advantage it does have over Nietzsche's alternative is that it is realistic enough to recognise that for salvation to be human salvation it must incorporate and face up to our past as well as our present. While Christianity requires repentance of one's past the child image suggests its complete annihilation. And surely this represents a species of denial (a refusal to 'face up to') no less susceptible to the workings of *ressentiment*. Nietzsche, I think, recognises this, but his hatred for the idea of forgiveness is altogether too powerful. Thus Nietzsche desperately needs something equivalent to forgiveness which can function to 'redeem' the past. His answer to this, roughly speaking, will be that one can accommodate one's past into a potentially redeemed existence in so far as one can totally and absolutely affirm what one has been. In a sense his is the opposite answer to that of Christianity: one does not repent of one's past but one wholeheartedly celebrates it. As Nietzsche might put it, one does not say 'No' to one's past, but an emphatic 'Yes'. But if this is the case the child image breaks down completely, for surely the child represents the ultimate 'No-saying' to one's past since, obviously enough, the child does not have a past. To be born again as a child is to born again as an amnesiac.

Another disturbing feature of Nietzsche's celebration of the child is the idea that total unselfconsciousness is a sign of spiritual excellence. Nietzsche makes this point on a number of occasions. In a note recorded in *The Will to Power* he writes of 'the profound instinct that only automatism makes possible perfection in life and creation'.[12] Similarly in *The Anti-Christ*, when celebrating the spirituality of the Manu Law-Book, he writes:

> The higher rationale of such a procedure lies in the intention of making the way of life recognised as correct (that is demonstrated by a tremendous amount of finely-sifted experience) unconscious: so that a complete automatism of instinct is achieved – the precondition for any kind of mastery, any kind of perfection in the art of living.[13]

Heller argues that Nietzsche's idea that an unselfconscious automaton represents some sort of redeemed condition is forced upon him by his overly developed suspicion of all belief: 'What haunted Nietzsche . . . was the pervasive suspicion that the self-consciousness of the intelligence had grown to such a degree as to deprive *any* belief of its genuineness.'[14] Nietzsche speaks of 'man's ability to see through himself and history' as something too well-developed to out-wit.[15] And though it is precisely this talent for suspicion that has won out over Christianity, the price of that victory is the release of a corrosive spirit that no belief can possibly survive. Nietzsche's capacity to knock down has thus exceeded his capacity to build up and he is consequently left, as he thinks Christianity is left, celebrating nothingness. For how different is the lobotomised automaton to the anesthetised Christian? Indeed the idea that unselfconsciousness constitutes some sort of redemption sounds a little like the logic of the drunk for whom redemption is found in a bottle. But perhaps, by developing the capacity for suspicion above all else, Nietzsche has made the search for redemption impossibly difficult, so there seems little else but to retreat into drunkenness. And such is the intelligence of the drunk that he continues to persuade himself that salvation is to be found in that which helps him forget his failure (hence Nietzsche's frequent celebration of forgetfulness).[16] But Nietzsche did say there would be casualties; perhaps these are they.

Redeeming the past

Thus far we have yet to track down the core of Nietzsche's soteriology –
though it has been suggested that, in some way, this core is intended to
operate as an alternative to 'forgiveness'. In fact, it is not all that difficult to
work out where this core actually should be, for Nietzsche is very clear that
a great deal of his work rests upon his notion of the eternal recurrence of the
same. For instance, he calls the eternal recurrence the 'fundamental conception' of *Thus Spoke Zarathustra* and states that 'it represents the highest
formula of affirmation that is at all attainable'.[17] And while there is a consensus as to its importance, there has been little agreement among scholars
as to what this 'doctrine' is all about (even what it is to be called is itself a
disputed question, Heidegger, for instance, preferring 'thought'). A great
deal of the difficulty is generated by Nietzsche's multiple and very different
accounts of what the eternal recurrence consists in. And perhaps the idea
that there is one single eternal recurrence in Nietzsche's thought has to be
abandoned in the face of this puzzling diversity. For my purposes I do not
seek to provide an exhaustive account of the eternal recurrence, but rather to
offer a reading that brings out a particular, and as I hope to show, a particularly important dimension to it. However, in order to begin an examination
of the eternal recurrence directly a certain amount of groundwork has to be
done beforehand.

Soteriological schemes are determined, in part, by how one understands
who it is, or indeed what it is, that requires saving. Thus accounts of the
self, accounts of the nature of human identity, play a crucial role in shaping
one's understanding of redemption. For instance, it has been argued that, for
the people of Ancient Israel individual identity subsists within what has
been called 'corporate identity'. That is, the basic unit of identity among the
people of Ancient Israel is the people as a whole, so it is 'the people of
Israel', and not autonomous individuals, who are the subject of salvation. It
is the people who are redeemed from captivity, the people who are promised
a new land, etc. The corporate and public nature of salvation corresponds to
the corporate and public understanding of how identity is preserved and
maintained (so, in the Hebrew scriptures, there is very little emphasis on
salvation as the individual surviving death). On the other hand, for Descartes,
the so-called 'father of modern philosophy', personal identity is founded
upon the inner 'self', that sense of the self disclosed through the *cogito* and
described as the 'soul'. Given this basic anthropology, it is the private and
individuated soul that becomes the subject of redemption. The influence of
Descartes' conception of the self brings with it a very particular conception
of what salvation must consist in. Generally speaking, differing accounts
of identity produce differing accounts of the nature of salvation. Thus it is
important to ask, when exploring the nature of Nietzschean soteriology,
what is his conception of the self? How does Nietzsche understand the
construction and preservation of identity?

What is radical about Nietzsche's approach is that he does not believe there to be any 'X', whether that be soul, or internal mental state, or whatever, in virtue of which personal identity is maintained. Indeed he believes the whole idea of the 'self' to be a carefully constructed fiction. Anticipating Wittgenstein he argues that the idea of an objectively existing 'self' is a product of the mistaken assumption that the word 'I' is meaningful only in so far as it refers to some-thing in the world. We are, to use Wittgenstein's phrase, 'bewitched by language'. Thus, for instance, Nietzsche writes:

> There is no 'being' behind doing, effecting, becoming: 'the doer' is merely a fiction added to the deed – the deed is everything . . . our entire science still lies under the misleading influence of language and has not disposed of that little changeling, the subject (the atom for example is such a changeling as is the Kantian 'thing-in-itself').[18]

Nothing therefore underpins, or acts as a guarantor for, the identity of 'the self'. Rather, a person is the sum total of their effects, of what they do, of their experiences, of where they live and who they meet. There is no permanently abiding feature of a person in virtue of which a person continues to be the same person over time. There is no secret corner of our 'being' that is above and beyond the gratuity of change.

Consider two different cities as metaphors for two different accounts of the self.[19] The first city is built around a central square, from which the government, the police and the central administration rule over the outlying districts. In this city order is maintained and unified around a totally centralised core. The second city has a totally different plan. In this city things are largely decentralised with no central administration but with semi-independent, and often conflicting, locations of authority. This city does not have the order and symmetry of the first, but is a jumble of back-alleys and ramshackle dwellings. To use the post-modern jargon: this is a city of *difference*. Recently a number of philosophers have come to argue that understanding the self on the basis of this second city model helps us understand various features of our experience that on the basis of the first model do not and cannot make sense. Amélie Rorty, for instance, has argued that if we take the self to be akin to the first city there is no way of providing a coherent account of *akrasia* (weakness of will) or of the experience of being 'at conflict' with oneself. How, for instance, is it possible to be 'in two minds' about something if the self is a fully integrated and totally centralised centre of authority? Surely the only way to make sense of such phenomena (phenomena which one recent Nietzsche commentator has dubbed 'the politics of the soul') is if we recognise the fundamental heterogeneity of 'the self'. But if we do go this way, as Nietzsche does, we give up the idea that there is some 'X' in virtue of which the city's identity is preserved.[20] If we consider cities of the second sort – say Los Angeles – we can see that no one feature or geographical location constitutes and secures its identity. It can grow, change, have various features destroyed, and yet remain substantially the same city. The identity of the centralised city, however, is maintained by one (set of) institution(s), and thus if that institution(s) was to change radically, so too would the identity of the whole city. Change is therefore threatening to the homogeneous city in a way that it is not to the heterogeneous city. Given that Nietzsche believes all things are in a constant state of flux, and that nothing is invulnerable to change, the centralised city is in danger of collapse at any point.

But although the decentralised city is not threatened by change in the same way as the centralised city (because its authority and power do not remain in one place) it faces the opposite problem: how is its identity actually established? What is it about this city that makes it this particular city? Nietzsche's answer, perhaps unsurprisingly, returns us to genealogy. For if, as Foucault has suggested, genealogy is Nietzsche's 'alternative' to ontology, so too identity does not reside in something permanently abiding, but is caught up with its changing and varied historical development. To return to the self: I am not myself because I posses some soul or spirit that abides over time, but rather I am what I have become, what I have come to be. And this coming-to-be is the central characteristic of who I am.

Now we are in a better position to see why Nietzsche is so keen to redeem the past. For, given that the 'subject' of redemption is inseparable from that person's past, in order that one be redeemed, redemption must, somehow, extend retrospectively to cover all that one has been – for what one has been constitutes what one is (again we see evidence of Nietzsche's desire to develop an alternative functional equivalent to Christian forgiveness). Coupled with Nietzsche's insistence that redemption is achieved through an act of will, we are left contemplating the seemingly bizarre idea that the will has to 'will backwards'. Nietzsche, in a chapter of *Thus Spoke Zarathustra* entitled 'On Redemption' phrases it thus:

> To redeem the past and to transform every 'It was' into an 'I wanted it thus!' – that alone do I call redemption! Will – that is what the liberator and bringer of joy is called: thus I have taught you my friends! But now learn this as well: The will itself is still a prisoner. Willing liberates, but what is it that fastens in fetters even the liberator? 'It was': that is what the will's teeth-gnashing and most lonely affliction is called. Powerless against that which has been done, the will is the angry spectator of all things past. The will cannot will backwards: that it cannot break time and time's desire – that is the will's most lonely affliction.[21]

This, Nietzsche tells us in *Ecce Homo*, is the central purpose of Zarathustra:

> On one occasion Zarathustra strictly defines his task – it is also mine – the meaning of which cannot be misunderstood: he is affirmative to the point of justifying, of redeeming even the entire past.[22]

Prima facie this idea is quite ridiculous. The past cannot be changed, what's done is done, and the will, however assertive, cannot make it otherwise. And though there are moments when one wonders whether Nietzsche is actually claiming that an ability to change the past would be soteriologically advantageous and that this impossibility is some sort of lack, one needs to understand that Nietzsche's 'answer' to the problem of the past is not to try and find some way of changing the past by some act of will, in fact quite the opposite, he challenges us to have the courage to affirm the totality of our past as it stands. With one very important qualification (which we shall come to) the challenge of the eternal recurrence has much in common with the question 'If you could have things all over again would you do anything different?' To say and wholeheartedly believe that one would have things the same way again is to have passed the test posed by the eternal recurrence and to have achieved redemption. Nietzsche phrases this ultimate test in the form of a striking parable. It is worth quoting in full:

> The heaviest burden – What if some day or night a demon crept into your loneliest loneliness and said to you: 'This life as you live it now and have lived it, you will have to live again and again time without number: there will be nothing new in it, but every pain and every joy, every thought and every sigh and the unspeakably small and great in your life must return to you, and everything in the same series and sequence – and in the same way this spider and this moonlight among the trees, and in the same way this moment and I myself. The eternal hour-glass of existence will be turned again and again – and you with it, you dust of dust!' – Would you not throw yourself down and gnash your teeth and curse the demon who spoke thus? Or have you experienced a tremendous moment in which you would have answered him: 'You are a god, and never did I hear anything more divine!' If this thought gained power over you it would, as you are now, transform and perhaps crush you: the question in all and everything, 'do you want this again and again, times without number?' would lie as the heaviest burden on all your actions. Or how well disposed towards yourself and towards life would you have to become to have no greater desire than for this ultimate eternal confirmation and seal?[23]

This expression of the eternal recurrence takes the form of a test: Can you affirm the totality of your life? Nowhere here does he suggest that time actually is circular. He begins, significantly, 'What if', as though he were telling a story. In this context the cosmological question of time is quite beside the point; what Nietzsche seeks to focus upon is whether one has the strength (the strength of will, as it were) to respond to the demon's suggestion with gratitude. To desire that one's past be wholly different, or indeed just slightly different, is to have failed Nietzsche's test of spiritual strength.

At the age of thirteen, and while still a Christian, Nietzsche wrote:

> But thy holy will be done! I want to accept joyfully everything there is, happiness and unhappiness, poverty and wealth and even look death daringly in the eyes.[24]

The doctrine of eternal recurrence is, in a sense, the atheistic rendition of the desire to experience with joy all that comes one's way. Whereas for the young Nietzsche a failure to 'accept joyfully everything there is' is a blasphemy against God, for the mature Nietzsche it became a blasphemy against life.

It is very easy to become fooled by Nietzsche's language of strength and will and thereby misunderstand what he means by 'affirmation'. All too often those who read Nietzsche come to his work with a pre-formed caricature of the *Übermensch* that conceives of him as some Teutonic super-hero with a proclivity for egomaniacal assertiveness and dangerously fascist leanings. And expressions like 'will-to-power' tend to support such a view. From such a perspective 'affirmation' can be seen as a form of will-driven self aggrandisement, an attempt to redeem the world by reshaping it according to one's own wishes and design. Coupled with Nietzsche's liking for images of power – philosophising with a hammer, as it were – we can gain the impression that the *Übermensch* is saved by imposing himself on his surroundings; that Nietzsche's approach to his world is to bulldoze it into a form he finds acceptable, that is, worthy of affirmation. On this account Nietzsche's 'salvation' is the spiritual equivalent of the despot who, in an attempt to make the view from his palace more pleasing, levels entire villages, removes unwanted mountains, replacing them with landscaped gardens. But this is not Nietzsche's way at all. Indeed, as his early desire to accept all that comes his way with gratefulness suggests, Nietzsche's approach is quite the opposite. 'Salvation' is about learning to love the view, whatever it is and however ugly.

Often commentators miss the central significance of love for Nietzsche. Indeed 'affirmation' functions in Nietzsche's text grammatically much closer to the language of love than to the language of power. The eternal recurrence is principally a test of one's capacity for *amor fati*, love of fate. It is in loving who we are that we are redeemed.

> I want to learn more and more to see as beautiful what is necessary in things; then I shall be one of those who make things beautiful. *Amor fati*: Let that be my love henceforth! . . . some day I wish only to be a Yes-sayer.[25]

As a test of one's *amor fati* the eternal recurrence is a test of one's capacity for love. It asks: is your self regard sufficiently free from regret that it enables you to affirm (that is, love) all about yourself and your personal history and the world in which you live, including especially all those moments of pain and heartbreak, of fear and anxiety? Especially these, for in loving them they are redeemed and overcome. Thus Nietzsche shares with Christianity the sense that love is the active ingredient in the process of salvation.

The problem with the way I have explained it, however, is that I have made it look as though Nietzsche is out to promote indiscriminate affirmation – loving the view, however ugly, etc. The thinker most associated with the claim that the eternal recurrence is not an instruction to affirm indiscriminately life in its totality is Gilles Deleuze. For Deleuze the eternal recurrence discriminates between what he calls 'active' and 'reactive' forces. 'Reactive' forces are products of *ressentiment* and are to be resisted, whereas 'active' forces are free from *ressentiment* and are to be affirmed. On this account the eternal recurrence does not call us simply to affirm all that life brings one's way, it is a criterion of judgement which sifts that which is worthy of affirmation from that which is not. Many, however, have argued that Deleuze's reading of Nietzsche is incompatible with an understanding of the eternal recurrence which sees it as an encouragement to the affirmation of all things. Ansell-Pearson puts it thus:

> Deleuze's reading of eternal return is instructive because it exposes two dimensions of the teaching which do not cohere, and which might explain why it continues to baffle and to generate different interpretations. On one level, it provides an experience of the affirmation of life in its totality and unity (providing a feeling of cosmic oneness with the universe); on another level, which is brought out by Deleuze's reading, it exists as a kind of ethical imperative. My argument is that if the eternal return is to be viewed in the latter terms, then it cancels out the attitude of total affirmation implied in the cosmic view, and imposes upon human beings the necessity, as moral beings, of making judgments on life: not only saying yes, I will that again and again, but also saying, no, never again.[26]

What counts against Deleuze's reading is Nietzsche's insistence that all things are tied together and ultimately inseparable. Nietzsche insists 'If we affirm one single moment, we thus affirm not only ourselves but all existence.'[27] And again:

> Have you ever said yes to a single joy? O my friends, then you have said Yes to all woe. All things are entangled, ensnared, enamoured: if ever you wanted one thing twice, if you ever said 'You please me, happiness! Abide, moment!' then you wanted all back. All anew, all eternally, all entangled, ensnared, enamoured – oh, then you have loved the world. Eternal ones. Love it eternally and evermore.[28]

If what Deleuze calls 'active' and 'reactive' forces cannot be finally separated, if all things are indivisibly 'entangled', then the idea that the eternal recurrence is a means of separating that which is worthy of affirmation from that which is to be resisted has to be mistaken. But before we dismiss Deleuze's approach too soon we must recognise that the textual basis of his reading is strong. Often Nietzsche speaks of the need for both a 'Yes' and a 'No'. For instance: 'Formula of my happiness: a Yes, a No, a straight line, a goal.'[29] And even more clearly:

> It has been my good fortune, after a thousand years of error and confusion, to have recovered the path that leads to a Yes and a No. I teach the No to all that makes weak – which exhausts. I teach a Yes to all that makes for strength.[30]

What then are we to make of this apparent contradiction? Does Nietzsche want us to affirm everything or to affirm some things and reject others?

An important clue is given in a passage quoted a little earlier, 'some day I wish only to be a Yes-sayer'. By this I take Nietzsche to imply that while unqualified Yes-saying is his goal, the means to this goal involves a process of discrimination, of both Yes and No saying. The *Übermensch*, Nietzsche's image of redeemed humanity, is an unqualified affirmer. However *becoming übermenschlich* requires a process of both affirmation and denial, that is, of judgement. What the test of the eternal recurrence does is to provide some sort of progress report on one's spiritual journey. *And in doing so it presses one on towards the attainment of that perspective from which total affirmation of life is made possible.* Thus Nietzsche's question becomes: What sort of person do I have to be in order to meet all things with gratitude, joy and affirmation? How can I become a person who meets all with love? The *Übermensch* is the one who has found the place from which he or she can respond to the demon's suggestion that all will come again 'in exactly the same sequence' with gratitude and joy.

This spiritual journey is a journey of re-invention. Nietzsche's understanding of the self is, as we have seen, wholly plastic. Like the city of *difference*, Nietzsche's 'self' is capable of re-configuring itself around wholly different perspectives. And in doing so it continually adjusts its sense of its own history and thereby of who it is. In a sense then, the eternal recurrence is about 'finding oneself'. Not that oneself is waiting to be discovered, but that, through the promptings of the eternal recurrence, a self worthy of affirmation is created, forged out of the continual interplay between one's capacity for affirmation and the reality of one's 'history'.

Earlier we noted that the heterogeneous city, while able to survive change, is tasked with the problem of supplying its own identity. The same problem exists for an understanding of the self whose identity is not secured around some fixed (metaphysical) point of reference. On what basis is unity to be achieved? What criteria of convergence will suit? The eternal recurrence is, as it were, Nietzsche's convergence criterion for the self. It is the means by which one becomes the sort of person capable of emphatic self-affirmation and thus self-justification. It is Nietzsche's articulation of being 'born again'.

For in the process of (unqualified and non-delusional) self affirmation one saves oneself. As Nietzsche puts it:

> Love yourselves as an act of clemency – then you will no longer have any need of your god and the whole drama of fall and redemption will be played out to the end in yourselves.[31]

The present tense of eternity

The test described by the eternal recurrence differs in one important way from the more commonplace 'Would you do the same if you could do it all over again?' in that the eternal recurrence requires one to affirm an infinite repetition of 'pasts' and not simply the affirmation of one single past. What difference, however, could this possibly make? Given the way Nietzsche sets up the eternal recurrence, that each 'past' remains wholly identical to all the others, what more can one be affirming in affirming an eternity of identical pasts rather than one single past? If we grant for a moment, as a thought experiment, that the eternal recurrence is a cosmological possibility, and that, as I sit in my study reflecting upon my life, I have done so an infinite number of times before in exactly the same way, there can be, in principle, no difference between this instance and one that occurred in a previous cycle. Indeed invoking Leibniz's principle of the identity of indiscernibles (the principle that if x has every property of y, and y every property of x, then x and y are identical) these cycles are not different cycles but exactly the same. And though one may quibble and say that these various loops are different from each other in sequence (that is, one loop differs from another in that one is before/after another) it is surely clear that such a 'difference' (if that it be) fails to make any psychological difference to me in my study, and thus cannot at all contribute in any way to the act of affirmation. If these objections are in order why does Nietzsche choose to invoke *eternal* recurrence rather than simply the affirmation of one's entire past?

Here we need to return to Heidegger, for he claims that it is precisely at this point that Nietzsche betrays his desire to think beyond metaphysics and, by invoking the eternal in the way he does, Nietzsche compromises his much vaunted affirmation of becoming. There are, Heidegger insists, two general positions on the question of the nature of being:

> The one answer – roughly speaking, it is the answer of Parmenides – tells us that being is. An odd sort of answer, no doubt, yet a very deep one, since that very response determines for the first time and for all thinkers to come, including Nietzsche, the meaning of is and Being – permanence and presence, that is, the eternal present. The other answer – roughly speaking, that of Heraclitus – tells us that being becomes. That being is in being by virtue of its permanent becoming, its self-unfolding and eventual dissolution.[32]

Nietzsche, as we noted in Chapter 3, wants to articulate a sense of salvation consistent with the claim that all things exist in a state of constant flux. However, the problem with an ontology premised upon continual change is that it does not seem to be able to supply a secure basis on which value can establish itself. This, of course, is the motivation behind Plato's doctrine of Forms. Amid troubled and changing times human beings look for something secure and permanent around which to establish a sense of what makes human life important, worthwhile, valuable, etc. And if nothing 'of the earth' is capable of supplying a suitably secure basis, the criteria for a worthwhile life have to be established 'in heaven', or meta-physically. In attacking this line as cowardly and impossible, and in urging us to 'remain true to the earth', Nietzsche is faced with the task of generating criteria of value amid the shifting sands of time. It is this problem that the idea of eternal recurrence is designed to meet. It is, as Heidegger seeks to emphasise in his reading of Nietzsche, the closest approximation to 'being' in a world of becoming. Thus for Heidegger the give-away passage, found in Nietzsche's manuscripts, is *The Will to Power* 617:

> To impose upon becoming the character of being – that is the supreme will-to-power. Twofold falsification, on the part of the senses and of the spirit, to preserve a world of that which is, which abides, which is equivalent, etc. That *everything recurs* is the closest *approximation of a world of becoming to a world of being:* – high point of the meditation.[33]

But isn't this simply a subtle and clever way of returning to Parmenides? – or, at the very least, the invention of a third position somehow between that of Heraclitus and Parmenides? This, at least, is what Heidegger claims: the eternal recurrence is 'Nietzsche's fundamental metaphysical position'. In short, 'The sense is that one must shape Becoming as being in such a way that *as becoming* it is preserved, has subsistence, in a word, is.'[34]

As touched upon already, the problem with Heidegger's *Nietzsche* is that it is too much about Heidegger. What makes one uncomfortable about the applicability of Heidegger's argument at this point is that, by focusing upon Nietzsche's use of 'being' in the way he does, one suspects that he is seeking to draw Nietzsche into his own philosophical *mondo*. I think there is something basically right about what Heidegger says but that it is obscured by his insistence in seeing everything Nietzsche writes as representing some twist and turn in the history of metaphysics. I want, therefore, to look at the eternal recurrence from an altogether different perspective, and return to Heidegger's interpretation in a short while. First, I want to turn to the work of the Czech novelist, Milan Kundera – and, in particular, to the treatment Nietzsche receives throughout the pages of what is perhaps Kundera's best-known novel *The Unbearable Lightness of Being*. Even so, as this title suggests, in turning from Heidegger to Kundera we continue our investigation of what both writers call 'Being'.

Kundera begins his novel by asking the meaning of the eternal recurrence:

> The idea of eternal return is a mysterious one, and Nietzsche has often perplexed other philosophers with it: to think that everything recurs as we once experienced it, and that the recurrence itself recurs ad infinitum! What does this mad myth signify?[35]

Kundera goes on to explain the purpose of the eternal recurrence in terms of 'lightness and weight' – the title of the first chapter. A whole range of contrasts can, for Kundera, be explored under this rubric. For example, communist Czechoslovakia is a place of oppression, a totalitarian state in which one's very life is put at risk in exercising what might seem the smallest human freedom. This, so to speak, is a place of 'weight'. Western Europe, however, is a place where 'everything is permitted', a place without the oppressive presence of the state, and yet, in some way because of that, a place where things don't seem to matter as much. This is what Kundera calls 'the unbearable lightness of being'. Much of Kundera's novel explores the complex emotional consequences of being liberated from communist oppression. Without the 'weight' of communist oppression, one's emotional and spiritual life lacks gravity. Kundera puts it thus:

> But is heaviness truly deplorable and lightness splendid? The heaviest of burdens crushes us, we sink beneath it, it pins us to the ground. But in the love poetry of every age, the woman longs to be weighed down by the man's body. The heaviest of burdens is therefore simultaneously an image of life's most intense fulfillment. The heavier the burden, the closer our lives come to the earth, the more real and truthful they become. Conversely, the absolute absence of a burden causes man to be lighter than air, to soar into the heights, to take leave of the earth and his earthly being, and become only half real, his movements are as free as they are insignificant. What shall we choose? Weight or lightness?[36]

Nietzsche is faced with an analogous problem following the death of God. Nietzsche considered God to be an instrument of oppression, a great burden upon human lives. And there is no doubt that, on one level, Nietzsche celebrates the liberation from oppression brought about by the death of God. Nonetheless he fully appreciates that this freedom is, potentially, just as difficult to bear. For, without God, nothing seems to matter quite as much as it did. Whereas before God's death the weight of divine judgement bore down upon each and every human choice, the felt presence of heaven and hell rendered human decision making of ultimate significance, freedom from divine judgement means that what human beings choose to do no longer carries the same significance. What is required by Nietzsche is some way of generating gravity, of introducing judgement, without returning to divine judgement or divine weight. This is the purpose of the eternal recurrence. The thought of eternal recurrence sets out to become a moral centrifuge, a way for the self to generate its own gravity. Kundera answers his own question as to the significance of Nietzsche's 'mad myth' thus:

> Putting it negatively, the myth of the eternal return states that a life which disappears once and for all, which does not return, is like a shadow, without weight, dead in advance, and whether it was horrible, beautiful, or sublime, its horror, sublimity, and beauty mean nothing.[37]

On the other hand . . .

> If every second of our lives recurs an infinite number of times, we are nailed to eternity as Jesus Christ was nailed to the cross. It is a terrifying prospect. In the world of eternal return the weight of unbearable responsibility lies heavy on every move we make. This is why Nietzsche called the eternal return the heaviest of burdens.[38]

It looks, then, as if Nietzsche invents the eternal recurrence as a way of having his cake and eating it – of having liberation from divine oppression and also having the sort of moral and spiritual *gravitas* or gravity that comes from the presence of divine judgement. A number of commentators have noted the proximity of the eternal recurrence to Christian notions of eternal life[39] – a superficial and ultimately unrewarding comparison, I think. It is no coincidence that the articulation of the eternal recurrence in *The Gay Science* bears more than a passing resemblance to those passages in the Gospels which anticipate the intrusion of eschatological judgement. Consider, for instance, Matthew 24: 42–51:

> Therefore keep watch, because you do not know on what day your Lord will come. But understand this: If the owner of the house had known at what time of night the thief was coming, he would have kept watch and would not have let his house be broken into. So you also must be ready, because the Son of Man will come at an hour when you do not expect him. Who then is the faithful and wise servant, whom the master has put in charge of the servants in his household to give them their food at the proper time? It will be good for that servant whose master finds him doing so when he returns. I tell you the truth, he will put him in charge of all his possessions. But suppose that servant is wicked and says to himself, 'My master is staying away a long time', and he then begins to beat his fellow servants and to eat and drink with drunkards. The master of that servant will come on a day when he does not expect him and at an hour he is not aware of. He will cut him to pieces and assign him a place with the hypocrites, where there will be weeping and gnashing of teeth.

The image of the 'thief in the night' and Nietzsche's demon ('what if some day or night a demon were to steal into your loneliest loneliness') are clearly cousins of sorts. Both come unbidden, and both represent the intrusion of judgement, indeed eternal judgement, into the everyday. Indeed it is surely the very purpose of the master/servant story to illustrate the fact that the anticipated coming of Christ should 'lie upon your actions as the greatest weight' – what will the master find the servant doing when he comes? Something of which he is proud or ashamed? What will the demon find when he asks you of your life? Something of which you are proud or ashamed? Will you be able to affirm or not? When the demon comes will you be able to pass his test of judgement – or will you be crushed? Will this *weight* be too much to bear?

This Biblical comparison also adds an important dimension to the understanding of time and temporality in Nietzsche's thought of eternal recurrence. We have already noted Nietzsche's sensitivity to the Christian narration of salvation history and his awareness that this story loads time with a particular purpose and direction. Hence for Christianity there is a sense of time that is never the neutral succession of events as measured by calendars and clocks. The distinction that is often used to distinguish between the time of clocks and calendars and the theologically charged 'opportune' time is that between *chronos* and *kairos*. *Chronos*-time refers to the regular flow of measured time, *kairos*-time to times-of-opportunity or times-of-decision-making. In Greek to seize the moment is *kairon lambanein*. Throughout the LXX attention is drawn to the key events of salvation history with the stereotyped phrase *to kairo ekeino*, 'at that time'. And, to draw upon an example from recent history, when a group of liberation theologians and Church leaders in South Africa called their collection of essays *The Kairos Document* their meaning was emphatic: now is the time to rise up against apartheid. It was intended as a bugle call, urging people not to miss the opportunity. *Kairos*-time is that time in which God intervenes in human lives and calls for human response. The whole energy and tension of the Gospels is created by the sense that God's dramatic intrusion into the human realm is immanent. Jesus' central message is of the proximity of the kingdom of heaven: the eternal is close upon you, the eternal is all about you, the eternal is upon you now. This is a time of the most dramatic liminality. Joachim Jeremias summarises Jesus' message thus: 'The hour of fulfillment has dawned, the reign of God is already being manifested here and now: soon the catastrophe introducing its definitive coming will arrive. Make use of the time before it is too late: it is a matter of life and death.'[40] In the same way we can say that the temporality of the eternal recurrence is *kairos*-temporality rather than *chronos*-temporality.

The suspicion we gained from Heidegger was that the eternal recurrence, in as much as it sought to stamp becoming with the character of being, was some sort of sell-out to Platonic or Parmenidean metaphysics – that the eternal recurrence sought to grasp the flow of becoming and, for a moment at least, hold it fast. My anxiety was that Heidegger drew Nietzsche into a philosophical debate that was, to a worrying extent, of Heidegger's own making. Having introduced Kundera's perspective we can begin to gain a certain critical distance from Heidegger's interpretation. For we begin to see Nietzsche's purpose as seeking to find some sort of non-foundational foundation (centrifuge) for the generation of value or, to put it in Kundera's idiom, for making weight (and, of course, a centrifuge only generates artificial 'gravity' when it is constantly rotating, as it were, eternally recurring). Heidegger's analysis seems to lose sight of the eschatological dimension of the eternal recurrence; the sense that its message 'is a matter of life and death'.

One of the key ideas held within Nietzsche's concept of the eternal recurrence is that of 'the moment'. The articulation of the eternal recurrence which gives most prominence to the notion of moment is, however, also the most enigmatic:

> 'Behold, this gateway, dwarf!' I went on: 'it has two aspects. Two paths come together here: no one has ever reached their end. This long lane behind us: it goes on for an eternity. And that long lane ahead of us – that is another eternity. They are in opposition to one another: and it is here at this gateway that they come together. The name of the gateway is written above it: "Moment" . . . Behold this moment!' I went on. 'From this gateway Moment a long, eternal lane runs back: an eternity lies behind us. Must not all things that can run have already run along this lane? Must not all things that can happen have already happened, been done, run past? And if all things have been here before: what do you think of this moment, dwarf? Must not this gateway, too, have been here – before? And are not all things bound fast together in such a way that this moment draws after it all future things? Therefore – draws itself too? For all things that can run must also run once again forward along this long lane. And this slow spider that creeps along in the moonlight, and this moonlight itself, and I and you at this gateway whispering together, whispering of eternal things – must not all have been here before?'[41]

Nietzsche is trying to portray a sense that 'the moment' is loaded with the weight of eternity. One is reminded of the well-known last words of Bultmann's *History and Eschatology:* 'In every moment slumbers the possibility of being the eschatological moment. You must awaken it.'[42] Nietzsche likewise is calling his reader to awaken the eschatological moment, to recognise in the present the presence of the eternal. Nietzsche's insistence on the interconnectedness of all things makes the same point a different way: the present 'moment' is intrinsically linked to all else, to the eternal. Note also that the *The Gay Science*, 341 version of the eternal recurrence asks 'or have you experienced a tremendous *moment* in which you would have answered him: "You are a god, and never did I hear anything more divine!"' It is this sense of 'moment' with which Nietzsche is concerned – the *kairos* of the eternal recurrence. The eternal recurrence is the decisive moment in which one is faced with possibility of redemption. It is the fulcrum of Nietzsche's alternative soteriology. This dimension to Nietzsche's thought is what Heidegger fails to appreciate in charging the eternal recurrence with re-introducing the metaphysics of Parmenides. For the eternal recurrence does not work according to the temporality of *chronos*, but of *kairos*. Nietzsche is using time-language to illuminate fundamental questions of human growth and self-regard. And just as the significance of those parables which speak of impending judgement is not rendered obsolete by the non-arrival of the expected Parousia, so too the eternal recurrence must be seen as much more than, and not logically reliant upon, its bizarre cosmology.

The idea that both the eternal recurrence and the Christian expectation of the coming of the kingdom are about (moral and evaluative) weight-creation can easily mislead one into thinking that the eternal recurrence is necessarily a return to *oppressive* (rather than gravitational) weight, replacing the oppression of divine judgement with a post-Christian weight creator which is no less oppressive than the original. In fact, Nietzsche's deeper purpose in constructing the eternal recurrence is to seek an articulation of joy.[43] Erich Heller is right to prefer *The Joyous Science* to Kaufmann's (now canonical) translation *The Gay Science*.[44]

And it is through the invocation of eternity that joy is brought to frui-tion. 'But all joy wants eternity . . . wants deep, deep, deep eternity', Nietzsche insists.[45] And again, at the concluding section of part III of *Also Spoke Zarathustra* the following antiphon is repeated seven times:

> Oh how should I not lust for eternity and for the wedding ring of rings – the Ring of Recurrence! Never did I find the woman by whom I wanted children, unless it be this woman whom I love: for I love you, O Eternity! For I love you Eternity.[46]

The eternal recurrence is, for Nietzsche, a way of describing the irruption of the eternal into the all-too-human; a moment of pure ecstasy in which one is able to shout out a 'Yes' to everything. At this point Nietzsche's work crosses over into mysticism. In a letter to his friend Peter Gast he writes:

> The intensity of my feelings makes me shudder and laugh – already a few times I could not leave the room for the laughable reason that my eyes were inflamed – from what? I had cried too much the day before each time on my walks, and indeed not sentimental tears, but tears of jubilation; wherein I sang and talked nonsense, filled with a new glimpse that I have in advance of all men.[47]

And again in *Ecce Homo*:

The concept of revelation – in the sense that suddenly, with indestructible certainty and subtlety, something becomes visible, audible, something that shakes one to the last depths and throws one down – that merely describes the facts.[48]

Julian Young, in his examination of *The Gay Science*, makes a point against Nehemas that is similar to the one I have been making against Heidegger. Nehemas, Young claims, is wrong to consider Nietzsche's insistence that all things are tied together 'eternally enamoured, ensnared' etc. to be a metaphysical claim. For Young, Nietzsche's affirmation of all things has to be understood as a wholly *intoxicated* 'Yes' – not 'the cautious, qualified discerning "Yes" of, as Nietzsche would be likely to say, the scholar'[49] – but the 'Yes' that calls out from a moment of ecstasy and intoxication. We saw the same attraction to the ecstatic exhibited in *The Birth of Tragedy* and I have made the comparison between Dionysian joy, rave culture and the connotations of the drug ecstasy. Nietzsche's 'Damascus road' experience, walking along a forest path next to the lake at Silvaplana when the idea of the eternal recurrence came to him, is described as '6,000 feet beyond man and time'.[50] Likewise he speaks of 'future souls' for whom 'elevated moods', being 'on a high' so to speak, will be more than just an exceptional condition:

> What has so far entered our souls only now and then as an exception that made us shudder, might perhaps be the usual state for these future souls: a perpetual movement between high and low, the feeling of high and low, a continual ascent as on stairs and at the same time a sense of resting on clouds.[51]

Young claims, and I think correctly, that to affirm something ecstatically is to affirm it both unquestioningly and unconditionally. It is the affirmation of the intoxicated lover for his or her beloved: it does not affirm some aspects of the loved one and not others. The intoxicated lover loves everything about the other. She is engrossed, totally absorbed. Moreover the affirmation of the lover for the beloved is clearly an affirmation 'beyond good and evil' – the beloved can 'do no wrong' as it were. Nietzsche speaks of 'a Dionysian affirmation of the world as it is, without subtraction, exception, or selection'.[52]

Nietzsche himself is aware of the dangers of spiritual rapture. In a section in which he is seeking to illuminate the degree to which religious 'truths' are generated by the power and intensity of feeling he concludes:

> None of these holy epileptics and seers of visions possessed a thousandth part of that integrity in self criticism with which a philologist today reads a text or proves the truth of an historical event – Compared to us they are moral cretins.[53]

As Leslie Thiele puts it: 'The saint whose mysticism is not matched with skepticism remains a holy fool, duped by his own spiritual infatuation.'[54]

And Theile seems to think that Nietzsche achieves this balance. But can you really have it both ways? Is it really possible to embrace the ecstatic so enthusiastically and, at the same time, insist that one's rational/sceptical/critical integrity is not thereby compromised? Surely not. For the whole point about the intoxicated lover and intoxicated seer is that they affirm unconditionally. The state of intoxication does not allow the capacity for critical judgement to take place. One way of putting this is to say, with Nietzsche himself, that 'rapture' works through 'intuitions' rather than 'the rope ladder of logic'.[55] The ecstatic demands that one give oneself over completely to its power. It is this feature of the ecstatic that makes it such a dangerous phenomenon, one that is all too often used to manipulate people to do things that otherwise – that is, when their critical faculties are fully engaged – they would never dream of doing (the murder of Pentheus, for instance, is clearly an ecstatic murder; otherwise peaceable women whipped up into some homicidal fury by the destructive power of Dionysus). And to believe that one is able to give oneself over to the ecstatic while retaining one's capacity of critical judgement is a dangerous naïveté.

For Young the centrality of the ecstatic returns Nietzsche to the divine.[56] Nietzsche is not just an atheist evangelical, if that makes any sense, he is an atheist charismatic evangelical. Nietzsche's 'Yes' is a close relative of those expressions of affirmation witnessed at revivalist meetings and charismatic evangelical churches. Nietzsche's 'Yes' is the 'Yes' of praise – his own Dionysian Alleluia. But, though a relative of the charismatic evangelical 'Yes', Nietzsche's post-Christian affirmation is, as I am now going to suggest, closer in spirit to something much more sinister – to the highly charged, emotionally intoxicating 'Yes' of the Nazi rallies at Nuremberg. Aping the Christian revivalist rally, and seeking to re-focus the instinct for reverence upon the Führer himself, the genius of the Nazi propaganda machine was to have appreciated the political possibilities of harnessing the power of 'spiritual' intoxication – 'Evermore shall your brow drip with the sweat of applause' wrote the underground poet Friedrich Georg Jünger.[57] Both the pseudo-religion of Nazism and Nietzsche's post-Christian soteriology draw upon the spirit of charismatic intoxication. Is this just a historical coincidence, or is there a deeper affinity at work here? It is to this comparison that we now turn our attention.

6 Salvation, kitsch and the denial of shit

On the way to becoming an 'angel' (not to use a stronger word here), man has upset his stomach and developed a furry tongue so that he finds not only that the joy and innocence of animals is disgusting, but that life itself is distasteful: – so that every now and again, he is so repelled by himself that he holds his nose and disapprovingly recites a catalogue of his offensive features, with Pope Innocent the Third ('conception in filth, loathsome method of feeding in the womb, sinfulness of the raw material of man, terrible stench, secretion of saliva, urine and excrement'.)

Nietzsche, *On the Genealogy of Morals*, II: 7

Shit

Thus far I have sought to reveal various manifestations of Nietzsche's attempt to articulate a convincing post-Christian soteriology. My next move will be to say why I think his soteriological experiments fail. Broadly, my contention will be that Nietzsche's soteriology is incapable of facing the full horror of human suffering, in particular, the evil as revealed in the Nazi death-camps. I will argue that after Auschwitz Nietzsche's soteriology looks like the imaginings of a more comfortable and innocent age.

Part of my reason for turning to the holocaust is that it forces us to think less abstractly, as it were, less philosophically about what Silenian wisdom might actually mean. 'Oh, wretched ephemeral race, children of chance and misery, why do you compel me to tell you what it would be expedient for you not to hear? What is best of all is utterly beyond your reach: not to be born, not to be, to be nothing. But the second best for you is – to die soon'[1]: this is Silenian wisdom. Life is horror. Nietzsche's whole soteriology, his successive experiments in redemption are all designed to overcome this wisdom without avoiding it. My contention will be that he does, in fact, avoid it and that, therefore, Nietzsche's soteriology fails by its own standards. He avoids it by failing to register the fulness of its extent, the full horror of true evil. And, for many people of my generation, the name of true evil is Auschwitz.

There is a problem here, however. For Nietzsche, to speak of something as 'evil' is to express one's own *ressentiment* (and, of course, this is why Nietzsche's own re-formed value system is cast as beyond good and evil). Therefore, if I am to demonstrate that Nietzsche's work fails to face up to the sort of horror witnessed in the holocaust, and do so in such a way that Nietzsche constructs the case against himself, then the concept of evil has to be avoided. Also, for some, 'evil' has too many theological associations to be acceptable.

There is, I think, a way of circumventing this problem. In his important study of evil Paul Ricoeur carefully distinguishes two wholly different senses of evil; what he calls 'blame' and 'lament'.[2] In one sense to speak of something as evil is to declare blame. It is to claim that a person is guilty of wrongdoing. It is this sense of evil, the blaming/punishing sense, which Nietzsche believes to be infused with *ressentiment*. However, to speak of something as evil in the sense of lament is something significantly different. It is to understand evil as that which describes the horror of human pain, the cry of the afflicted. And though, as Nietzsche himself has acutely observed, this sense of 'lament evil' very easily spills over into 'blame evil' – the sufferer looking for the provenance of his suffering – this does not collapse Ricoeur's distinction. It ought, perhaps, to make us cautious about relying upon it too heavily. With this in mind, I want to charge Nietzsche with avoiding and misrepresenting lament evil. And to avoid confusion I will not speak of the problem of evil but of the problem of shit. I hope to show that there are further good reasons for speaking of it thus.

In his extraordinary essay 'Excremental Assault', Terrence Des Pres writes of the pervasiveness of excrement within the Nazi death camps, of how 'dirt and excrement were permanent conditions of existence'.[3] All the camps stank of it. Prisoners lived in blocks where commonly 'the whole floor was awash with urine and faeces'. Diarrhoea and dysentery were widespread:

> Those with dysentery melted down like candles, relieving themselves in their clothes, and swiftly turned into stinking repulsive skeletons who died in their own excrement.[4]

One of the most disturbing aspects of Des Pres' study is his exploration of the use made by Nazi guards of shit as a means of torture and humiliation. Prisoners were commonly not allowed to relieve themselves during work periods other than by doing so as they stood working. One woman writes:

> If any of us, tormented by her stomach, would try to go to a nearby ditch, the guards would release their dogs. Humiliated, goaded, the women did not leave their places – they waded in their own excrement.[5]

Another writes of the death marches where any prisoner who stopped, for whatever reason, was immediately shot:

> Urine and excreta poured down the prisoners' legs, and by nightfall the excrement, which had frozen to our limbs, gave off its stench. We were

really no longer human beings in the accepted sense. Not even animals, but putrefying corpses moving on two legs.[6]

One of the 'favourite games' of the guards at Buchenwald was to catch men relieving themselves in the latrines, which were holes twelve feet deep, full, often to the point of overflowing, with human excrement, and throw them in. At Buchenwald many were drowned in this way. Relieving oneself thus became an extraordinarily dangerous activity and for many something that had to be achieved secretly.

> Many women with diarrhoea relieved themselves in soup bowls or the pans for 'coffee'; then they hid the utensils under the mattress to avoid the punishment threatening them for doing so: twenty five strokes on the bare buttocks, or kneeling all night long on sharp gravel holding up bricks. These punishments often ended in the death of the 'guilty'.[7]

'Shit', for Des Pres, therefore becomes a symbol of the Nazi camps and of the horror of the holocaust. Drawing on Ricoeur's *The Symbolism of Evil* he notes the extent to which shit and excreta have been employed throughout history as ways of referring to evil:

> In *The Symbolism of Evil*, Paul Ricoeur defines 'dread of the impure' as the special kind of fear we feel in relation to 'a threat which, beyond the threat of suffering and death, aims at a diminution of existence, a loss of the personal core of one's being'. That, I think, is a good description of what survivors feel when threatened by excremental assault. Ricoeur goes on to argue that the feeling of defilement underlies concepts like 'sin' and 'guilt', and finally that as 'the oldest of the symbols of evil' defilement 'can signify analogically all the degrees of the experience of evil'. And indeed, why does imagery of washing and physical purgation underlie our ideas of sanctity and spiritual purification? Why do we use images associated with excrement – imagery of corruption and decay, of dirt and contagion, of things contaminated, rotting or spoiled – to embody our perceptions of evil?[8]

In the context of an academic thesis, however, the word 'shit' is, in one sense, wholly out of place. And that, perhaps, is one of its principal virtues. For maybe the shocking vulgarity of 'shit' is the only way properly to open up academic discourse to the reality of genocide? If 'shit' is awkwardly juxtaposed to the measured vocabulary of critical discourse then so much the better. For if that discourse believes itself able to apprehend the full dimensions of Auschwitz then it has committed the most terrible hubris. 'Shit' is valuable in so much as it is so thoroughly resistant to any form of philosophical appropriation; it cannot be readily co-opted into a philosophical system or distorted into a technical term.[9]

To those who suspect that my use of 'shit' is a cheap and vulgar trick I note the words of Emil Fackenheim. 'I never use the word *shit*', Fackenheim comments, 'but the way Terrence Des Pres uses it, it becomes a holy word.'[10] Shit is a sacrament of ultimate seriousness.

'Kitsch is the absolute denial of shit'

Milan Kundera's *The Unbearable Lightness of Being* can be read as a sustained reflection upon the pathological nature of kitsch. Kundera is concerned to illustrate that kitsch is a natural ally of totalitarianism and a means of its control. Kitsch, for Kundera, is the enemy of independent mindedness, it seeks to standardise our spiritual, emotional and political life, and, by the indiscriminate promotion of sentimentality, represents a powerful, though insidious threat to public life.

The objection to kitsch as launched by Sabina, the heroine of *The Unbearable Lightness of Being*, is, Kundera informs us, 'aesthetic rather than ethical'. In creating Sabina, Kundera clearly had Nietzsche in mind: Sabina is the free-spirited artist, the wanderer, and (because her criticisms are aesthetic rather than ethical) the one who operates 'beyond good and evil'. Nevertheless Kundera recognises that Sabina's use of 'kitsch' and her 'aesthetic' criticisms of totalitarianism(s) are themselves profoundly moral. One is reminded of Dewey's comment that 'art is more moral than the moralities'. Both Sabina and Nietzsche seek to go 'beyond good and evil' not because they wish to be moral monsters, far from it, but rather because they believe, as it were, morality to be insufficiently moral. What they seek is an order of moral seriousness that is 'beyond' the dictates of conventional morality. Both seek to articulate alternative configurations of virtue.

In a purely aesthetic sense to speak of something as kitsch is to say that it is cheap, gaudy and crass; that it employs sentiment as a way of hiding its lack of aesthetic content. But what great harm is there in that? Is the attack upon kitsch art simply an expression of aesthetic snobbery; those with 'good taste' sneering at those with 'poor taste'? For Sabina the problem with kitsch has nothing to do with taste, but rather to do with truth. Kitsch art is a lie, it wholly distorts reality by denying the perspective of the afflicted, by denying the horror, by denying shit. Kitsch is a beautifying gloss, and as a gloss a strategy of denial. As Kundera defines it 'kitsch is the absolute denial of shit'.[11] The sculptor Edward Robinson, from a Christian perspective, reaches a similar conclusion:

> Bad art does not just fail to tell the truth; it substitutes a lie. When Christ is portrayed as a characterless figure of sentimental benevolence surrounded by cuddly lambs in a romantic landscape, what effect does such representation have on the prayers, let alone the theology, of those for whom he is a focus of worship? Kitsch degrades by satisfying the heart or mind with an inadequate or false image of reality. It is this, and

not in its failure to appeal to the finer feelings of a cultivated mind, that makes it an enemy of true spirituality.[12]

This idea that the problem with kitsch is that it fails to speak the truth, that it is insufficiently honest, that it prefers, wherever possible, sentimental fantasy to painful reality, connects Kundera's sense of kitsch to Nietzsche's understanding of truth. Nietzsche believed 'truth' to be realised only through complete honesty and by opening up one's experience of the world to as many different perspectives as possible. It is upon this premise that Nietzsche's soteriology is founded. Kitsch is therefore the great enemy of truth and the great enemy of salvation. Edward Robinson, after having defined kitsch as 'sentimental art', discloses this important connection when he writes:

> Sentimentality is more accurately defined as partiality; its fault is that it does not tell the whole truth, but only that part of it we want to see . . . sentimentality . . . is the attitude of those who cannot bear to look at life in its wholeness. Sentimentality . . . is blind to the evil in the world.[13]

For Nietzsche the ability to 'look at life in its wholeness', in all its horror, is a pre-condition of redemption. And Nietzsche clearly prides himself on his ability to out-face horror. My contention, however, is that Nietzsche's work is shaped considerably by the effects of kitsch – and thus is, at least partially, 'blind to the evil in the world'. If I am right then Nietzsche's soteriology is profoundly flawed and many of his soteriological exhortations are revealed as empty rhetoric. The value of this approach is that it evades Nietzsche's defences by challenging him on his own terms and at that point where he believes himself to be the most courageous. Indeed to accuse Nietzsche of kitsch, that is, of a certain sort of dishonesty, is to use his own arguments against him. Thus before we go on to mount this case against Nietzsche let us first of all consider an instance of Nietzsche mounting a version of this same case against one of his opponents. What I want to achieve thereby is Nietzsche's endorsement of the sort of case I want to mount against him.

Wagnerian decadence

Kundera clearly counts Nietzsche among the enemies of kitsch: 'Nietzsche's hatred for Victor Hugo's "petty words" and "ceremonial dress" was a disgust for kitsch *avant la lettre*.'[14] Nietzsche does not, to the best of my knowledge, use the word kitsch in his published writings. However a word he often does employ and, on the surface at least, to similar effect is 'decadence'. Like kitsch, Nietzsche's use of decadence has a strongly aesthetic orientation. And like Kundera's use of kitsch, its aesthetic focus is intended to make possible a critique of the prevailing culture that is at once both aesthetic and moral. The target of Nietzsche's charge of decadence is, in his later works, most frequently Wagner – though in condemning Wagner Nietzsche is also condemning the culture of his day.

Nietzsche's relationship with Wagner was undoubtedly a complicated one, and the reasons for their acrimonious separation have as much to do with differences of personality as they do with philosophy. Two such enormous egos were almost bound to fall out. Nonetheless, Nietzsche's claim that Wagner is decadent cannot be explained simply as the continuation of a personal feud. At the heart of Nietzsche's charge is that Wagner betrayed his artistic vocation by the indiscriminate promotion of sentiment and passion as a means of generating mass appeal. He traded the hazardous quest for beauty for the instant gains of theatricality, or rather he dressed up his own theatricality with the gravitas of beauty, and by doing so trivialised the full potential of art.

> The theatre is a form of demolatry [worship of the people] in matters of taste; the theatre is a revolt of the masses, a plebiscite against good taste. – This is precisely what is proved by the case of Wagner: he won the crowd, he corrupted taste, he spoiled even our taste for opera.[15]

For Nietzsche, *'Pulchrum est paucorum hominum.'*[16] Wagner is kitsch in as far as he has substituted the emotional intensity of passion – 'Nothing is cheaper than passion' says Nietzsche – for the rigours of the aesthetic search for truth. With Wagner art becomes popular entertainment.

> Let us never admit that art 'serves recreation'; that it 'exhilarates'; that it 'gives pleasure'. Let us never give pleasure! We are lost as soon as art is again thought of hedonistically.[17]

Nietzsche believes that art-as-recreation is a betrayal of art because he takes it to be the central virtue of art that it is able to search out the truth. And given that Nietzsche believes the truth to be ugly and terrifying, Wagner's approach to art is intrinsically unable to speak the truth. Silenian wisdom cannot be a basis for entertainment. So Wagner's art becomes 'the absolute denial of shit'. Wagner's art, Nietzsche continually insists, becomes 'a lie'.

Moreover, for Nietzsche, Wagner's art lies the most where it promises the most; that is, in its pretensions to become theology. For Nietzsche the guiding theme running in various guises throughout Wagner's work is redemption.

> The problem of redemption is certainly a venerable problem. There is nothing about which Wagner has thought more deeply than redemption: his opera is the opera of redemption. Somebody or other always wants to be redeemed in his work: sometimes a little male, sometimes a little female – this is his problem – and how richly he varies his leitmotif! What rare, what profound dodges! Who if not Wagner would

teach us that innocence prefers to redeem interesting sinners? (The case of *Tannhäuser*.) Or that even the Wandering Jew is redeemed, settles down, when he marries? (The case in *The Flying Dutchman*.) Or that old corrupted females prefer to be redeemed by chaste youths? (The case of Kundry.) Or that beautiful maidens like best to be redeemed by a knight who is Wagnerian? (The case of Meistersinger.) Or that married women, too, enjoy being redeemed by a knight? (The case of Isolde.) Or that 'the Old God', after having compromised himself morally in every respect, is finally redeemed by a free spirit and immoralist? (The case in *The Ring*.) Do admire this final profundity above all![18]

Nietzsche is, of course, being sarcastic. Nonetheless Nietzsche and Wagner both occupy very similar conceptual space (and Nietzsche's name-calling ought not to disguise his continued closeness to his one-time mentor – indeed perhaps it even emphasises it). Nietzsche's quest for redemption begins with the wisdom of Silenus; how is one able to live with a recognition that the world is ugly and terrifying and human life without meaning? Nietzsche's answer in *The Birth of Tragedy* requires a combination of Dionysus and Apollo. To oversimplify: Dionysus is that pole of the duality which keeps us pressed up against Silenian wisdom, and Apollo that pole which, by transforming Silenian wisdom into art, enables us to encounter Silenian wisdom without despair. It is a fragile balance, and the temptation to overplay the Apollonian pole, thus transforming Silenian wisdom into something so beautiful as to be wholly unobjectionable, remains strong. Nietzsche recognised, however, that to do so was not to offer redemption from Silenian wisdom, but simply to avoid it. Hence Nietzsche uses the Apollonian motif less and less in his later writing while continuing with the Dionysian. Wagner, however, has simply cast the Dionysian aside. This observation is borne out in Wagner's own reflections upon his own work. In *Art and Revolution*, for instance, Wagner concentrates almost exclusively upon Apollo as the redemptive deity. For instance, *Art and Revolution* concludes thus:

> Thus would Jesus have shown us that we all alike are men and brothers; while Apollo would have stamped this mighty bond of brotherhood with the seal of strength and beauty, and led mankind from doubt of its own worth to consciousness of its highest godlike might. Let us therefore erect an altar of the future, in Life as in the living Art, to the two sublimest teachers of mankind: – Jesus, who suffered for all men; and Apollo, who raised them to their joyous dignity.[19]

Nietzsche thinks it quite ridiculous that one person's suffering can achieve redemption for another. And while Nietzsche seems to concede that Jesus himself counts as 'redeemed' – indeed Jesus on the cross out-faced the wisdom of Silenus; nonetheless, redemption cannot be vicarious. To suppose that Jesus' own redemption in some way constitutes our own is simply an evasion of the journey by which we are called to transformation through pain and suffering. The question is, as Christ put it, 'Are you able to drink from the cup that I drink?': thereby the strong and the weak are discriminated. Wagner's use of Christ's vicarious suffering as the topological counterpoint to Apollo is therefore, for Nietzsche, simply an act of cowardice. An act of cowardice that leads his art into a systematic avoidance of pain and suffering, eliding Silenus, and so constructing itself on the basis of kitsch.

Before we return to Nietzsche and examine the case that he too is undone by a residual weakness for kitsch I want to shift the focus away from Nietzsche and back onto the holocaust. By an exploration of Nazi ideology I will seek to elucidate the conceptual links between 'shit', 'kitsch' and 'redemption' as well as to demonstrate something of what is at stake in the ways these concepts relate to each other. I am aware, of course, that in making this move I invite the interpretation that I am claiming Nietzsche's work to be, in some way, bound up with preparing the ground for the holocaust. Though this is not the principal focus of this chapter it is sufficiently important to demand comment.

Kitsch soteriology and the final solution

Hitler, who believed himself to know something about art, having once been an aspiring artist, detested what he called 'so-called modern art'. Intent on demonstrating the inherent superiority of 'true German art' over the corrupt art of Bolsheviks and Jews, he arranged two exhibitions, one entitled 'Degenerate Art', the other the 'Great Exhibition of German Art', both of which opened in Munich in the summer of 1937 (two years later the modernist art guru Clement Greenberg was famously to baptise this cultural opposition 'avant-garde and kitsch').

That Hitler took the cultural and aesthetic 'health' of Germany with enormous seriousness cannot be doubted. Concluding the speech with which he opened the Great Exhibition of German Art, Hitler gives clear notice of his intent:

> I do not want anybody to have false illusions: National-Socialism has made it its primary task to rid the German Reich, and thus, the German people and its life of all those influences which are fatal and ruinous to its existence. And although this purge cannot be accomplished in one day, I do not want to leave a shadow of doubt as to the fact that sooner or later the hour of liquidation will strike for those phenomena which have participated in this corruption. But with the opening of this exhibition the end of German art foolishness and the end of the destruction of its culture will have begun. From now on we will wage a war of purification against the last elements of putrefaction in our culture.[20]

The sort of art Hitler liked – Romantics such as Caspar David Friedrich and Phillip Otto Runge (and, of course, in music, pre-eminently Richard Wagner) – were, he believed, able to express timeless values that were clear and accessible to the German people. In the same speech Hitler reveals the centre of his moral and aesthetic evaluations.

> But we National-Socialists know only one morality, and that is the morality of the people itself. Its causes are known to us. As long as a people exists, however, it is the fixed pole in the flight of fleeting appearances. It is the being and the lasting permanence. And, indeed, for this reason, art as an expression of the essence of this being, is an eternal monument – in itself the being and the permanence.[21]

Another of Kundera's claims in *The Unbearable Lightness of Being* is that kitsch 'has its source in the categorical agreement with being',[22] that is with the intoxicating conviction that one is standing in a relationship of unity with the ultimate nature of things. For Kundera, the very essence of kitsch is demonstrated not in art-works but in the dynamics of the political rally, in particular in the May Day parade. During these parades the streets are full of flags and brass bands, all participants marching together in step with each other, all seeking to express a sense of communal joy. This expression of joy is misinterpreted if it is understood as an act of support for Communism (indeed many of those who participated so enthusiastically in the parade were 'indifferent to the theses of Communism'); rather the enthusiasm of the parade was a reflection of the sense in which the members of the parade saw themselves as united with each other and united with life. The parade was a celebration of the 'categorical agreement with being'.

The rhetoric of 'the people', and the construction of a sense of folk identity was, as Grunberger rightly emphasises in *A Social History of the Third Reich*, a crucial constituent of Nazi propaganda. The ethos of the May Day parade was tirelessly evoked in the furtherance of the spirit of folk community. The promotion of 'One Volk, one Reich, one Führer' as the national rallying cry served to enhance the sense of a community at one with itself. And, with the sustained exploitation of mass communication, the self-image of Nazi Germany became, to an exceptional extent, one of a people united in pursuit of the common good. Grunberger, for instance, writes:

> Proof of folk community was provided by the miners donating half their shift per month for the benefit of colleagues who were still unemployed, by pupils of girl's secondary schools 'adopting' deprived children, and by students replacing workers so as to give them additional paid holidays. Such acts, when suitably embroidered and magnified, gave the impression that the whole nation was finding itself through mutual aid.[23]

Nothing morally questionable was allowed to intrude upon the community's sense of its own moral wholesomeness.

Kitsch, Sabina discovers, is not confined to Communism (there are, Kundera notes, 'various kitsches: Catholic, Protestant, Jewish, Communist, Fascist, democratic, feminist').[24] Some years after her escape from the east Sabina experiences a different expression of kitsch, this time from an American senator.

> The senator stopped the car in front of a stadium with an artificial skating rink, and the children jumped out and started running along the large expanse of grass surrounding it. Sitting behind the wheel and gazing dreamily after the four bounding figures, he said to Sabina, 'Just look at them.' And describing a circle with his arm, a circle that was meant to take in the stadium, grass, and children, he added, 'Now that's what I call happiness.'[25]

Kundera reflects:

> Kitsch causes two tears to flow in quick succession. The first tear says: How nice to see children running on the grass! The second tear says: How nice to be moved, together with all mankind, by children running on the grass! It is the second tear that makes kitsch kitsch.[26]

And what is sinister about all of this? In the past few weeks a small story has been running in a tabloid newspaper. The paper noticed that one of its rivals had printed a photograph of the English cricket team, jubilant after having won the Test series against South Africa, in which a girl in a wheelchair, who was with the team as they celebrated, had been 'removed' from the printed photograph. This is how kitsch works to exclude. Of course, there are more violent ways of excluding than airbrushing out a disabled child from a photograph, though metaphorically, this is violent enough. What is so sinister about the American senator's kitsch is that his own lens ('describing a circle with his arm') lays the foundation for this act of exclusion, and, at its most extreme, the logic of this exclusion leads to the 'final solution'. It is, of course, no coincidence that the techniques used in the death-camps were principally developed by Die Gemeinnützige Stiftung für Heil und Anstaltspflege – The General Foundation for Welfare and Institutional Care – better known as T-4, an organisation set up to effect the 'mercy death' of those who were disabled and had 'hereditary diseases'.[27]

Nothing is more kitsch than the image of a perfect society dreamed up by Hitler and promoted through the Nazi propaganda machine. His vision of creating living space for the racially pure is shot through with a sense of its own moral wholesomeness.[28] It was to be a place where beautiful Aryan children could grow up happy and strong. The blond-haired, blue-eyed stereotype was a vision of perfect innocence – an innocence premised upon the total exclusion of shit. And for Hitler it was the Jews who were responsible for the presence of shit, indeed they were shit.

> The vileness of the Jew, he claimed, resided in the blood of the race and was evident in the Jew's physical, mental and cultural being. This vileness, Hitler declared, had permeated nearly every aspect of modern society. Over and over again he kept on describing the Jews in terms of filth and disease. 'If the Jews were alone in this world, they would stifle in filth and offal.'[29]

Kundera writes: 'we can regard the gulag as a septic tank used by totalitarian kitsch to dispose of its refuse.'[30] Likewise the concentration camps and ultimately the death camps. Hitler's final solution was a solution to the problem of how to rid the world of shit, a solution to the problem of how to create heaven on earth. In this light the excremental assault described by Des Pres is not just one form of barbarity among others, it is a barbarity perfectly consistent with the economics of kitsch soteriology.

To speak of the final solution in terms of the pursuit of salvation is supported by Hitler's own rhetoric. As Lucy Davidowicz comments:

> *Mein Kampf* is a vision of the apocalyptic conflict between the Aryans and the Jews, of two world streams struggling for domination. It was his own Manichaean version of the conflict between good and evil, between God and the devil, Christ and the Antichrist. He saw himself as the Messiah who would bring deliverance from the Devil: 'Hence today I believe I am acting in accordance with the will of the Almighty Creator: by defending myself against the Jew, I am fighting for the work of the Lord.' . . . A saviour was needed to come forth and slay the loathsome monster. In Hitler's obsessed mind, as in the delusive imaginings of the medieval millennarian sectarians, the Jews were the demonic hosts whom he had been given a divine mission to destroy.[31]

So Yehuda Bauer concludes 'The Nazis viewed the destruction of the Jews as a quasi-apocalyptic redemptive event.'[32] The 'uniqueness' of the holocaust does not reside in the quantity of suffering or in the numbers dead, but in the sense in which (and I tentatively offer this as a definition) the holocaust is the implementation of genocide for the purposes of salvation.

I am not, of course, arguing that kitsch is responsible for the holocaust, but rather that the way in which kitsch works is perfectly consistent with the ideology of the final solution. Grunberger puts this particularly well:

> The new art canon enjoined the banishment of all evocations of human anguish, distress and pain – in other words all ugliness from people's consciousness. (In the Nazi's own subconscious the aesthetic defeat of

ugliness by beauty dovetailed with the extermination of the Jews –
ugliness incarnate – by the Nordics.)[33]

Nietzsche's aristocratic kitsch

Since Walter Kaufmann's ground-breaking re-assessment of Nietzsche was
published in 1950 a consensus has gradually emerged that Nietzsche was not,
as Nussbaum puts it, a 'boot-in-the-face-fascist'. It is now common knowledge that his work was vastly distorted by those, not least his sister, who
were keen to conscript him to the cause of National Socialism. Once damned
as an anti-Semite, Nietzsche is now, more often than not, hailed as an anti-
anti-Semite. Indeed there is considerable textual evidence to support such a
claim. For example, Nietzsche suggests 'it would perhaps be a good idea to
eject the anti-Semitic ranters from the country'.[34] Nonetheless, those who
have sought to depict Nietzsche as mounting a sustained campaign against
anti-Semitism often miss the sense in which his attack upon anti-Semitism
is largely an attack upon vulgarity. It is not that Nietzsche was opposed to
racism *per se* – he hated the English, for example – what he despised was the
sort of vulgar anti-Semitism whipped up by such people as his brother-in-
law. It is significant, for instance, that he condemned anti-Semitism as 'taste-
less'. Yirmiyahu Yovel is correct in stating that, first and foremost, Nietzsche's
problem with anti-Semitism was that it was a sentiment of the mob:

> Anti-Semitism is a mass movement, vulgar, ideological, a new form of
> slave morality and of the man of the Herd.[35]

No one would have been as emphatically opposed to the Nazi promotion of
folk identity as Nietzsche. Indeed Nietzsche is consistently one of the fiercest
critics of the pathologies inherent within mass movements. And yet it is
here, at the point where Nietzsche looks to have set himself so much against
kitsch that he is most disposed towards it. Initially such a claim may look
perverse; surely that which despises the herd mentality with such vigour
cannot be sympathetic to the nurture of sentimentality, or inclined to celebrate that which is cheap and tawdry. Indeed Nietzsche's work demands so
much mental effort, is so consistently 'high-brow', that it looks *prima facie*,
to be the very opposite of kitsch. And Nietzsche's critique of Wagner surely
confirms this. Nonetheless, in Kundera's sense, kitsch is not about low-brow
art or poor taste, it is about the denial of shit. Thus Nietzsche's strenuous
affirmation of the aristocratic and the high-brow does not necessarily make
his work immune to kitsch. Indeed, I will argue, it is precisely in and
through this affirmation of the aristocratic that Nietzsche's work most dis-
poses itself to kitsch. That is, Nietzsche's work reveals a very different level
of kitsch – what I will call 'high-brow' kitsch.

Central to the case against Nietzsche is that in founding his moral perspective upon the pursuance of aristocratic virtues Nietzsche resists any

exploration of what he considers base or somehow beneath him. Take, for instance, Nietzsche's celebrated affirmation of the body. Martha Nussbaum is correct to point out the irony that a philosopher so concerned with celebrating the body, is at the same time so seemingly unconcerned with the issues of material welfare. Nietzsche's concern is not for the reality of human bodily needs, but with celebrating the physical beauty of those bodies for whom the question of bodily functions does not arise, that is, the 'aristocratic' body; and this is physicality only in the aesthetic sense. Nietzsche's celebration of the body is a celebration of the sort of bodies one sees in Greek sculpture. Like the author of St. John's gospel, the author of *Zarathustra* has a rather suspect take on the fulness of incarnation.

Nietzsche's unrepentant elitism, his indifference to the concerns of the ordinary person, are most obviously expressed in his almost total lack of concern for the politics of everyday life. I hesitate to claim that Nietzsche was wholly uninterested in politics (though, in fact, I do believe this also to be substantially the case) because I do not want to break off here to consider those numerous books that seek to isolate a political dimension to his thought. Sufficient for my purpose is the claim that Nietzsche was unconcerned with the politics of the everyday. That is, he was wholly uninterested in exploring (any further than the ubiquitous throw-away comment) the politics of food, of housing, of taxation, of land law, of marriage, of welfare, etc.

This is an important point and is worth exploring further. Charles Taylor, in his superb *Sources of the Self*, makes a good deal of the transition of Western culture from an ethic which celebrates glory and heroism, that is, which affirms the *extraordinary* as being the paradigm moral exemplar to what he calls 'the affirmation of ordinary life'. Taylor argues that this 'affirmation of ordinary life finds its origin in Judaeo-Christian spirituality'.[36] In particular, Taylor associates this transition as bound up with the paradigm shift expressed through the Reformation. Taylor argues that in premising salvation upon the faith of the individual believer alone, and in attacking the idea that one could achieve a closeness to God through the mediation of those who absented themselves from the profanity of the ordinary (i.e. monks, celibate clergy, etc.), the locus of the spiritual life is shifted to the ordinary. Thus, for instance, not a separate priesthood, but a priesthood of all believers. The idea of 'vocation', associated in the Roman Catholic tradition with priesthood or monasticism is, for the Protestant, something that can be acted out within even the humblest of employments. Think, for instance, of George Herbert's famous hymn 'Teach me, my God and King, In all things thee to see; and what I do in anything To do it as for thee!' Verse four is particularly relevant: 'A servant with this clause Makes drudgery divine; Who sweeps a room, as for thy laws, Makes that and the action fine.' Taylor likes the phrase, used by Joseph Hall, that 'God loveth adverbs'. Meaning: 'The highest in life can no longer be defined by an exulted *kind* of activity; it all turns on the spirit in which one lives whatever one lives, even the most mundane existence.'[37] These, I imagine, are precisely the sort of sentiments shared by

Nietzsche's parents and against which he came to react so strongly. Nietzsche's subsequent affirmation of 'aristocratic values' is, on one level, associated with his rejection of claustrophobic domesticity and antipathy towards 'ordinary life'.

Therefore, the reason Nietzsche has no desire to task himself with a major and sustained consideration of the politics of everyday life is that they are not the issues that face the sort of person whose perspective Nietzsche is keen to promote. That is, they are not the concerns of the privileged aristocracy. If Nietzsche is interested in politics it is only in what he calls 'grand politics'. For him, the majority of society's members have simply an instrumental function in providing the right conditions in which that aristocracy can flourish. Hence Nietzsche claims the aristocracy, for their part, have to accept 'with a good conscience the sacrifice of untold human beings who, for its sake, must be reduced and lowered to incomplete human beings, to slaves, to instruments' (we will look at the significance of Nietzsche's use of sacrificial language in the next chapter). He continues:

> Their fundamental faith has to be that society must not exist for society's sake but only as the foundation and scaffolding on which a choice type of human being is able to raise itself to a higher task and to a higher state of being.[38]

In order to understand his work, Nietzsche claims, 'one must be accustomed to living on mountains – to seeing the wretched ephemeral chatter of politics and national egoism beneath one'.[39] And again:

> For a few must first of all be allowed, now more than ever, to refrain from politics and step a little aside: . . . these few must be forgiven if they fail to take the happiness of the many, whether by many one understands nations or social classes, so very seriously and are now and then guilty of an ironic posture; for their seriousness lies elsewhere, their happiness something different.[40]

To put it in the idiom of 'shit': the aristocracy are to be left unsoiled from the dirty business of political life. They are to be separated from shit, at least that is, separated from the shittiness of ordinary life, in order that they can ponder great things and undergo heroic adventures of the spirit. It is thus, in Nietzsche's continual celebration of the aristocratic, that kitsch, 'highbrow' kitsch, is present throughout the twists and turns of Nietzsche's soteriological experimentations.

The obvious objection to this charge is to point out that few philosophers have been as concerned as Nietzsche with the investigation of pain and suffering – surely the most un-kitsch of concerns. This has to be the heart of the question of Nietzsche's disposal to kitsch, for if this objection stands then the claim that Nietzsche succumbs to kitsch all but collapses. If, however, this claim can be rebutted, if moreover it is precisely through his depiction of pain and suffering that Nietzsche is most disposed to kitsch, then Nietzsche is shown to be a most dangerous thinker; one who writes of suffering in such a way that much of the reality of suffering is actually hidden.

The very idea of the Apollonian, as we have seen in relation to Wagner, does suggest a desire to refract the experience of suffering so as to produce an aestheticised version of pain. Significantly, Kundera speaks of kitsch as the 'beautifying lie' which could almost be a text-book definition of the function of the Apollonian in the soteriology of *The Birth of Tragedy*.[41] It is as if the Apollonian idea is there to filter out the very painfulness of pain, leaving us simply with the idea of pain. Arguably, the sort of pain Nietzsche writes about is the pain of a hero in a novel, the sort of overly aestheticised pain experienced by the eponymous hero of Goethe's *The Sorrows of Young Werther*.

Nietzsche claimed a great spiritual affinity with Goethe. Indeed Nietzsche was often to suggest that in order to understand his own work one had to understand Goethe first. So it is not implausible that a consideration of a book such as *The Sorrows of Young Werther* will provide us with a clue as to the provenance and thus the true moral weight of Nietzsche's depiction of human suffering. The sorrows referred to in the title of Goethe's *The Sorrows of Young Werther* are those of a well-to-do adolescent who falls in love with a girl who is engaged to someone else. Of course there is nothing wrong with this as a subject for a novel. What there is something wrong with, however, is dressing up the pain of unrequited adolescent love as if it were the epitome of human affliction. This is how Werther speaks about the sufferings engendered by his unhappy infatuation.

> It is as if a curtain had been drawn from before my soul, and this scene of infinite life had been transformed before my eyes into the abyss of the grave, forever open wide. Can you say that anything is, when in fact it is all transient? and all passes by as fast as any storm, seldom enduring in the full force of existence, but ah! torn away by the current, submerged beneath the waves and dashed against the rocks? . . . all I can see is a monster forever devouring, regurgitating, chewing and gorging.[42]

The language and the ideas are very similar to Nietzsche's own. Werther is clearly articulating what Nietzsche would call a *ressentiment* against time, a fear of the radical impermanence of things. *The Sorrows of Young Werther* charts Werther's increasing mental anguish which leads him eventually to suicide. And it surely says something about the collective mind of nineteenth-century Germany that Werther's suicide was to make suicide fashionable.

The Sorrows of Young Werther, and the impression it made, cannot be understood without taking account of what Charles Taylor has called 'the moral consecration of sentiment' in the eighteenth century.[43] Following Richardson's *Clarissa*, and particularly Rousseau's *La Nouvelle Héloïse*, the depiction of pain and suffering came to be linked to the exultation of noble sentiments and purity of feeling. Many of the novels of this period celebrate the pain of renunciated or unrequited love as an expression of heightened sensibility. 'Love transmuted by suffering seems to offer the way to the highest in life.'[44] In this way pain and suffering come to be seen as something to be valued, the melancholy of unrequited love something worthy of admiration. Taylor writes:

> There is something tremendously consoling about melancholy, a beguiling pleasure, which can make suffering strangely enjoyable, a source of 'les rêveries mélancholiques et les voluptueuses tristesses' ('melancholy revery and voluptuous sadness'). This recourse had been available in all ages. But it was only in an age which valued sentiment that melancholy could be cherished. If distinction attached to the loftiness of one's sentiments, and if the highest were inseparable from renunciation and suffering, then the very savouring in melancholy of a nobly felt misfortune could be seen as admirable. Not everyone would have the sensibility to feel such misfortune, but those who did must be superior beings. The conditions had been created for the tremendous success of *The Sorrows of Young Werther*.[45]

Taylor's account demonstrates that kitsch is not something exclusive to mass movements. From the eighteenth century and throughout the nineteenth there developed a powerful association of sentimentalised suffering with nobility. In the novels of this period suffering is characteristically portrayed in terms of the romantic disappointments of aristocratic young men. It is therefore perhaps unsurprising that the very concept of kitsch originates in the cultural atmosphere of nineteenth-century Germany.

It is in this same atmosphere that Protestant theological kitsch begins to take off. From about 1840 onwards the revivalist presses of Calw and Stuttgart began to produce large numbers of copies of cheap and sentimental popular devotional literature for home consumption, illustrated with woodcuts or copperprints of a loving and mild Jesus.[46] This is precisely the sort of literature that would have been read in a Pietistic household like that of the Nietzsches.

The other significant literary development of mid-nineteenth-century Germany was that of realism. Realism, unlike Romanticism, saw itself not as the literature of the nobility but as that of the bourgeoisie. As Boeschenstein writes: 'Realism and bourgeois merge into one concept, and the latter is all but identical with the significant writing of this period.'[47] (The period referred to is 1830–85, during which many of Nietzsche's important works were produced.) It might be suspected, then, that a literary movement known as realism would be concerned to depict the grim reality of human suffering. And in the realm of the visual arts such is the case; one thinks, for instance, of the depiction of manual labour by Millet and Courbet, of Trübner's brutal 'The Dead Christ' (1874) and of Degas' paintings of prostitutes and those poisoned by absinthe. Nietzsche, however, is largely indifferent to painting as an art-form. In the literary realism of nineteenth-century Germany, however, the theme of suffering is conspicuously avoided. Take for instance the work of Adalbert Stifter. Stifter, again, was an important literary influence upon Nietzsche and acknowledged by him as such. Indeed Stifter, Goethe and the realist writer Godfried Keller are counted by Nietzsche as his three favourite novelists.[48] Erich Auerbach, in his monumental study of the way reality is depicted in Western literature writes of Keller:

> He too stylises the language of his characters, making it so simple, pure, and noble that we never find a coarse expression, hardly ever a hearty colloquialism. His language touches on the common things of life with delicate, innocent, somewhat timid refinement. This has a direct bearing on the fact that his characters too live in a world with hardly a trace of historical movement. Everything which forces its way in from the bustle of contemporary history, from the modern life of the world, politics, business, money matters, professional concerns (unless it is in the domain of agriculture or the crafts), he expresses in simple and noble, extremely general, allusive and cautious terms, so that nothing proceeding from that ugly and impure confusion shall reach him and his reader.[49]

Again we have here a banishment of the ugly. A banishment that Grunberger claims 'dovetails' with the Nazi programme of mass murder. A banishment that concedes cultural ground to the workings of kitsch.

What then of Nietzsche's fiction? What of Nietzsche's Zarathustra? Within the context of Nietzsche's fantasy world, the world of *Thus Spoke Zarathustra*, Zarathustra reigns supreme, and readers, in as much as they are able to suspend their disbelief in Zarathustra's world, are tempted to go along with Nietzsche and agree that Zarathustra is indeed capable of redeeming all that is about him. But there is the rub: what is about him? What sort of world does Zarathustra inhabit? With what does he do battle?

A *dramatis personae* of *Thus Spoke Zarathustra* would contain a range of different people – the fool, the ignorant, the cripple, the disappointed, the gullible, the easily led, even the ugly – but where is the presence of brutality, where the horrific, where violence, where the portrayal of shit? Among the extraordinary dream-like situations in which Zarathustra finds himself when does he come into contact with that darkness he claims with such alacrity to be able to overcome? Of course there are a number of passages where Nietzsche seeks to portray the horror of the nihil. But since then we have looked into the pit and instead of seeing emptiness we are faced with piles of bodies. Compared to that Nietzsche's own version of the nihil looks pale and self-obsessed.

In juxtaposing 'emptiness' with 'piles of bodies', and intending to suggest by that juxtaposition that the realities of Auschwitz or Srebrenica are of an altogether different order from concepts such as emptiness or meaninglessness, an enormous question is thereby raised as to the capacity or incapacity of philosophy for thinking human suffering. For in tending towards the general and the abstract philosophy becomes intrinsically disincarnate. Human suffering, on the other hand, is always the suffering of a particular person at a particular moment in time. It is bound up with specific stories. And that is why, for example, a documentary such as Lanzmann's 'Shoah', by attending to the detailed descriptions of those who witnessed the holocaust, is able to think human suffering in a way of which philosophy is incapable. Of course Nietzsche is hailed as resisting the metaphysical imperative to generalise wherever possible, but this instinct is preserved in his preference for dealing in types and tropes. The characters in *Zarathustra* always stand for generalised approaches to the world. They are little more than sophisticated cartoons representing types of human failure or weakness. Zarathustra himself has no history, no wider context. We do not find it appropriate to ask of his childhood or of his sexuality because Zarathustra only exists to the extent that he expresses the twists and turns of Nietzsche's spiritual journey. In such a milieu authentic thinking about suffering becomes all but impossible. For any thinking about suffering that does not attend to its incarnation thinks only the idea of suffering, that is suffering without pain.

For Christians the success of the attempt to think through the nature of suffering is bound up with the story of a particular person at a particular moment in time. Philosophy, of course, condemned this particularity as a scandal. However, I would argue that, precisely because of this attitude, philosophy is unable to generate a genuine encounter with the necessary particularity of human pain. This is not to rubbish philosophy. We do not, for instance, condemn physics for being unable to attend to suffering. What is condemned is not philosophy *per se* but the use to which Nietzsche puts it. For in seeking to express suffering philosophically Nietzsche takes suffering away from its locatedness in particular contexts and stories, thereby rendering it kitsch. When Zarathustra ascends to his mountain top he leaves the shittiness of the world far behind.

My overall objection to Nietzsche is that he glamorises suffering. His sense that suffering has the capacity to edify the noble spirit is only possible from the perspective of one who knows not the destructive power of excremental assault. Following the holocaust, Nietzsche's prescriptions for redemption can only be looked on as those of a more comfortable age. The holocaust re-defines nihilism in such a way that Nietzsche's strategy for overcoming it is rendered obsolete.

Christianity and shit

Does Christianity fare any better than Nietzsche in its capacity to encounter human suffering? Milan Kundera thinks not. Indeed for Kundera, Christianity is premised upon an unassailable dualism between God and shit which inevitably renders Christianity kitsch.

When I was small and would leaf through the Old Testament retold for children and illustrated by engravings by Gustave Doré, I saw the Lord God standing on a cloud. He was an old man with eyes, nose and a long beard, and I would say to myself that if he had a mouth, He had to eat. And if he ate, He had intestines. But that thought always gave me a fright, because even though I came from a family that was not particularly religious, I felt the idea of a divine intestine to be sacrilegious. Spontaneously, without any theological training, I, a child, grasped the incompatibility of God and shit and thus came to question the basic thesis of Christian anthropology, namely, that man was created in God's image. Either/or: either man was created in God's image – and God has intestines! – or God lacks intestines and man is not like Him. The ancient Gnostics felt as I did at the age of five. In the second century, the great Gnostic master Valentinus resolved this damnable paradox by claiming that Jesus 'ate and drank, but did not defecate'.[50]

The problem with Kundera's charge is surely obvious: Valentinus was declared a heretic, his views emphatically shunned by what came to be official Christian doctrine. And for precisely the reason Kundera suggests: he could not think of God and shit together – or, to put it in more traditional language, he did not recognise the full reality of the incarnation. It is symbolically important that Christ was born in a stable, amid the stench and mess of animal dung (though, all too often, the nativity scene is imagined all cleaned up – and this act of cleaning it up is precisely the beginnings of Christian kitsch). The *prima facie* offensiveness of the intimate juxtaposition God/shit recaptures something of the original offensiveness of the incarnation itself, which offence, incidentally, points to Athens and not Jerusalem as the original purveyor of kitsch. Valentinus' mistake, one could say, was to prefer Platonism (and hellenised Zoroastrianism) to authentic Christianity, and like so many Christian Platonists of the first and second centuries he found John 1: 1 more conducive than John 1: 14. Ultimately nothing is less kitsch than the idea of the crucifixion (Kundera has also described kitsch as 'a folding screen to curtain off death'; that is, kitsch cannot face death, still less one as horrific as crucifixion). Of course, as in the case of the stable, there are kitsch depictions of the crucifixion: Christ smiling on the cross and so forth. And these depictions are often more popular because the kitsch versions are more easily marketable (but how is it possible to market the crucifixion?). The power of Good Friday is that as He is crucified Jesus meets and takes upon Himself the full horror and darkness of the world. The fulcrum of Christian soteriology is the point at which God and 'shit' meet.

7 Sacrifice and the logic of exclusion

Every day, without exception, the community as a whole provided two male yearling lambs that were offered to God as burnt (that is, entirely burnt) sacrifices, along with flour, oil and wine (Ex. 29: 40), one in the morning, to open the temple service, and one in the evening, just before its conclusion . . . The lamb was tied 'with its head to the south and its face to the west'; that is, it was laid on a table on its left side. The priest who wielded the knife 'stood to the east with his face to the west', behind the animal. He slit the throat, and another priest received the blood in a vessel, then sprinkled part of it on the altar. The rest was poured out at the base of the altar, where it ran into a channel and was flushed out of the temple area . . . The carcass was hung up by its hind leg and partially flayed. Apparently it was taken down and again laid on the table, where the priest removed the hide completely, slit the heart and cut off the legs. He laid the underside open and removed the innards, which another priest took and washed. The carcass was then carefully cut into parts, following the natural divisions so that the bones were not broken, and the parts were washed and salted. The entirety was burnt.

E.P. Sanders, *Judaism: Practice and Belief* [1]

Salvation and sacrifice

The practice of ritual sacrifice, the offering of a burnt carcass to God (a 'holocaust' no less), exhibits *in nuce* the violent economy of kitsch. Commenting on the suitability of describing these sacrifices as sin-offerings Sanders remarks: 'In some cases the English word "sin", which implies transgression, is inappropriate, and consequently some scholars prefer "purification offering". After childbirth, for example, a woman brought a "sin offering" (Leviticus 12: 6) even though she had done nothing wrong.' [2] The sacrificial mechanism is a way of dealing with ritual impurity – with shit, variously construed. One could argue along these lines that the book of Leviticus represents the codification of kitsch; the development of a systematic programme for the exclusion, or at least, for the management, of shit.

Given the way in which I described the incarnation at the end of the last chapter it must be obvious that I see the incarnation as instituting a wholly different theological spirit, moreover one totally at odds with the economics of ritual sacrifice. And indeed I will be arguing in the course of this chapter, following René Girard, that Jesus re-construes salvation as resistance to the workings of the sacrificial mechanism; that, roughly speaking, Jesus re-invents salvation as forgiveness. Part of the problem with taking this line is that one finds oneself in direct opposition to a powerful tradition of Christian thought which seeks to interpret the saving work of Christ in precisely those terms that I believe Christ himself rejected. When Jesus turns over the tables of the money changers in the temple he is, I think, commenting upon the practice of ritual sacrifice that the money changing sustained. On the Girardian model, salvation is only possible by rejecting the whole idea that salvation can be effected by sacrifice (and I want to splice into Girard's account my own concern with kitsch, for the rejection of the sacrificial mechanism can be seen as the rejection of that practice which sustains the activity of kitsch). On this account the violence inherent within sacrifice is precisely what we need saving from – at least, one of the important things we need saving from. On the other model (represented particularly by Anselm and Calvin), sacrifice remains the means by which we are saved. We are saved by Jesus' sacrifice of himself on the cross. Saved by the blood of the lamb, so to speak. There was no other good enough to pay the price of sin . . . etc.

How does all of this relate to Nietzsche? One of the things frequently missed about the famous 'death of God' passage in *The Gay Science* (aphorism 125) is that Nietzsche quite clearly speaks of it as a murder:

> 'Whither is God?,' he cried. 'I shall tell you. We have killed him – you and I. All of us are his murderers.'

The madman then continues with an increasingly bloody and clearly sacrificial description of this murder and its consequences:

> God is dead. God remains dead. And we have killed him. How shall we, the murderers of all murderers, comfort ourselves? What was holiest and most powerful of all that the world has yet owned has bled to death under our knives. Who will wipe this blood off us? What water is there for us to clean ourselves? What festivals of atonement, what sacred games shall we have to invent?

This passage illustrates much of the conflicted psychology I have been ascribing to Nietzsche. Only God – or something God-like – is able to forgive, or provide a basis for the atonement of God's murder. Only God – or something God-like – is able to fill the hole left by God's death. As Ofelia Schutte has noted, Nietzsche's mourning for God, his sense that God's death provides material for tragedy (rather than seeing it as something exclusively liberating and an occasion for undiluted joy) reveals Nietzsche's nostalgia for the dead God.[3] But it is not just God that Nietzsche misses: still more he misses (at the same time as being the most hostile critic of) the rites of atonement through which Christianity had dealt with human sin. Nietzsche's thought is shaped by these twin drives: a powerful, almost overwhelming sense of the need for redemption, coupled with a devastating critique of the provenance of that need and the pathologies inherent within it.

But in turning away from the Christian God Nietzsche does not turn away from sacrifice, indeed his alternative soteriology appeals to another great tradition of sacrificial practice – that of the Greeks and, in particular, to the Greek deity most closely associated with sacrificial practice, Dionysus.[4] Dionysus is, of course, an extremely complex figure, an enigma to generations of classicists and a subject of theological controversy even during the very height of the popularity of the Dionysian cult itself. Albert Henrichs, in an article on the use and abuse of Dionysus 'from Nietzsche to Girard' has observed 'no other god has created more confusion in the modern mind, nor produced a wider spectrum of different and often contradictory interpretations.'[5] It is (luckily) no part of my argument to set out in search of the historical Dionysus; sufficient for my purpose is to examine Nietzsche's Dionysus. So while I sympathise with Rainer Friedrich in his attack upon the Dionysus of 'bloodshed, cannibalism, savagery, violence, death-cult irrationalism, and madness' as a reflection of the post-Romantic preoccupation with the primitive and savage, agreeing also that too often the Dionysus of myth is superimposed upon the Dionysian cult, nonetheless, in as much as this is a study of Nietzsche, it is precisely with this dark malevolent Dionysus of myth that we are concerned.[6] This is the Dionysus who is seduced, cooked and eaten by the Titans (from which death Dionysus is subsequently 'resurrected'). This is the Dionysus whose cults incorporated the ritual dismemberment (*sparagmos*) of a sacrificial victim. And for all Nietzsche's hostility to Euripides, it is also the Dionysus of *The Bacchae*. When the maenad women, driven by religious ecstasy, rip Pentheus apart with their bare hands, they are worshipping the same divinity which tears down the *principium individuationis* in *The Birth of Tragedy*, the same god of *Rauch* 'worshipped' by Nietzsche – the god of the rave, the god of dance, the god of intoxication, the god of violence. But, above all, this Dionysus is the divinity who stands for 'salvation' by sacrifice or violent exclusion (this, as we have seen, is the shadow side of kitsch). Nietzsche uses Dionysus to articulate a post-Christian soteriology parallel to 'traditional' atonement theology. He presses Dionysus into the service of re-creating an understanding of salvation that, *prima facie*, looks nothing like the Christian equivalent, but in fact borrows the fundamental shape of traditional atonement theology and shares its fundamental fault: that it is a pretext for violence and exclusion.

Girard's work on sacrifice is premised upon an analysis of violence as the inevitable outcome of the workings of what he calls 'mimetic desire'. We learn, Girard insists, by imitation. Indeed, it is not just that we learn things like speech by copying those around us, for Girard our very desires are learned by copying. This means that all desire is imitation of the desire of another. And this means that desire leads to conflict. As I work, my two children are squabbling in the background. They both want to play with the same Barbie doll. Isabella desires to play with Barbie according to the desire of her elder sister, Alice. For Girard, this familiar domestic squabble occasioned by sibling rivalry can be seen as a model for a whole range of violent conflicts that erupt within communities as a result of the workings of mimetic desire. Mimetic desire renders all communities unstable and prone to violent conflict.

Sacrifice, according to Girard, is a mechanism by which a society saves itself from the potentially devastating effects of communal violence which is consequent upon mimetic desire. Sacrifice is an outlet for violence which otherwise would perpetuate itself in a never-ending cycle of tit-for-tat reprisals.[7] 'Violence' Girard claims 'is not to be denied, but can be diverted onto another object, something it can sink its teeth into.'[8] That something is the sacrificial victim; the one upon whom violence can be vented without unleashing further violence which would threaten to consume society. Sacrifice is a means of avoiding war. Instead of striking his wife the angry husband kicks the dog – his marriage is (supposedly) thereby protected and his anger assuaged.

As Richard Seaford has argued, quite independently of Girard, the Dionysian cult becomes a way of protecting the *polis*. It encourages civic solidarity by the casting out of a sacrificial victim(s). For Girard, communal unity is re-established after a dangerous crescendo of violent rivalry by picking on a weak and ineffectual other (such as the dog) and scapegoating them, sacrificing them. Only thus is 'peace' restored. Seaford claims 'Greek tragedy is the dramatisation of aetiological myth shaped by the vital need to create and sustain the *polis*.'[9] He goes on to argue that the mythology of Dionysus reveals the very basis of Greek tragedy:

> Dionysos is not involved in many myths in the archaic and classical periods. But there is one that is told of various places in roughly the same form. Dionysos arrives from abroad but is rejected by the ruler or ruling family, and so he inflicts upon the family a frenzy which results in the females becoming maenads in the wild, in one member of the family killing another in a perversion of animal sacrifice, and finally in the establishment of Dionysos' cult . . . I would suggest that this pattern is common in all tragedy: kin-killing, often in a kind of frenzy and involving the perversion of ritual, concluded by the prefigurement of establishment of communal cult.[10]

'Religion' has a key role in this 'sustenance' of the city. According to Girard, the purpose of religion, indeed the founding purpose of religion, is to conceal the violence of this means of sustenance, of the sacrificial mechanism, by mythologising it, by making it 'sacred'. 'Religion' is the means by which a community launders its own violence. It is why the temple is so obsessed with purification and washing – just like Lady Macbeth, in fact. Temple religion is a cover and legitimisation of the sort of violence that cements civic solidarity by a controlled detonation of violence manifest as the exclusion of an ineffectual innocent. The ceremonial dimension of religion not only offers a suitably rule-bound context in which this controlling is made possible, but it also disguises the violence that is being discharged, dressing it up, and thus not reflecting back to the community the violence that is being ritually expressed and enacted. Milbank puts it thus:

> The mystification of the socially beneficial effects of scapegoating constitutes the precise point of birth of religion, whose real function is to legitimate and conceal acts of founding violence. By the same token religions are machines for the forgetting of history and the substitution of mythology.[11]

Nietzsche himself writes: 'all religions are, at their most fundamental, systems of cruelty.'[12] Even so, if Seaford is right about the shape and purpose of tragedy, Nietzsche hardly escapes the charge of cruelty in preferring tragedy to religion.

Girard's unique genealogy of religion when applied to Nietzsche has remarkable consequences. For Nietzsche's soteriology is premised upon exclusion, it too is premised upon the rejection of the victim, though in his case the victims are many and the redeemed very few. His preparedness to sacrifice the herd in the formation of the *Übermensch* is, on the Girardian model, a religious move, a move which calls for the invention of new 'festivals of atonement' and 'sacred games'. For Girard, these games need to be partially invisible; sacrifice needs to be dressed up in such a way that its violence is disguised. And because Nietzsche has already unmasked the violence hidden within the Christian priest, a new way of hiding soteriological violence is required. 'Religion' no longer serves its purpose of disguising violence. Being an 'atheist' is therefore a useful alibi in Nietzsche's construction of an alternative scheme of salvation. The reason I have spent some time rehearsing Girard's argument is that through it (and once again) one can come to see Nietzsche as a dangerous unreconstructed religious obsessive.

Nietzsche's philosophy is in a sense about the founding of a new sort of religion; at least, he invents a new and very exclusive conception of salvation, which is disguised as anti-religion. Indeed, though it has become largely invisible to the modern reader, Nietzsche is clearly a religious thinker, and not just in the obvious sense that he is one who thinks about 'religion'. Nietzsche has a faith, his faith is Dionysian. His hostility is not to religion *per se* (whatever one might actually mean by the very slippery term 'religion') but hostility to Christianity. The fight Nietzsche is conducting is not, as it were, anti-religion vs. religion, or atheism vs. Christianity; it is, as he clearly says it is, Dionysus vs. the Crucified. It is about the spiritual superiority of

Nietzsche's faith to that of Christianity. It is not, as so many commentators readily assume, a battle against faith, but a battle between faiths, or rather, a battle between competing soteriologies.

A few sentences back I described Nietzsche as a dangerous unreconstructed religious obsessive. What do I mean by unreconstructed? Basically, following Girard, I see the theological significance of the Gospels as being a full-scale attack upon 'religion' as I have just described it. Jesus' attack upon the Pharisees, the religious establishment as represented by the Temple, and so on, is an attack upon religion as scapegoating. Jesus reinvents salvation as forgiveness. Jesus reconstructs religion on the basis of the perspective of the one excluded. It is here that Christianity and the religion of Nietzsche find themselves utterly opposed to each other.

Jesus contra Dionysus

The one important difference with Christianity, Girard insists, is that Jesus is not the agent of casting out, but the one cast out, not the victimiser but the victim. This is the sense in which it is acceptable to speak of Jesus' death as a sacrifice. And the difference between this sacrifice and that conducted in the name of Dionysus or at the Temple is not that it inverts the pattern: not the sacrifice of the weak to save the strong nor (as Nietzsche thinks of Christianity) the sacrifice of the strong to save the weak, rather it is a rejection of the violence inherent within the whole sacrificial mechanism itself. It is a rejection of Dionysian soteriology.

For Girard, Jesus is the only true opponent of 'religion' (which we might define as the sacralisation of sacrifice). The Gospels, he insists, represent a full-frontal attack upon this whole sacrificial mechanism. 'Go away and learn what this means: I desire mercy, not sacrifice' (Matt. 9: 13) quotes Jesus from the Hebrew scriptures.[13] Jesus reveals the violence hidden within a society built upon sacrificial exclusion by his readiness to become a wholly innocent victim of it. Too often the radical nature of Jesus' response to violence is lost by interpreting the significance of his life and death in the very sacrificial terms he rejects; that is, Jesus is the 'lamb of God who takes away the sins of the world'. Just as in Anselm's theory of the atonement, the God-man is required in order to provide a suitable sacrifice to appease the angry God. On this account Jesus takes upon himself the sins of the world and takes them with him to the cross, thus cleansing humanity of its sinfulness and restoring a right-relationship between God and humanity. This, for Girard, is precisely the sort of thinking that Jesus attacks. The 'sacrifice' of Jesus is a sacrifice only in a very particular sense. It is a way of revealing to humanity its own violence, and specifically the violence implicit within sacrificial soteriology. As such it calls for a rejection of the whole sacrificial mechanism, urging humanity to found itself upon a mimesis of the innocent victim as the only way of rejecting, once and for all, the violence generated by mimetic desire. The new mimesis is *Imitatio Christi*. This is, for example, exactly what is being described in the Sermon on the Mount. Not an eye for an eye, but a preparedness to suffer violence without returning it.

The sacrificial theology of the Gospels is, therefore, wholly different from, indeed opposed to, the sacrificial theology implicit within the sacrificial practices of the Jewish religious establishment and which classic doctrines of the atonement, such as Anselm's, perpetuate. Whereas on this latter model, the community in general is 'saved' or cleansed by the sacrifice of the scapegoat, the Gospels, on the other hand, reveal the sacrificing community to be damned, or at least indicted, not saved, by its involvement with sacrificial practices. And this revealing takes place precisely at the point at which the sacrificing community sacrifices one who has no complicity in the violence of society. As Jesus is cursed, spat upon, beaten and then strung up, the brutality of sacrifice pierces the religious gloss and is seen for what it is. This, then, is the sense in which the cross is judgement upon the wicked.

Nietzsche, of course, develops an ethic based upon the opposite ideal. For Nietzsche 'victims' are the real enemy. Powerlessness does not wipe out the desire of the 'victim' for vengeance, indeed it amplifies it. Moreover, because of this powerlessness, vengeance becomes sublimated into value and, eventually, into self-hatred. This is the birth-story of *ressentiment* and, according to Nietzsche, the root cause of the moral and spiritual turmoil of late nineteenth-century post-Christian Europe. Nietzsche would surely reject Girard's soteriology as the epitome of the Christian glorification of the victim and celebration of weakness.

But is Nietzsche's charge against Christianity entirely fair (not, of course, that he is ever interested in being fair)? Jesus does not set out to become a victim, and Jesus does not believe victims are in any sense necessarily virtuous *per se*. Rather it is Jesus' capacity to resist violence and vengeance without thereby perpetuating it that constitutes the centre of his ethical imperative; it is simply that this resistance is only effective if it totally eschews violence, a consequence of which is that one becomes vulnerable to it. As Simone Weil puts it: 'Whoever takes up the sword shall perish by the sword. And whoever does not take up the sword (or lets it go) shall perish on the cross.'[14]

But Nietzsche is partially correct. The non-violent resistance of evil often has for those who seek to practise it the psychological consequence of increasing and magnifying feelings of hostility towards the 'evil' they resist and Christians are often insufficiently honest about this. For Girard, what Nietzsche is pointing out is the way in which the instinct for vengeful reciprocity continues to assert itself when violent retribution is denied. I may respond to your striking me by turning the other cheek, but in my guts I still want to punch you back. That instinct may, of course, have all sorts of morally significant consequences, and Nietzsche is right to point them out. But even so, such consequences are surely a price worth paying for calling a halt to retributive violence. Girard puts it thus:

Ressentiment is the interiorisation of weakened vengeance. Nietzsche suffers so much from it that he mistakes it for the original and primary form of vengeance. He sees *ressentiment* not merely as the child of Christianity, which it certainly is, but also as its father, which it certainly is not. *Ressentiment* flourishes in a world where real vengeance (Dionysus) has been weakened. The Bible and the Gospels have diminished the violence of vengeance and turned it to *ressentiment* not because they originate in the latter but because their real target is vengeance in all its forms, and they succeeded in wounding vengeance, not eliminating it. The Gospels are indirectly responsible; we alone are directly responsible. *Ressentiment* is the manner in which the spirit of vengeance survives the impact of Christianity and turns the Gospels to its own use.[15]

Ressentiment is what is left of vengeance once one sets out on the road for peace. Nietzsche is at his best in seeking out and revealing the instinct for vengeance that hides behind the false Christian smile or the pathos of the victim. In times of peace and prosperity it is easy to miss the bigger picture and confuse this interiorised weakened vengeance with the real thing. Girard continues:

Nietzsche was less blind to the role of vengeance in human culture than most people of his time, but nevertheless there was blindness in him. He analysed *ressentiment* and all its works with enormous power. He did not see that the evil he was fighting was a relatively minor evil compared to the more violent forms of vengeance. His insight was partly blunted by the deceptive quiet of his post-Christian society. He could afford the luxury of resenting *ressentiment* so much that it appeared a fate worse than real vengeance. Being absent from the scene, real vengeance was never seriously apprehended. Unthinkingly, like so many thinkers of his age and ours, Nietzsche called on Dionysus, begging him to bring back real vengeance as a cure for what seemed to him the worst of all possible fates, *ressentiment*.[16]

Girard's claim that in Nietzsche 'real vengeance was never seriously apprehended' is parallel to my accusation that Nietzsche's account of suffering is prone to kitsch. In the last chapter I suggested an association between kitsch and the political aesthetics of the fascist appeal to the mob. Girard helps me to continue this line of thought, for what Girard reveals is that Dionysus is the God of the mob, of the herd, the God of mass hysteria. As he puts it: 'Dionysus is the God of decisive mob action'. It is the mob who bay for the blood of the sacrificial victim. It is the frenzied mob of women who tear Pentheus to pieces under the charm of Dionysus. Indeed it is the mob who cry 'Crucify him' at Jesus. And whereas Jesus stands against the mob – revealing their hatred by his very innocence – Nietzsche, in siding with Dionysus, is surely siding with the mob. And what Girard could have gone on to spell out more clearly is that the vengeance Nietzsche called upon to remedy *ressentiment* turned out to be the vengeance of the mob as expressed by fascism. That through Nazism the horrific logic of the sacrificial mechanism reached its climax with the systematic murder of six million Jews. Dionysus is not the divinity of the strong self-contained individual, but the divinity of mob vengeance. Dionysus is the patron saint of mass extermination. And if Nietzsche is implicated in the holocaust it is not because he was anti-Jewish – he wasn't – but because he too was a worshipper of Dionysus, the god who effects salvation by way of exclusion.

Nietzsche's appeal to Stoicism

It could be objected that I have not been entirely fair on Nietzsche in another respect. For there is an alternative way of positioning Nietzsche vis-à-vis Girard in which Nietzsche is read as anticipating the insights made by Girard and of offering an answer to the same basic problem, namely the way in which violence perpetuates itself.

Nietzsche, like Girard, is awake to the ways in which the desire for retribution is the engine of a good deal of cultural activity. In the second chapter of *On the Genealogy of Morals* Nietzsche elaborates this idea with reference to the institution of creditor and debtor. In order to secure his loan the creditor enters into a bargain with the debtor that gives the creditor various legally secured powers over the debtor if the debtor is unable to repay the loan. However 'legal', this retributive system licenses vengeance and makes it socially acceptable.

> But in particular, the creditor could inflict all kinds of dishonour and torture on the body of the debtor, for example, cutting as much flesh off as seemed appropriate to the debt: – from this standpoint there were everywhere, early on, estimates which went into horrifying detail, legally drawn up estimates for individual limbs and parts of the body . . . Let us be quite clear about the logic of this whole matter of compensation: it is strange enough. The equivalence is provided by the fact that instead of an advantage directly making up for the wrong (so, instead of compensation in money, land or possessions of any kind), a sort of pleasure is given to the creditor as repayment and compensation – the pleasure of having the right to exercise power over the powerless without a thought, the pleasure *de faire le mal pour le plaisir de la faire*, the enjoyment of violating . . . So, then, compensation is made up of a warrant for and entitlement to cruelty.[17]

Nietzsche believes this 'enjoyment of violating' has come to be written into the very social fabric of human life. Moreover, and perhaps more importantly, this 'entitlement to cruelty' becomes the basis for many of our fundamental moral benchmarks, not least those which inform Christian conceptions of salvation. It has become a familiar observation among theologians that there is an important connection between the way in which the law is understood to work, in particular of the place and purpose of punishment, and the way in which the atonement is understood to work. Anselm's *Cur Deus Homo?*, it is commonly observed, is a theological extension of the basic retributive principles of Roman law. It is no coincidence that, as the reception of Roman law took place in Europe during the late eleventh and early twelfth centuries, so too retributive theologies of atonement became increasingly popular. Nietzsche observes that the legal pretext for violence informs much of Christian soteriology. In return Christianity baptises the violence inherent within the legal system. Nietzsche calls this the 'spiritualisation of cruelty'. For Nietzsche, God and the law form a pact of mutual support steeped in blood.

> In this sphere of legal obligations then, we find the breeding-ground of the moral conceptual world of 'guilt', 'conscience', 'duty', 'sacred duty', – all began with a thorough and prolonged blood-letting, like the beginning of all great things on earth. And may we not add that this world has really never quite lost a certain odour of blood and torture?[18]

Nietzsche goes on to suggest that the cruelty upon which society is founded expresses itself in a whole range of social guises:

> not so long ago it was unthinkable to hold a royal wedding or full-scale festival for the people without executions, tortures or perhaps an auto-da-fé, similarly, no noble household was without creatures on whom people could discharge their malice and cruel taunts with impunity.[19]

This cruelty provokes the need for revenge. As Zarathustra puts it: 'The spirit of revenge, my friends, has so far been the subject of man's best reflection; and where there was suffering, one wanted punishment also.' In the following passage, which prefigures Girard's work to an extraordinary extent, Nietzsche demonstrates that he too recognises the pathologies of that sacrificial mechanism by which society deals with its own violence.

> The anger of the injured creditor, the community, makes him return to the savage and outlawed state from which he was sheltered hitherto: he is cast out – and now any kind of hostile act can be perpetrated on him. 'Punishment' at this level of civilization is simply a copy, a mimus, of normal behaviour towards a hated, disarmed enemy who has been defeated, and who has not only forfeited all rights and safeguards, but all mercy as well; in fact, the rules of war and the victory celebration of *vae victus*! In all their mercilessness and cruelty: – which explains the fact

that war itself (including the warlike cult of the sacrificial victim) has given us all forms in which punishment manifests itself in history.[20]

For both Girard and Nietzsche the central question is how one breaks the cycle of self-perpetuating violence. Girard's answer, his way of getting beyond the logic of the blood-feud, is the answer of the victim; Nietzsche's answer is the answer of the victor – or, at least, it seeks to demonstrate that the need for a sacrificial mechanism is overcome by the confidence and security brought about by power and not powerlessness. In effect his answer is that mercy is only possible through strength.

> As a community grows in power, it ceases to take the offence of the individual quite so seriously, because they do not seem to be as dangerous and destabilising for the survival of the whole as they did earlier: the wrongdoer is no longer . . . cast out . . . instead the wrongdoer is carefully shielded by the community from this anger, especially from that of the immediate injured party, and given protection.[21]

This, of course, is another answer to the problem set up by Girard and, on the face of it at least, a far more practicable one. Girard himself acknowledges that the problem with retributive violence is that it threatens the stability, indeed the very viability, of communal living. Nietzsche believes that a society that has sufficient power and authority over itself is able to absorb a degree of violence without self-destructing or needing to cast out a scapegoat. Mercy, he contends, is only possible from a position of strength: 'mercy; it remains the prerogative of the most powerful man'.[22]

One of the principal influences upon Nietzsche's thinking about strength is that of Stoicism. For the Stoic, the most important thing for a human being to develop, indeed the *only* thing worth developing, is virtue. Virtue is, in itself, sufficient for happiness. The happy man is the one who seeks nothing other than his own virtue. This means that one must treat with equal indifference wealth or poverty, illness or health; in fact anything which is beyond the remit of self-sufficient virtue (though the Stoics do develop a theory of 'preferred indifferents').

A number of commentators use the following example: returning home to find his house on fire and his child inside, the Stoic sage seeks to save the child from the flames – because that is the virtuous thing to do. If, however, he is unable to save his child the Stoic sage will have no regrets. This for three reasons: 'First, because the sage did the right thing . . . Second because death is not an evil but an "unpreferred indifferent" . . . And, third, everything that happens is ordered for the best by Providence.'[23] It is interesting to note, with Nietzsche in mind, that the 'hardness' of Stoicism is connected with a cosmological view which enables the sage to treat with equal affirmation whatever Providence might bring, even the death of a child. This, as I have argued, is the sort of state Nietzsche believes is suggested by the eternal recurrence: an affirmation of life in its totality, so-called tragedies and all. And it is no coincidence that the Stoics (arguing from the impossibility of a 'first cause') themselves believed that history endlessly repeated itself in identical cycles.

The civic virtue of Stoicism, the social usefulness of Stoic 'hardness', is well expressed by Seneca in his *De Ira*. Seneca's interlocutor, his brother Novatus, says a number of things about anger which tie in with our theme of self-perpetuating violence. He says, for instance, 'But anger has some pleasure, and it is sweet to return pain for pain' (2.32) and 'We shall be less despised, if we avenge a wrong' (2.33). Here we glimpse what Girard and Nietzsche, as well as Seneca, believe to be the engine of self-perpetuating violence. Having brought Novatus to see the pathological nature of these expressions of anger, Seneca proceeds to demonstrate how they are to be overcome. One has, in a sense, to make oneself 'hard'; give up attachments, particularly emotional ones, which generate such anger, and seek to found one's life upon virtue alone. One must be 'above' the need to respond to violence with violence. One must have the strength to see slights against one's person – indeed even to loved ones – as a matter of total indifference, save how such slights intersect with one's sense of virtue.

Here, then, is another way of breaking the cycle of violence and vengeance. What is to be made of it? Firstly, surely this: it must be the case that this sort of 'hardness' is some unrealistic fantasy. Can the Stoic sage really remain indifferent to the screams of his burning child? And if he does, if indeed he is prepared to affirm these screams as a necessary condition of the full affirmation of life, surely he is not to be admired. Nussbaum argues that the 'hardness' of the Stoics and Nietzsche is a symptom of their weakness, not of their strength. It is the 'hardness' of one who wishes to become, or fantasises he can become, something other than (more than? less than?) human. Deafness to the screams of the child is the deafness of one who has lost sight of humanity. Nussbaum argues:

> Finally, we arrive at what perhaps is the deepest question about the antipity tradition: is its ideal of strength really a picture of strength? What should we think about a human being who insists on caring deeply for nothing that he does not control . . . who cultivates the hardness of self-command as a bulwark against all the reversals that life can bring? We could say, with Nietzsche, that this is a strong person. But there is clearly another way to see things. For there is a strength of a specifically human sort in the willingness to acknowledge some truths about one's situation: one's mortality, one's finitude, the limits and vulnerabilities of one's body, one's need for food and drink and shelter and friendship . . . There is, in short, a strength in the willingness to be porous rather than totally hard, in the willingness to be a mortal animal living in the world. The Stoic, by contrast, looks like a fearful person, a person who is

determined to seal himself off from risk, even at the cost of the loss of love and value . . . He fails, that is, to see what the Stoicism he endorses has in common with the Christianity he criticises, what 'hardness' has in common with otherworldliness: both are forms of self-protection, both express a fear of this world.[24]

Nussbaum thereby charges the anti-pity tradition with a disloyalty to the earth; a cardinal crime in Nietzsche's book, of course. But what about the idea that this disloyalty is generated out of fear? Fear of what? Or of whom? This is the question we will turn to in the next chapter.

8   Fear of the other

Honesty

What is supposed to be so wrong with pity? For the Stoic tradition that Nietzsche endorses, pity belittles the one pitied as well as the pitier. The quality of mercy is not twice blessed but twice cursed. It is patronising to the person who is pitied and smugly self-congratulatory on the part of the pitier. It is a cheap and easy response to the suffering other in which emotionalism becomes the false currency of human care. Pain has to be endured, conquered and overcome by strength of spirit – pity only weakens the strength of that spirit and leads the person pitied into mournful self-disappointment. This simply adds to the sum total of unhappiness in the world.

Nietzsche's sympathies for this sort of argument grow out of his sense of moral honesty. Pity ultimately misrepresents. It substitutes bedside manner for a clear-eyed encounter with painful reality. Pity stands in the way of tough-mindedness about the human condition. As we have already seen, honesty is one of Nietzsche's core values and in rejecting pity Nietzsche is seeking a more honest encounter with the world. Rejecting pity is about rejecting palliatives. Nussbaum argues that Nietzsche's pseudo-hardness is a subtle form of otherworldliness – a betrayal of this earth. Nietzsche sees it the other way round: hardness is honesty.

My argument in this chapter will be that Nietzsche's sense of honesty is too narrow in focus and insufficiently aware of the levels of honesty revealed in the more ordinary and communal activities of everyday life. In one key respect, as I have already argued, Nietzsche was not a child of the Reformation: he continued to think of vocation as being something extra-ordinary, something that required one to be set apart from the domestic and the humdrum. For all his condemnation of religious asceticism, Nietzsche continually sought out the habitat of monks; the empty wilderness or the solitude of the mountaintop. His whole energy seeks the cultivation of the individual self (in this, of course, he is supremely a thinker of the Reformation), a cultivation that is premised upon a sense of scrupulous honesty about his own spiritual journey. The battle conducted by Nietzsche is a battle conducted on his own, and with himself, in which he employs the demands of absolute honesty as a way of establishing or generating his true identity in the full awareness of the horrors of life. It is, as Nietzsche sees it, these 'horrors', the horrors of human suffering, that stand in the way of full self-realisation, for constantly they tempt one to betray the vocation of absolute honesty in favour of self-comforting. But there are more ways in which one can be deceived, or tempted to self-deception, than by the desire to avoid the full reality of human suffering. This is important, because Nietzsche is so focused upon this particular source of dishonesty that he fails fully to recognise the power of any other. Dishonesty has many motives. And Nietzsche's preoccupation with himself, with the state of his own spiritual health, has about it another powerful form of dishonesty which his great sensitivity to the pathologies of self-comforting does not prepare him to recognise or combat. For Nietzsche's struggle to be honest is a struggle to be honest about himself. He is not really concerned with whether he is honest about others – hence his shocking misrepresentations. But is it, in the end, really possible to be fully honest about oneself without being honest about others and with others? What of the idea that many of us 'become who we are' in and through a relationship with others? What of the idea that relationships make possible (and require) a level of honesty about oneself that is not possible in isolation? If so, then Nietzsche's self-focus, for all its intensity, may turn out to be a strange form of dishonesty. A dishonesty which, as Nussbaum suggests, is motivated by a fear of vulnerability, of dependency, of not being fully in control.

Stanley Cavell and 'skepticism'

In the last few chapters I have sought to construct a picture of Nietzsche's soteriology as being built upon, indeed perhaps, as being constituted by, his willingness to exclude; by a certain sort of denial. I have examined this denial, in particular, in terms of the desire to purify and in terms of the workings of sacrifice. At various points I have, albeit *sotto voce*, sought to contrast this excluding soteriology with an including soteriology which is built around the notion of forgiveness. In what follows I want to offer a reading of the motivational forces that lead Nietzsche to an excluding soteriology. Though I have no wish to over-psychologise Nietzsche's thought – that is, I do not want to suggest that Nietzsche's philosophy is undermined simply by calling into question the forces that motivate it – nonetheless, such an approach may open up new and potentially important ways of understanding that philosophy, and, of course, ways that open up new levels of criticism. At least, this is precisely the sort of strategy developed to such powerful effect by Nietzsche himself in attacking Christianity. My reading of the motivational forces behind Nietzsche's excluding soteriology is generated by the application of a seam of thought developed by the philosopher Stanley Cavell concerning what he calls 'skepticism'.[1] Before I can go on to apply this thought to Nietzsche I need to give a synopsis of Cavell's complex and multi-layered strategy of argument.

By 'skepticism' Cavell means various things, linked, so to speak, by family resemblance. At the analytic end of the philosophical tradition this 'skepticism' is represented by 'other minds' skepticism and skepticism concerning the existence of the world. But this is only one dimension of the phenomenon which also includes, for example, the skepticism of Leontes concerning his wife's fidelity, the failure to recognise (or refusal to admit) the humanity in another human being, the suspicion I have that you don't like me and the puzzlement I feel in working out how I might come to know what you really think. In a sense, Cavell uses 'skepticism' as a way of confronting what one might call the 'problem of the other'. And this so-called 'problem' is not simply, or even primarily, a philosophical concern, but, for Cavell, is to be pursued across such diverse terrain as literature, psychoanalysis, and cinema, thus illuminating the 'innumerable particular manifestations of this endemic skeptical impulse'.[2]

Cavell's interest is not, however, in 'solving' the problem of the other. He is not, as are many of his fellow Wittgensteinians, seeking to defeat the skeptic by appealing to the commonality implicit within 'ordinary language', though neither is he out to give support to the skeptic's claims not to know whether the other *really* exists. According to Cavell, the problem with the skeptic's position is that it is a displaced and misplaced expression of a fundamental and genuine human concern. Cavell asks what it is the skeptic wants to know, what sort of evidence would count as sufficient, when the skeptic asks after the existence of another. Unlike those thinkers who begin with a sense that human beings are essentially alien to one another, Cavell insists that the actual practice of social intercourse reveals quite the opposite, that human beings exhibit a considerable attunement to one another. He begins with a sense of the effortless intimacy of two people sharing a joke or having a row. How then does skepticism with regard to the other come to be? What is behind the skeptic's claims not to 'know' that others exist? How do we come to the belief that we are 'trapped' inside our own perspective?

Cavell argues that what is going on in thinking such as this is a translation of the complex demands of social intercourse into the language of philosophy, thus effectively de-problematising the emotionally sensitive questions of human contact by rendering them metaphysical or philosophical. In a sense, skeptical philosophy avoids the more difficult, one might say human-all-too-human 'problem of the other', by making the uncertainty inherent within human contact some sort of philosophical puzzle to be solved intellectually. Thus Cavell writes:

> In making the knowledge of others a metaphysical difficulty philosophers deny how real the practical difficulty is of coming to know another person, and how little we can reveal of ourselves to another's

gaze, or bear of it. Doubtless such denials are part of the motive which sustains metaphysical difficulties.[3]

The sense of a gap that divides us from our fellow human beings is generated by a desire to avoid the vulnerabilities, the openness and consequent risk, inherent within genuine human encounter. As one commentator has put it: 'Our turning from others – and not, say, simply being uncertain about them – points to something in us (shame, for example, or embarrassment) and not something missing in them.'[4] Cavell dubs this 'avoidance'.

How then are we to respond to the skeptic and to the demand that unless we have some cast-iron proof of the existence of the other, or of the other's faithfulness, then such things can never be said to be fully known? Cavell suggests the following:

> Mightn't it be that just this haphazard, unsponsored state of the world, just this radiation of relationships, of my cares and commitments, provides the milieu in which my knowledge of others can be best expressed? Just this – say expecting someone to tea; or returning a favour; waving goodbye; reluctantly or happily laying in groceries for a friend with a cold; feeling rebuked, and feeling it would be humiliating to admit the feeling; pretending not to understand that the other has taken my expression, with a certain justice, as meaning more than I sincerely wished it to mean; hiding inside a marriage, hiding outside a marriage – just such things are perhaps the most that knowing others comes to, or has come to for me.[5]

For Cavell skepticism should not be explained away – because there *is* something legitimate and real in puzzling over the otherness of the other – but neither ought it to be generalised into a philosophical principle. And in order to halt the pressure to generalise the puzzlement, Cavell seeks to undermine the idea that it makes any sense to speak of a 'best case' scenario for knowing others; that is, there isn't anything that could do the sort of work required by the skeptic: by Descartes as well as by Leontes or Othello.

For Cavell, our sense of human commonality is sustained by two things: a participation in the 'ordinary' and our sense of 'empathic projection' (the very things, of course, that Nietzsche so despises). By emphasising the 'ordinary', Cavell means to draw attention to the role of our everyday (going-about-our-) business in weaving us together in a way that makes the expression of generalised skepticism seem disingenuous (and there is, of course, more than an echo of Wittgenstein's notion of forms of life in Cavell's use of the term 'ordinary'). Michael Fisher claims that 'In Cavell's account, the skeptic deprives himself of our ordinary links with the world and each other and then tries – unsuccessfully – to repair those links all by himself.'[6]

Empathic projection is, for Cavell, the name for a sense of kinship that one acknowledges between oneself and another; that sense in which we identify with another and recognise what is shared and common to us both. It is not that empathic projection is some reliable way of *answering* the skeptic's problem (it is not some epistemic bridge). Rather, empathic projection is the name for what actually goes on every day in human contact, it is the name for our acknowledgement of our kinship with the other; it simply describes what happens, rather than provides foundations for its justification. (For Cavell the extraordinary thing about this sense of kinship is not how flimsy it is but how pervasive and powerful it is.) To anticipate a little the connections with Nietzsche it is worth noting that Wittgenstein's word for empathic projection is, sometimes, 'pity': 'Pity, one might say, is the form of conviction that someone else is in pain.'[7] In this light Nietzsche's rejection of pity is brought alongside the skeptical 'problem of the other'. In what ways, one wonders, is Nietzsche's famous suspicion analogous to Cavell's skepticism?

Applying what might have been learned from Cavell's deconstruction of skepticism to Nietzsche is problematic in a number of ways, not least because it seems that Cavell's skepticism has an overridingly Cartesian format; and whatever else Nietzsche is, he is not a skeptic of the Cartesian variety. Nietzsche is not interested in questions of other minds or the existence of the external world. Cavell, however, is the first to recognise that the skeptical recital takes a variety of forms, not all of which are reducible to those which issue from Descartes. Indeed, for Cavell, the skeptical problematic – the 'problem of the other' – is something which re-asserts itself in a whole variety of very different philosophical traditions. Though he does not mention Nietzsche by name, the following passage surely has Nietzsche somewhere in view:

> It should be considered also that an initiating form for the achievement of privacy would be the convulsion of sensibility we call the rise of Protestantism. From then on, one manages one's relation to God alone, in particular one bears the brunt alone of being known to God . . . As long as God exists, I am not alone. And couldn't the other suffer the fate of God? It strikes me that it was out of the terror of this possibility that Luther promoted the individual human voice in the religious life. I wish to understand how the other now bears the weight of God, shows me that I am not alone in the universe. This requires understanding the philosophical problem of the other as the trace or scar of the departure of God.[8]

In understanding the problem of the other thus we can begin to see a relatedness between the skeptical recital and the sorts of issues that occupy Nietzsche; and this suggests that the arguments formulated by Cavell in response, principally to Cartesian skepticism, may be, at least partially, transferable.

The foregoing excursus into the philosophy of Stanley Cavell is intended to provide a platform for the argument that Nietzsche's rejection of pity and his antipathy towards 'ordinary life' are linked to his 'azure isolation' and his desire for self-authoring, for self-salvation. I will suggest that from this perspective the motivational psychology of Nietzsche's outcasting is shown to issue from a certain sort of fear. Finally, I will return to Cavell, and to his examination of the film genre he calls 'comedies of remarriage', and look at how through that genre we see how vengeful reciprocity is overcome through what one might call cycles of eternal forgiveness – or remarriage.

Ecce Homo

In his excellent *Friedrich Nietzsche and the Politics of the Soul: A Study of Heroic Individualism* Leslie Thiele situates the source of Nietzsche's 'heroic individualism' in the realm of epistemology:

> The road to radical individualism, which has its greatest ramifications in the realms of politics and morality, finds its origin in epistemology. The starting point is the limitations of man's mind. Nietzsche's individualism is above all an extension of his skepticism.[9]

I would like to be able to agree with Thiele; indeed it would make the construction of my 'Cavellian' argument against Nietzsche all the more straightforward. Unfortunately, I think Thiele oversimplifies and thus misrepresents the complexities of Nietzsche's position. Nonetheless, I think it true to say that the references Thiele finds to epistemological skepticism are telling – though more as symptoms than as causes of the radical individualism Nietzsche promotes. That is, for Nietzsche the rejection of pity is logically anterior to the expression of epistemological skepticism. To use Cavell-type language: it is the denial of empathic projection that initiates the skeptical recital and not the other way around.

Part of my disagreement with Thiele is that, on his account, the 'personal' dimensions to Nietzsche's individualism are made subservient to the philosophical – for Nietzsche is always at pains to insist that, first and foremost, his philosophy begins in the personal. Thus, for instance, Nietzsche writes in *Ecce Homo*: 'At an absurdly early age, at the age of seven, I already knew that no human word would ever reach me.'[10] I do not believe that Nietzsche was taken with ideas of *epistemological* skepticism at the age of seven. Consider also the following. In a passage of extraordinary sadness, Nietzsche expresses his deepest loneliness, his desperate need for the comfort of another:

> The last philosopher I call myself, for I am the last human being. No one converses with me beside myself and my voice reaches me as the voice of one dying. With the beloved voice, with thee the last remembered breath of human happiness, let me discourse, even if it is only for another hour. Because of thee I delude myself as to my solitude and lie

my way back to multiplicity and love, for my heart shies away from believing that love is dead. I cannot bear the icy shivers of loneliest solitude. It compels me to speak as though I were Two.[11]

Nietzsche's answer to loneliness was to imagine himself as two persons who can then comfort each other. Nietzsche became his own imaginary friend. It can be no surprise then that the sort of salvation he sought to design for himself was a form of self-salvation.

Nietzsche's 'individualism' is made up of many elements. On one level it is about his being lonely, on another about his rejection of the mob. It is bound up with his Protestant inheritance, with his rejection of politics, as well as with his admiration for Greek heroes and a penchant for high mountains and the solitude of caves. I'm not sure how one goes about disentangling these complex tributaries or how one decides which of them is primary. I have said that I believe Nietzsche's individualism begins with his rejection of pity because I think of Nietzsche as one who uses philosophy as a tool to explore his own personality. But I do not feel entirely confident in mapping out the full topology of Nietzsche's individualism; perhaps that is something we should never feel all that confident about.

Nonetheless, although I disagree with Thiele's claim that Nietzsche's individualism finds its *source* in his epistemological skepticism, Thiele is right to highlight the existence of epistemological skepticism in Nietzsche's texts. Consider, for instance, the following:

> The habits of our senses have woven us into lies and deceptions of sensation: these again are the basis of all our judgments and 'knowledge' – there is absolutely no escape, no backway or bypath into the real world! We sit within our net, we spiders, and whatever we catch in it, we catch nothing at all except that which allows itself to be caught precisely in our net.[12]

In seeking to sort out some sort of classification for Nietzsche's various 'individualisms' I want to make a distinction between two sorts of claim. There is a great deal of difference between Nietzsche's typically over the top claim 'He shall be the greatest who can be the most solitary'[13] – a claim that cannot be absorbed into the skeptical recital – and the claim that 'In the final analysis one experiences only oneself.'[14] It is claims of this latter sort that chime in with those of Cavell's skeptic. And what Thiele does achieve is to bring to the fore this dimension of Nietzsche's work. It is on this basis that Thiele is justified in claiming of Nietzsche's anthropology: 'The individual, like the species, cannot see around his own corner. Each is locked into a world of his own.'[15]

Karl Barth suggests a related tack upon Nietzsche's 'individualism'. One of Barth's favourite targets, arguably *the* target of much of his *Protestant Theology in the Nineteenth Century*, is Pietism, and beginning with Pietism

Barth outlines a genealogy of the pathologies that have built up within Protestant thought, the weaknesses of which culminate in the ease with which that tradition sells out to the Nazis and the German Culture movement. According to Barth, one of the key root causes of the failure of Protestant resistance was the considerable influence Pietism exerted upon the Protestant imagination and in particular the influence of Pietist individualism. The importance of Nietzsche for Barth is that Nietzsche's thought, his celebration of the 'azure isolation' of the solitary individual, represents an inevitable consequence of Pietism.[16] Barth writes: 'In its basic form, in so to speak the original Pietist, it is *individualism.*' He goes on:

> This Pietist is to be seen as a fighter, a conqueror. The one who fights and conquers here is the man who had discovered himself or in himself that ultimate reality, related to God; who thus knows no object which is not in the first place really within him and which must therefore, if he sets himself against it, be brought in, be made inward, be transposed where it originally and authentically belongs . . . The sought-for goal is the appropriation of Christianity, which is regarded as complete when all that is not one's own as such is dissolved and made one's own.[17]

The Pietist rejection of all that stands over against the sovereign human individual, its rejection of any authority other than the authority of the human heart, made a lasting impression upon Nietzsche. And Nietzsche's ultimate rejection of God is nothing less than a continuation of Pietist logic; either God can be sucked into, and put in the service of, the human will, or God has to be destroyed. It wasn't so much that God had to die in order for humanity to flourish (as so many followers of Nietzsche understand him to be saying) but that God had to die in order for the individual to assume what had been hitherto divine sovereignty. Nietzsche claimed for the individual the place traditional Christianity had ascribed to God: 'The "ego" subdues and kills: it operates like an organic cell: it is a robber and violent. It wants to regenerate itself – pregnancy. It wants to give birth to its god and see all mankind at his feet.'[18] Luce Irigaray (picking up the image of birthing) puts it another way. In setting up an imaginary dialogue with Nietzsche, and accusing him of *ressentiment* against life and specifically a *ressentiment* against women (as having a 'womb-envy' expressed in his desire to give birth to himself), she writes:

> To overcome the impossible of your desire – that surely is your last hour's desire. Giving birth to such and such a production, or such and such a child is a summary of your history. But to give birth to your desire itself, that is your final thought. To be incapable of doing it, that is your highest *ressentiment*. For either you make works that fit your desire, or you make desire itself into your work. But how will you find material to produce such a child? And going back to the source of all

your children, you want to bring yourself back into the world. As a father? Or child? And isn't being two at a time the point where you come unstuck? Because to be a father, you have to procreate, your seed has to escape and fall from you. You have to engender suns, dawns, twilights other than your own. But in fact isn't it your will, in the here and now, to pull everything back inside you and to be and to have only one sun? And to fasten up time, for you alone? And suspend the ascending and descending movement of genealogy? And to join up in one perfect place, one perfect circle, the origin and end of all things?[19]

This is a stunning (though perhaps characteristically, somewhat oblique) passage. Irigaray's point and the argument that Nietzsche seeks and fails to find self-salvation are, at base, quite the same. Nietzsche's attempt *to give birth to himself* is the ultimate logical consequence of his atheistic evangelicalism; that is, of his desire to be 'born again' but not 'born from above'.

Enough of a link has been established between Cavell's skeptic and Nietzsche's own philosophy for us to take Cavell's argument on another stage. For Cavell the acknowledgement implicit within empathic projection is necessarily reflexive. To recognise and acknowledge the other as like oneself is, at the same time, to recognise oneself as like the other. The emotional fantasy to which we readily succumb is that of the panopticon – the achievement of a position from which we can see, but cannot be seen. But the logic of acknowledgement works in another way. The other is open to our gaze only to the extent that we are open to the gaze of the other. There are, according to Cavell, certain types of skepticism that are motivated not by the demand for absolute and incontestable knowledge of the other, but rather out of the fear of its very possibility; the fear of being known. This, for instance, is how Cavell reads *King Lear*:

> My hypothesis will be that Lear's behaviour . . . is explained by – the tragedy begins because of – the same motivation which manipulates the tragedy throughout its course, from the scene which precedes the abdication, through the storm, blinding, evaded reconciliations, to the final moments: by the attempt to avoid recognition, the shame of exposure, the threat of self-revelation.

Self-exposure is resisted even if it means (and it always does) that one has to deny, or refuse to acknowledge, another. The power of the resistance to self-exposure is such that one would rather will madness or the death of loved ones than be exposed. Similarly, Cavell reads *Othello* as being about a certain sort of quasi-skeptical narcissism, by which he means 'a kind of denial of an existence shared with others' and 'the murderous lengths to which narcissism must go in order to maintain its stand of ignorance, its fear or avoidance of knowing, under the color of a claim to certainty'.[20] Could this be what underpins Nietzsche's 'sacrificial' atheology and his repression of pity?

Indeed, isn't his 'kind of denial of an existence shared with others' linked to 'the murderous lengths to which' Nietzsche will go in order to repress the claim the other has upon him? Could it be that Nietzsche's unwillingness to enter into the suffering of another, that is, his objection to the empathic projection involved with pity, represents an unwillingness not simply to see, but to be seen? Karl Barth seems to be tracking Nietzsche down in precisely this way when he writes:

> And the true danger of Christianity . . . on account of which he had to attack it with unprecedented resolution and passion . . . was that Christianity – what he called Christian morality – confronts the real man, the superman . . . with a form of man which necessarily questions and disturbs and destroys and kills him to the very root. That is to say, it confronts him with the figure of the suffering man. It demands that he should see this man, that he should accept his presence, that he should not be man without him but man with him, that he must drink with him at the same source. Christianity places before the superman the Crucified, Jesus, as the Neighbour, ignoble and despised in the eyes of the world (of the world of Zarathustra, the true world of men), the hungry and thirsty and sick and captive, a whole ocean of human meanness and painfulness. Nor does it merely place the Crucified and his host before his eyes. It does not merely will that he see Him and them. It wills that he should recognise in them his neighbours and himself.[21]

For Barth, what Nietzsche feared in the other was a reflection of his own suffering humanity. Nietzsche preferred fantasies of (super-human) strength and self-sufficiency to the recognition of human-all-too-human need and fragility. Throughout *Zarathustra*, Nietzsche's hero is haunted by the crippled dwarf, the little man, the small man. In one of the great emotional climaxes of *Thus Spoke Zarathustra*, as Zarathustra comes to feel the full force of eternal recurrence, that is, as he is faced with the reality of what he can and cannot affirm about himself, it is the *weight* of the dwarf (note especially that Nietzsche speaks of the eternal recurrence as 'the greatest weight') that restricts his full self-affirmation. In the climax of the passage Zarathustra turns on the dwarf: 'Dwarf! You! Or I!' Stanley Rosen interprets this exclamation in this way: 'The immediate sense of the image is as follows. Zarathustra can rise no higher until he overcomes the pity for humanity that still pulls him back to the earth below.'[22] In this way Nietzsche's rejection of pity (in so far as Nietzsche and Zarathustra are of a common mind at this point) represents a rejection of, a refusal to acknowledge, any sense of identity between himself and the crippled dwarf figure, suffering humanity. Better to murder the dwarf, to oust him, to sacrifice him even, than to have him make me face my own dwarfness – thus spoke Zarathustra. In rejecting suffering humanity, in casting people as the herd, Nietzsche is seeking to set himself free from the earth below. This begins Nietzsche's disloyalty to the earth; a 'murderous' disloyalty which, for all Nietzsche's emphasis on honesty, is motivated by an unwillingness fully to face the pains and disappointments of his own humanity.

Reciprocity, intimacy and marriage

As a choice for a final thought on the failures of Nietzschean soteriology 'marriage' may seem odd and strangely out of place. I am aware that some may suspect that this theme introduces an unwelcome spirit of exclusiveness associated with the more conservative elements of Church teaching. This is not my intention at all. I employ marriage, following Cavell, as a way of speaking about the ordinariness of human intimacy that is shared over time and has come to be caught up in a whole pattern of life. Cavell puts it thus: 'questions about marriage . . . are meant as questions about weddedness as a mode of human intimacy generally, intimacy in its aspect of devotedness'.

There is, nonetheless, an important theological connection between marriage and ordinariness that is worth underlining. As we have already seen, one of the key dimensions of the Protestant revolution is the celebration of what Charles Taylor calls 'ordinary life'. This revolution marks the transition from a sense of the holy based upon separateness and being set aside, to one in which the holy is seen to be enmeshed in the ordinary and the everyday. And a crucial moment in this transition is the abandonment of clerical celibacy. It is highly relevant that many of the key reformers, including Luther and Cranmer, got married while remaining priests. According to Oberman it is Luther's theology of marriage gained through an exegesis of Genesis 2: 18 that 'is truly epoch making' and at the heart of the Reformation. The celebration of marriage (rather than seeing it as occasion for regret), at least historically, constitutes a definitive moment in the celebration of the ordinary.

In Cavell's thought the ordinary everyday human intimacy that is characteristic of (Cavell's sense of) marriage is counterposed to the tragedy of avoidance. He points to a genre he calls 'comedies of remarriage' – films such as *The Philadelphia Story* and *Bringing up Baby* – which pursue the logic (and glitches) of acknowledgment. For whereas avoidance 'does violence to others, it separates their bodies from their souls, makes monsters of them; and presumably we do it because we feel others are doing this violence to us', acknowledgment is the 'release from this circle of vengeance'.[23] And here we are back to Girard.

Cavell speaks of marriage as *re*marriage to emphasise the sense in which 'redemptive' marriage, marriage that institutes cycles of acknowledgement and forgiveness, is constituted by the desire and willingness of each partner repeatedly to remarry each other. Reminding us of the connections with skepticism he writes: 'marriage is an emblem of the knowledge of others not solely because of its implication of reciprocity but because it implies a devotion, in repetition, to dailiness.'[24] This quality of repetition Cavell finds in Nietzsche's notion of eternal recurrence. Of the title 'remarriage' Cavell comments:

> The title registers, to my mind, the two most impressive affirmations known to me of the task of human experience, the acceptance of human relatedness, as the acceptance of repetition. Kierkegaard's study called *Repetition*, which is a study of the possibility of marriage; and Nietzsche's Eternal Return, the call for which he puts by saying it is high time; this is literally *Hochzeit*, German for marriage, with time itself as the ring.[25]

I have argued that Nietzsche betrays this vision by what I have called a *ressentiment* against ordinary life. It is a betrayal which leads him away from honesty, away from 'the awful truth' (significantly the title of what Cavell takes to be the most impressive of the remarriage comedies). But the 'cyclical' dimension to Nietzschean soteriology is, I think, tremendously important and in speaking of remarriage Cavell reclaims this without succumbing to Nietzsche's own brand of *ressentiment*.

Circling around a similar idea to that explored by Cavell, Rowan Williams, in a sermon preached at the wedding of John and Alison Milbank, speaks of the relationship between truth and love. Williams begins thus:

> One of the great dramatic points in an old-fashioned wedding was the moment when the bride removed her veil from her face; and whatever the original symbolism of this, it's a remarkably telling sign of what marriage involves. Unveiling, undeception – clear and just vision. John and Alison are promising to look at each other for the rest of their lives, and to be looked at by each other: lovingly, faithfully and, above all, truly and honestly.[26]

To begin with, it is worth noting that Williams is speaking here about truth-as-honesty in much the same way as Nietzsche. For Nietzsche, total honesty is only possible alone – for Williams honesty comes through relationship; there can be no 'total' honesty about oneself that completely by-passes the gaze of the other. Truth requires love just as much as love requires truth.

> Because there can be no love without truth. Without clear and just vision, love is a business of projection and fantasy. And there can be no truth without love. Without trust and tenderness and courtesy, truth will vanish behind the walls of fear and pain.[27]

Nietzsche clearly believes the first of these claims, that there can be no love without truth. As we have seen Nietzsche's own 'version' of love is affirmation, and he believes total affirmation of human life is only possible and meaningful on the basis of a full apprehension of life's horror. But Nietzsche never sees the point of the second claim – that there can be no truth without love. Truth can be had for Nietzsche by tough-minded determination, by a rigorous exercise of suspicion. But this suspicion, when pursued as an absolute demand, forecloses upon dimensions of honesty available only to those who are prepared to accept and trust the love of another. The one who is loved is more able to face the reality of their own pain and sense of worthlessness because admitting and facing all of that no longer seems so cataclysmic. Only thus is the wisdom of Silenus fully defeated. Williams sums up: 'Truth makes love possible; love makes truth bearable.'

Notes

1 Holy Nietzsche

1 Martin Heidegger 'The Self-Assertion of the German University' p. 474.
2 Erich Heller *The Importance of Nietzsche* p. 11.
3 BGE 53.
4 BT.
5 Quoted by Michael Tanner in his introduction to *Ecce Homo*.
6 Steven E. Aschheim *The Nietzsche Legacy in Germany 1890–1990* p. 202.
7 Albert Kalthoff *Zarathustrapredigten: Reden über die sittliche Lebensauffassung Friedrich Nietzsches* (Leipzig, Eugen Diederichs, 1904). See Aschheim *The Nietzsche Legacy* p. 208.
8 Aschheim *The Nietzsche Legacy* p. 207.
9 Eberhard Bethge 'The Challenge of Dietrich Bonhoeffer's Life and Theology' p. 27.
10 Dietrich Bonhoeffer *No Rusty Swords: Letters, Lectures and Notes from the Collected Works* p. 37.
11 BGE 164.
12 'The Christian himself creates his standards of good and evil for himself. Only he can justify his own actions, just as only he can bear the responsibility. The Christian creates new tables, new Decalogues, as Nietzsche said of the Superman. Nietzsche's Superman is not, as he is supposed, the opposite of the Christian; without knowing it Nietzsche has introduced many traits of the Christian made free, as Paul and Luther know and describe him.' From Bonhoeffer's Barcelona address (8 February 1929), Bonhoeffer *No Rusty Swords* p. 40.
13 Bonhoeffer *Ethics* p. 3.
14 AC 25.
15 Bonhoeffer *Letters and Papers from Prison* p. 279.
16 Ibid. pp. 280–1.
17 Ibid. pp. 285–6.
18 Bonhoeffer (from 1929 Barcelona address) *No Rusty Swords* p. 43.
19 Bonhoeffer *Letters and Papers from Prison* p. 286. It seems to me that Bonhoeffer must have had Nietzsche somewhere in his mind at the time of writing these words. It is surely no coincidence that the next day, writing another letter to Bethge, he is clearly thinking again of Nietzsche when he writes: 'I shall be writing next time about Christians' "egoism" ("selfless self-love"). I think we agree about it. Too much altruism is oppressive and exacting; "egoism" can be less selfish and less demanding.' (Ibid. p. 287.)
20 Ibid. p. 345. Nietzsche admires the Greeks who knew how 'to stop courageously at the surface, the fold, the skin, to adore appearance . . . Those Greeks were superficial – out of profundity!'

21 Ibid. pp. 344–5. See also Rowan Williams 'The Suspicion of Suspicion: Wittgenstein and Bonhoeffer'.
22 Bonhoeffer *Letters and Papers from Prison* p. 333.
23 Ibid. p. 286; see also pp. 328 ff.
24 Hans Urs Von Balthasar *The Theology of Karl Barth* p. 68.
25 Karl Barth *Epistle to the Romans* (trans. Hoskyns from the 6th edition) (Oxford University Press 1977) p. 43.
26 Ibid. p. 85.
27 Karen L. Carr *The Banalization of Nihilism: Twentieth-Century Responses to Meaninglessness* p. 84.
28 Thomas J.J. Altizer *The Gospel of Christian Atheism* p. 25.
29 Altizer ibid. p. 103.
30 Altizer ibid. p. 72.
31 Altizer ibid. p. 81.
32 Altizer ibid. p. 51.
33 Gilles Deleuze *Nietzsche and Philosophy* p. 159.
34 Eberhard Jüngel *God as the Mystery of the World: On the Foundation of the Theology of the Crucified One in the Dispute between Theism and Atheism* p. 57.
35 Helmut Thielicke *The Evangelical Faith* vol. 1 p. 251.
36 Karl Barth *Church Dogmatics* III/2 p. 231.
37 Alasdair MacIntyre and Paul Ricoeur *The Religious Significance of Atheism*. In particular, see the first of these lectures.
38 Michael J. Buckley *At the Origins of Modern Atheism* p. 359.
39 Stephen Williams *Revelation and Reconciliation: A Window on Modernity* p. 100.
40 HAH 237.
41 AC 61.
42 Jüngel's 'Towards the Heart of the Matter' *The Christian Century* 1991.
43 G.O Mazur 'On Jüngel's Four-Fold Appropriation of Friedrich Nietzsche' in *The Possibilities of Theology: Studies in the Theology of Eberhard Jüngel in his Sixtieth Year.*
44 Heidegger 'The Word of Nietzsche: "God is dead"' in *The Question Concerning Technology and Other Essays* p. 61.
45 Heidegger *Nietzsche* vol. 4 p. 97.
46 Jacques Derrida 'Nietzsche and the Machine: An interview with Richard Beardsworth' p. 26.
47 Douglas Smith *Transvaluations: Nietzsche in France 1872–1972* pp. 225–6.
48 BGE 1 p. 16.
49 Mark C. Taylor *Erring: A Postmodern A/theology* pp. 12–13.
50 Ibid. p. 5.
51 Philippa Berry in *idem* and A. Wernick (eds) *Shadow of Spirit: Postmodernism and Religion* p. 4. It is worth noting that Berry herself is in danger of positioning Nietzsche and indeed the whole of 'postmodern religious thinking' within that oversimplified narrative discussed above; i.e. that Nietzsche's work is situated in the end-game of the Enlightenment. She begins her introduction to 'Postmodernism and Religion' thus: 'It seems strange to acknowledge, as this century draws to a close, that in several important respects twentieth-century thought is still positioned as it was at its inception. For much intellectual activity in the humanities and social sciences apparently continues to occupy that disturbing twilight zone which was evoked by Nietzsche in 1888, in *The Twilight of the Idols:* that indeterminate moment which ostensibly marks the limit of the bright day of the Enlightenment' p. 1.
52 Carl A. Raschke 'The Deconstruction of God' p. 27.
53 Graham Ward in *idem* (ed.) *The Postmodern God: A Theological Reader* p. xxviii.
54 Z p. 114.

55 Z p. 278.
56 Paul Tillich *The Shaking of the Foundations* p. 46 ff.
57 Merold Westphal 'Nietzsche as a Theological Resource' p. 213.
58 It is arguable, of course, that Greek thought was appropriated in the first few centuries AD primarily as an aid to mission rather than as a way of helping resolve doctrinal questions.
59 AC 51.
60 Jürgen Moltmann is rather good at keeping Nietzsche out of the picture in *The Crucified God*, though one is tempted to assume that the question he asks – 'The "Death of God" as the Origin of Christian Theology?' – at the beginning of the central chapter 6 has Nietzschean connotations. Certainly Moltmann does nothing to discourage this association. Nonetheless it is Moltmann's theological answer (the crucified God) that Nietzsche would have found more offensive than the problem it was an answer to (the existence of dysteleological suffering).
61 AC 42.
62 AC 58.
63 BGE 144.

2 The orientation of Nietzsche's question of God

1 From the young Nietzsche's poem: 'To the Unknown God' see Philip Grundlehner *The Poetry of Friedrich Nietzsche* p. 26.
2 John Locke *Essay Concerning Human Understanding* III: 10.
3 Iris Murdoch and Brian Magee 'Philosophy and Literature: Dialogue with Iris Murdoch' in *Men of Ideas* (ed.) Magee (New York 1978) p. 265.
4 John Locke *Essay Concerning Human Understanding* III: 10.
5 Martha Nussbaum *The Fragility of Goodness: Luck and Ethics in Greek Tragedy and Philosophy* p. 16.
6 BGE Preface p. 13.
7 Arthur C. Danto *Nietzsche as Philosopher* pp. 13–14.
8 EH p. 21.
9 Buckley *At the Origins of Modern Atheism* p. 341.
10 Richard Schacht *Nietzsche* p. 119.
11 WP 251.
12 AC 47.
13 Schacht *Nietzsche* p. 120.
14 Z p. 274.
15 BGE 48 p. 59.
16 TI p. 54.
17 BGE 58 p. 65.
18 BGE 58 p. 66.
19 HAH 292 p. 135.
20 Dietrich Bonhoeffer *Ethics* p. 71.
21 Carl Pletsch *Young Nietzsche* p. 18.
22 EH p. 14.
23 Pletsch *Young Nietzsche* p. 38.
24 *Historische-Kritische Gesamtausgabe* (ed.) H.J. Mette (Munich: Beck, 1934–40) II: 5.
25 Nietzsche has nothing to say about other important Reformation figures such as Zwingli and Calvin.
26 Duncan Large '"Der Bauernaufstand des Geistes": Nietzsche, Luther and the Reformation' unpublished paper given at Nietzsche Society Conference, St. Andrews 1996.

27　Tillich makes an interesting connection between Luther's realisation that he had come to hate God and the experience of the ugliest man in *Thus Spoke Zarathustra*. See Paul Tillich 'The Escape from God' in *The Shaking of the Foundations* p. 51.

28　The significant difference between Augustine's understanding of justification and that of Luther is that for Augustine justification is given a Platonising gloss, thus it is to be understood ontologically, that is, it is about being 'made righteous'. For Luther, however, it is about being 'declared righteous' and involves no ontological change. Hence, for Luther, those who are declared righteous by God are still nonetheless sinners.

29　Alister McGrath *Luther's Theology of the Cross* p. 153.

30　Martin Luther *Luthers Werke* Kritische Gesamtausgabe (Weimar 1883–) I.345.17–21 trans. McGrath p. 148.

31　Ibid. pp. 148–9 n. 3.

32　Ibid. 18; 164, 25–7 (1525).

33　Heiko Oberman *Luther: Man between God and the Devil* p. 156.

34　Martin Luther *Luther's Werke* 56; 371, 17–27 (1515–16) (quoted in Gerhard Ebeling *Luther: An Introduction to his Thought* (trans. Wilson) (Fontana 1972) p. 78).

35　Rowan Williams *The Wound of Knowledge* p. 146.

36　See Eberhard Jüngel *God as the Mystery of the World* p. 64.

37　Tertullian *Against Marcion* (Ante-Nicene Christian Library, T. and T. Clark, 1868) p. 89.

38　Nicholas Hope *German and Scandinavian Protestantism 1700–1918* p. 364.

39　See Albert C. Outler 'Pietism and Enlightenment: Alternatives to Tradition' in *Christian Spirituality III* (eds) Dupré and Saliers p. 243.

40　Martin Pernet 'Friedrich Nietzsche and Pietism' p. 477.

41　Ibid. p. 478.

42　R.J. Hollingdale Introduction to *Thus Spoke Zarathustra* p. 28. The two extracts which follow are also quotations from this title.

43　Outler 'Pietism and Enlightenment' p. 246.

44　AC 39 p. 151.

45　See Grundlehner *The Poetry of Friedrich Nietzsche* pp. 33–4.

46　Pernet 'Friedrich Nietzsche and Pietism' p. 475.

47　GS p. 283.

48　Lou Salomé *Friedrich Nietzsche in seinen Werken* p. 147.

3　Facing the truth, outfacing the horror

1　One might say, with Jaspers, that it is as old as the Axial Period.

2　Charles Taylor *Sources of the Self: The Making of the Modern Identity* p. 117.

3　Bernard McGinn *The Foundations of Mysticism* vol. 1 p. 27.

4　E.R. Dodds 'The *Parmenides* of Plato and the Origin of the Neoplatonic "One"' *Classical Quarterly* 22 1928 p. 141.

5　Plato *Theaetetus* 176b trans. F.M. Cornford in *The Collected Dialogues of Plato* (eds) Hamilton and Cairns (Princeton University Press 1961).

6　Arthur Schopenhauer *The World as Will and Representation* Volume 1 p. 525.

7　Schopenhauer *Essays and Aphorisms* p. 41.

8　Ibid. p. 51.

9　Ibid. p. 52.

10　By the time Nietzsche wrote *Human, All Too Human* he came to recognise the centrality of the principle of sufficient reason in the construction of Kantian and Schopenhauerian philosophy: 'Appearance and thing in itself – Philosophers are accustomed to station themselves before life and experience – before that which they call the world of appearance – as before a painting that has been unrolled once and for all and unchangeably depicts the same scene: this scene, they believe, has to be correctly interpreted, so as to draw a conclusion as to the nature of the being that produced the picture; that is, as to the nature of the thing in itself, which it is customary to regard as the sufficient reason for the world of appearances.' (HAH p. 19.)

11 Schopenhauer *Essays and Aphorisms* p. 7.
12 Schopenhauer *The World as Will and Representation* Volume 1 p. 179.
13 Iris Murdoch *The Sovereignty of Good* p. 84.
14 Schopenhauer *The World as Will and Representation* Volume 2 p. 628.
15 Brian Magee *The Philosophy of Schopenhauer* p. 223.
16 BT p. 35.
17 BT p. 36.
18 Paul De Man 'Genesis and Genealogy in Nietzsche's *The Birth of Tragedy*' p. 49.
19 BT p. 37.
20 E.R. Dodds *The Greeks and the Irrational* pp. 76–7.
21 BT p. 36.
22 BT p. 37.
23 Silk and Stern *Nietzsche on Tragedy* p. 287.
24 Max Baeumer 'Nietzsche and the Tradition of the Dionysian', quotation from p. 166; see also Silk and Stern *Nietzsche on Tragedy* pp. 209–16.
25 Cited in Baeumer 'Nietzsche and the Tradition of the Dionysian' p. 170.
26 BT 26.
27 WP 840.
28 Silk and Stern *Nietzsche on Tragedy* p. 287.
29 WP 17.
30 BT 10 p. 74.
31 BT 3 p. 42.
32 BT 7 p. 60.
33 BT p. 24.
34 BT 7 p. 60.
35 BGE p. 15.
36 BGE p. 17.
37 Augustine *Confessions* X: 24.
38 Augustine *Confessions* XI: 11.
39 There is clearly a good deal of evidence to support the claim that Christianity shares Plato's sense that the passage of time is something that salvation needs to save one from. For instance, as Isaac Watts puts it in his famous hymn: 'Time, like an ever-rolling stream, Bears all its sons away; They fly forgotten, as a dream dies at the opening day.' God, for Watts, is our 'shelter from the stormy blast and our eternal home', a place of refuge from the ravages of time. And again, as Henry Lyte puts it in another famous hymn: 'Change and decay in all around I see, O Thou who changest not, abide with me.' It supports Nietzsche's case that these are two of the most popular hymns chosen for funerals.
40 AC 18.
41 TI p. 35.
42 Martha Nussbaum 'Transcending Humanity' in *Love's Knowledge* p. 376. Immediately following this passage Nussbaum adds in parentheses 'Once again, the Christian idea that god is also fully human and has actually sacrificed his life is, if it can be made coherent, the most important element in the thought that god actually loves the world.'
43 Ibid. p. 377.
44 WP 822.
45 BT 7 p. 60.
46 TI pp. 40–41.
47 TI p. 40.

48 TI p. 41 This section ends with Nietzsche announcing the arrival of Zarathustra. Keith Ansell-Pearson in *Nietzsche contra Rousseau* connects this 'arrival' with a number of others in which Zarathustra comes with the promise of redemption: 'It cannot be without significance that the climactic points of several of Nietzsche's major works culminate in a pre-figuration of Zarathustra. In *Twilight of the Idols* Zarathustra appears at the end of Nietzsche's terse history of Western metaphysics which results in the abolition of any distinction between a true world and an apparent world. It is the moment at which man experiences the end of the longest error and the zenith of mankind. At the end of the second inquiry of the *On the Genealogy of Morals*, in sections 24 and 25, Zarathustra is referred to as "the redeeming man" who may bring home the redemption of man the sick animal; he is the man of the future who will redeem humanity from nihilism by teaching the liberation of the will; he is the victor over God and nothingness. The justification for reading *Thus Spoke Zarathustra* (1883–5) after the *On the Genealogy of Morals* (1887) stems from the key role Nietzsche assigns to Zarathustra as a teacher of redemption who appears at a certain juncture in man's evolution to deliver a teaching of redemption' p. 153.

49 WP 818.

50 D p. 48.

51 Thiele *Friedrich Nietzsche and the Politics of the Soul* p. 137.

52 WP 552.

53 Alexander Nehemas *Nietzsche: Life as Literature* p. 174.

54 GS 290.

55 I think Mark Warren is substantially correct when he likens Nietzsche's position on truth to that of Marx: 'Nietzsche's approach to truth is not fundamentally epistemological: he was not providing another answer to the question of how we know that our concepts correspond to the world outside our minds. He regards the question itself as disembodied from practice and therefore unintelligible [see BGE 15]. The very terms of the question concerning "truth" presuppose the reality of our life, and when we understand this, such questions become altogether different. This is essentially Marx's position in the second of his "Theses on Feuerbach", where he writes that "the question whether objective truth can be attributed to human thinking is not a question of theory but is a practical question. Man must prove the truth, i.e. the reality and power, the this-worldliness of his thinking in practice. The dispute over the reality or non-reality which isolates itself from practice is a purely scholastic question." In this respect Nietzsche's project is comparable to Marx's; whereas epistemological approaches presuppose a knowing subject and then ask how knowledge of the world is possible, Nietzsche and Marx presuppose the reality of worldly practices, and then ask how knowing subjects and worldly objects become categories of consciousness.' Mark Warren *Nietzsche and Political Thought* MIT Press 1988 pp. 94–5.

4 Redeeming redemption

1 Z pp. 114–15.

2 HAH p. 66.

3 EH pp. 3–4.

4 GM II: 24.

5 Keith Ansell-Pearson *An Introduction to Nietzsche as Political Thinker* p. 102.

6 Daniel W. Conway 'Overcoming the *Übermensch*: Nietzsche's Revaluation of Values' p. 212.

7 Maudemarie Clark *Nietzsche on Truth and Philosophy* pp. 273 ff.

8 See, for example, John McIntyre *The Shape of Soteriology: Studies in the Doctrine of the Death of Christ.*

9 Z p. 42.
10 Karl Barth *Church Dogmatics* III/2 p. 121. For a full discussion of Barth's Christo-centrism and the way it relates to issues raised by Nussbaum see Fergus Kerr *Immortal Longings: Versions of Transcending Humanity* Chapter 2.
11 Barth *Church Dogmatics* III/2 p. 103.
12 Homer *Odyssey* V 214 (trans. Shewring) (Oxford 1980).
13 Martha Nussbaum 'Narrative Emotions: Beckett's Genealogy of Love' in *Love's Knowledge* pp. 286 ff.
14 Ibid. p. 298.
15 Samuel Beckett *Molloy, Malone Dies, The Unnamable* (New York 1955) p. 15.
16 Nussbaum 'Narrative Emotions' pp. 297–8.
17 Stanley Cavell 'Ending the Waiting Game: A reading of Beckett's *Endgame*' in *Must We Mean What We Say?* p. 149.
18 Kerr *Immortal Longings* p. 7.
19 Martha Nussbaum 'Transcending Humanity' in *Love's Knowledge* pp. 375–6.
20 NB 27 April 1862.
21 Nussbaum 'Transcending Humanity' p. 380.
22 Z V4 For further discussion on this issue see Walter Kaufmann *Nietzsche: Philosopher, Psychologist, Antichrist* Chs 10 and 11.
23 AC pp. 135–6.
24 AC p. 136.
25 GM I: 7.
26 GM I: 7.
27 GM I: 15; Thomas Aquinas *Summa Theologiae* Supplement to the Third Part, question xcvii, article i, 'conclusio'.
28 GM I: 15; Tertullian *De Spectaculis*.
29 GM II: 16.
30 AC 158.
31 AC 139.
32 GM III: 15.
33 AC 22.
34 AC 26.
35 AC 29.
36 AC 33.
37 AC 42.
38 AC 153.
39 GM III: 15.
40 GM III: 15.
41 GM III: 15.
42 EH p. 39.
43 Letter to Malwida von Meysenburg 14 January 1880.
44 Letter to Overbeck 18 September 1881.
45 BGE 157.
46 NB 11 November 1887.
47 Arthur C. Danto 'Some Remarks on *On the Genealogy of Morals*' p. 19.
48 Ibid. p. 21.
49 Daniel Conway 'Genealogy and Critical Method' p. 320.
50 WP 222.
51 Simone Weil *Gravity and Grace* p. 73.
52 GM III: 17.
53 David Farrell Krell has noted the similarities of Nietzsche's line here with that of his boyhood hero Novalis.
54 GS pp. 35–6.
55 Malcolm Pasley 'Nietzsche's use of Medical Terms' in *idem* (ed.) *Nietzsche: Imagery and Thought* pp. 136–7.

56 Martha Nussbaum *The Therapy of Desire: Theory and Practice in Hellenistic Ethics.*
57 Epicurus Us. 221 = Porph. Ad Marc. 31. See Nussbaum *The Therapy of Desire* p. 13.
58 TI p. 30.
59 Paul Weindling *Health, Race and German Politics between National Unification and Nazism, 1870–1945* p. 1.
60 WP 685.
61 For a full discussion of the historical use of degeneracy see Daniel Pick *Faces of Degeneration: A European Disorder c.1848–c.1918.* For his brief though interesting observations on Nietzsche see pp. 226–7.
62 TI p. 45.
63 Some have sought to salvage Nietzsche's perspectivism from this unwanted intrusion of normativity by arguing that the concept of health is not being employed by Nietzsche in an absolute sense, but rather in a relative sense. Nietzsche is concerned therefore with the relative health of various perspectives. See, for example, Daniel Conway's 'Genealogy and Critical Method'. Conway argues that: 'Nietzschean genealogy gains access to the meaning of historical phenomena via the dominant interpretations of those phenomena . . . Nietzsche is therefore warranted in claiming for his genealogies a validity relative to the authoritative interpretations they discredit and supplant. Beyond the terms of this relation, however, he is entitled to stake no further claim to the validity of his genealogies, though he may occasionally do so; as a hermeneutic strategy, genealogy is entirely parasitic upon the interpretations it challenges' p. 318.
64 BGE 259.
65 GM II: 11.
66 Mark Warren *Nietzsche and Political Thought* pp. 227–8.
67 John Milbank *Theology and Social Theory: Beyond Secular Reason* in which Chapter 10 is entitled 'Ontological Violence or The Postmodern Problematic'.
68 I am reminded, for instance, of the way in which Scottish links golf courses are spoken of as 'natural' in distinction to the 'artificiality' of American-style golf courses. But, of course, links courses are designed and made by designers in just the same way as American ones are. 'Natural' is thus 'a look' – something constructed. Wayne Klein *Nietzsche and the Promise of Philosophy* p. 142 ff.
69 KSA 12, 9.116.
70 KSA 12, 10.53.
71 Milbank *Theology and Social Theory* p. 279.
72 Ibid. p. 289.
73 Ibid. p. 282.
74 Though I bracket out the question of objective reality here in order to make the point about the distinction between fantasy and reality, nonetheless it could be said that I have conceded too much in doing this and that the slide towards fantasy begins at the point where one denies an objective reality to the world. Another way of putting this would be to say that Nietzsche's demand of total honesty requires a maximal sensitivity to all aspects of reality, including the most disagreeable. From this perspective it is not the case, as Milbank would have it, that the 'despised desires for security, consolation etc' represent a *mythos* simply not to Nietzsche's taste. Nietzsche attacks the drive for consolation precisely because it threatens to subdue the quest for absolute honesty. And that honesty is about facing the full horrors of reality, of Silenian wisdom.
75 See Heller *The Importance of Nietzsche* p. 85.
76 For instance: 'From his early youth Nietzsche was able to preserve his inner equilibrium through flights of imagination, and it is evident from his juvenilia that he avoided the tedium of Naumburg or the routine of Pforta by indulging in escapist fantasies. Escapist lyrics such as "Ohne Heimat" ("Without a Home-

land") (1859) bear witness to the vivid world which became a refuge in the midst of an oppressive reality.' Philip Grundlehner *The Poetry of Friedrich Nietzsche* p. 103.

77 Martha Nussbaum 'Pity and Mercy: Nietzsche's Stoicism' p. 159.
78 Ibid. p. 159.
79 Ibid. p. 161.
80 David Farrell Krell *Infectious Nietzsche* p. 212.
81 I recognise that this has been an extremely aggressive passage of argument. Almost too Nietzschean in its style (indeed the subtitle of *On the Genealogy of Morals* is 'an attack'). But to take on Nietzsche on his own terms requires something like this style. Just as Milbank claims that the 'practical expression' of Nietzsche's thought 'must be fascism' (Milbank *Theology and Social Theory* p. 279) – the competition between rival mythologies takes the form of fisticuffs once the traditional criteria of judgement and discrimination have been subject to Nietzsche's philosophical 'hammer'.
82 Cosima Wagner said that the gift of a hundred cigars would have been more useful to the war effort than the presence of a 'dilettante' such as Nietzsche who would, most likely, be more hindrance than help. Letter from Cosima von Bülow, 9 August 1870.
83 These student bodies, originally set up to help promote a united Germany in 1815, became social groups where members would gather together, sing nationalistic songs, wear uniforms and go on marches with military bands. These groups were to be appropriated by Hitler to form the basis of the Hitler Youth.
84 From a testimony by Nietzsche's friend Paul Deussen in *Conversations with Nietzsche* (ed.) Sander Gilman pp. 22–3.

5 Parables of innocence and judgement

1 W.H. Auden *For the Time Being* Faber and Faber 1964 p. 66.
2 Stanley Cavell *The Claim of Reason* OUP 1979 p. 352.
3 Z pp. 90–91.
4 Alister McGrath *Luther's Theology of the Cross* Blackwell 1985 p. 153.
5 Luther *Luther's Werke* 4.449.35–7.
6 John Powell Clayton 'Zarathustra and the Stages on Life's Way: A Nietzschean Riposte to Kierkegaard' p. 179.
7 Z p. 55.
8 Z p. 55.
9 Erich Heller *The Importance of Nietzsche* p. 83.
10 The same misunderstanding (taking the 'born again' image too literally) is ridiculed in St. John's Gospel (John 3: 1–15). In order to get the joke one has to understand that the Greek word ανωθεν has the double meaning of 'from above' and 'again'. So, Jesus says to Nicodemus 'no one can see the kingdom of God without being born ανωθεν'. Nicodemus gets the wrong end of the stick, thinking Jesus means born 'again': 'how can a person re-enter his mother's womb?' he asks, puzzled. The author of the Gospel is clearly making fun of Nicodemus' stupidity. Translations of the Bible are unable to capture the double-meaning of ανωθεν and so the joke is often missed. Ironic then that so many 'Bible-believing' Christians believe that being 'born again' is a precondition of being saved.
11 Michael Tanner *Nietzsche* p. 53.
12 WP 68.
13 AC p. 177.
14 Heller *The Importance of Nietzsche* p. 85.
15 WP 68.

16 In a telling passage from Nietzsche's second *Untimely Meditation* he praises 'forgetting': 'A person who simply did not possess the power to forget, who would be condemned to seeing a becoming everywhere: such a person no longer believes in his own being, no longer believes in himself, sees everything flowing apart in moving points and loses himself in the stream of becoming: like the genuine student of Heraclitus, he will scarcely dare to raise a finger in the end. To all action there belongs forgetting.' UM I p. 213.

17 EH p. 69.

18 GM I: 13.

19 This metaphorical use of 'city' is, of course, reminiscent of Plato's *Republic* and has a long and distinguished philosophical history.

20 'The assumption of one single subject is perhaps unnecessary; perhaps it is just as permissible to assume a multiplicity of subjects, whose interaction and struggle is the basis of our thought and our consciousness in general . . . My hypothesis: The subject as multiplicity.' WP 270.

21 Z p. 161.

22 EH p. 80.

23 GS 34.1.

24 NB 21: 35.

25 GS 276 p. 223.

26 Keith Ansell-Pearson *An Introduction to Nietzsche as a Political Thinker* p. 115.

27 WP 532.

28 Z pp. 331–2.

29 TI p. 27.

30 WP 54.

31 D 48.

32 Martin Heidegger *Nietzsche* vol. 2 (trans. Krell) p. 200.

33 WP 617.

34 Heidegger *Nietzsche* vol. 1 p. 202.

35 Milan Kundera *The Unbearable Lightness of Being* p. 3.

36 Ibid. p. 5.

37 Ibid. p. 3.

38 Ibid. p. 4.

39 For instance 'The recurrence is a positive doctrine of an afterlife, and as such it is even more powerful than the Christian for getting men to change their values in the desired way once they have accepted the doctrine. As in the Christian, in the Nietzschean afterlife a person shall be rewarded or punished according to the values by which he had lived. But in the Nietzschean afterlife the eternal return of the quality of this life is at once reward or punishment for success or failure in developing the value of this life as Nietzsche advises.' Arnold Zuboff 'Nietzsche and Eternal Recurrence' p. 344.

40 Joachim Jeremias *New Testament Theology* p. 139.

41 Z pp. 178–9.

42 Rudolf Bultmann *History and Eschatology* p. 155.

43 But if Nietzsche's 'weight' (judgement) is recoverable and capable of being seen as a feature of joy, by the same logic the Christian articulation of judgement must also be recoverable – and thus the moral advantage of post-Christian soteriology (that it is non-oppressive compared with the clearly oppressive Christianity) is not as clear as is often suggested.

44 See Heller *The Importance of Nietzsche* p. 181.

45 Z p. 244.

46 Z p. 245 (see also pp. 246 and 247).

47 NB 14 August 1881.

48 EH p. 72.

49 Young *Nietzsche's Philosophy of Art* p. 114.
50 EH p. 69.
51 GS 288.
52 WP 1041.
53 WP 171.
54 Leslie Paul Thiele *Friedrich Nietzsche and the Politics of the Soul: A Study of Heroic Individualism* p. 157.
55 PTG 69.
56 This is the point at which Young makes the claim that Nietzsche's deeper purpose is 'proving that God, after all, exists'. The context of this claim is worth quoting in full: 'Why does Nietzsche believe ecstasy to be the ideal relationship to the world? Because, in a word, he wants something to *worship* and is aware once again, as he was in *The Birth of Tragedy*, that a sense of the holy, of the sacred is a fundamental human need. If the old God is dead then nature herself must be made divine, "perfect" (Z IV, 19). The non-ecstatic affirmation of life holds no interest for Nietzsche since it has no bearing on his problem; the problem of proving that God, after all, exists. Less provocatively: the problem of achieving a state of mind, "feel[ing] oneself 'in heaven . . . eternal'" (A 33), in which a naturalised object is the target of all those feelings and attitudes that used to be directed towards the (no longer believable) transcendent.' Young *Nietzsche's Philosophy of Art* p. 115.
57 See Grunenberger *A Social History of the Third Reich* p. 105.

6 Salvation, kitsch and the denial of shit

1 BT 3.
2 Paul Ricoeur *Figuring the Sacred: Religion, Narrative and Imagination* p. 250.
3 Terrence Des Pres 'The Survivor: An Anatomy of Life in the Death Camps' in *Holocaust: Religious and Philosophical Implications* (eds) Roth and Berènbaum.
4 Alexander Donat *The Holocaust Kingdom* (Holt, Rinehart and Winston 1965) p. 269.
5 Krystyna Zywulska *I Came Back* (trans. Cenkalska) (Dennis Dobson 1951) p. 67.
6 Reska Weiss *Journey Through Hell* (Vallentine, Mitchell 1961) p. 211.
7 Halina Birenbaum *Hope Is the Last to Die* (trans. Welsh) (Twayne, 1971) p. 134.
8 Des Pres 'The Survivor' pp. 216–17.
9 It could be argued, of course, that to speak of 'shit' is to invite a conceptual takeover from Freudian psychology. Bruno Bettelheim in *The Informed Heart* has suggested that the obsession with toileting so prevalent within the camps is inherently regressive; that it corresponds to fixation upon pre-oedipal stages in human development. For Bettelheim, excremental assault reduces prisoners to 'the level they were at before toilet training was achieved'. Des Pres is right to resist this line of interpretation. He notes, correctly, that the important difference between the child's behaviour and that of prisoners in the camps is that prisoners were forced to soil themselves. The obsession with toileting was the product of a carefully designed strategy for human degradation. Shit was a means of torture. The obsession with lavatorial functions was not therefore a symptom of neurosis but a consequence of fear.
10 See *Holocaust: Religious and Philosophical Implications* (eds) Roth and Berènbaum p. 202.
11 Kundera *The Unbearable Lightness of Being* p. 242.
12 Edward Robinson *The Language of Mystery* p. 62.
13 Ibid. pp. 62–3.
14 Milan Kundera *The Art of the Novel* pp. 135–6.
15 CW p. 183.

16 CW p. 167 'What is beautiful belongs to the few.'
17 CW p. 169.
18 CW p. 160.
19 Richard Wagner 'Art and Revolution' in *The Art-Work of the Future and Other Works* p. 65.
20 See Herschel B. Chipp *Theories of Modern Art* p. 482.
21 Ibid. p. 478.
22 Kundera *The Unbearable Lightness of Being* p. 256.
23 Richard Grunberger *A Social History of the Third Reich* p. 77.
24 Kundera *The Unbearable Lightness of Being* p. 250.
25 Ibid. p. 243.
26 Ibid. p. 244.
27 Nietzsche expresses similar thoughts to those of T-4 when he writes: 'In numerous cases society ought to prevent procreation: to this end it ought to hold in readiness, without regard to descent, rank, or spirit, the most rigorous means of constraint, deprivation of freedom, in certain circumstances castration. – the Biblical prohibition "thou shalt not kill!" is a piece of naiveté compared to the seriousness of the prohibition of life to decadents: "thou shalt not procreate!" – Life itself recognizes no solidarity, no "equal rights," between the healthy and the degenerate parts of an organism: one must excise the latter – or the whole will perish.' WP 734.
28 It is important to note that Hitler's appreciation of the art-works on show at the 'Great Exhibition' of 1937 was primarily a moral one. 'A walk through this exhibition will allow you to find quite a few things that will impress you as beautiful and, above all, as decent, and which you will sense to be good.' Chipp *Theories of Modern Art* p. 482.
29 Lucy Davidowicz *The War against the Jews 1933–45* p. 45.
30 Kundera ibid. p. 245.
31 Davidowicz ibid. pp. 47–8.
32 Yehuda Bauer 'The Place of the Holocaust in Contemporary History' in *Holocaust: Religious and Philosophical Implications* (eds) Roth and Berènbaum.
33 Grunberger *A Social History of the Third Reich* p. 532.
34 BGE 251 p. 163.
35 Yirmiyahu Yovel 'Nietzsche and the Jews: The Structure of an Ambivalence' p. 122.
36 Taylor *Sources of the Self* p. 215.
37 Ibid. p. 224.
38 BGE p. 174 (258).
39 AC p. 114.
40 HAH 438.
41 Kundera *The Art of the Novel* p. 135.
42 Goethe *The Sorrows of Young Werther* (trans. Hulse) (Penguin 1989) p. 66.
43 Taylor *Sources of the Self: The Making of the Modern Identity* p. 194.
44 Ibid. p. 295.
45 Ibid. p. 296.
46 See Hope *German and Scandinavian Protestantism* p. 367.
47 Herman Boeschenstein *German Literature of the Nineteenth Century* p. 114.
48 HAH p. 336.
49 Erich Auerbach *Mimesis: The Representation of Reality in Western Literature* pp. 518–19.
50 Kundera *The Art of the Novel* p. 239.

7 Sacrifice and the logic of exclusion

1 E.P. Sanders *Judaism: Practice and Belief 63 BCE–66 CE* pp. 104–5.
2 Ibid. p. 108.
3 Ofelia Schutte *Beyond Nihilism: Nietzsche without Masks* p. 3.
4 Sanders concludes his description of Judaic sacrificial practice with which I began this chapter with the remark: 'The general principles were the same as in Greek sacrifice' (Sanders *Judaism* p. 105). Helene Foley in *Ritual Irony: Poetry and Sacrifice in Euripides* describes a typical Greek sacrifice thus: 'The participants began by purifying themselves (washing their hands) and sprinkling the victim with water. The victim was made to nod its head in consent to the sacrifice. The sacrificial knife, hidden beneath the barley in the basket, was then uncovered . . . The animal, now fully dedicated to death, had its throat cut with its neck turned towards the sky; the women screamed (*ololuzein*), marking the moment of religious intensity at which the animal's life departed its body (*Odyssey* 3.449–55). The *aulos* (Greek pipe) was played and the blood was caught in a vessel and poured on the altar. Chosen participants flayed the animal, cut out the thigh-bones, wrapped them in fat, and burned then with incense on the altar for the gods . . . The rest of the animal was butchered in accordance with precise procedures and distributed in different ways determined by the context' (pp. 29–30). Greek religiosity is founded upon the logic of sacrifice no less than that of the Hebrew scriptures. Frances Young, in her examination of the different types of sacrifice in *Sacrifice and the Death of Christ*, compares the role of sacrifice in *The Bacchae* to that of the eucharist. She writes: 'There were communion-sacrifices of another type. The classic example of these is found in Euripides' play *The Bacchae*. Here we see ecstatic and frenzied worshippers wandering over the mountains, tearing at the raw flesh of a bull. The bull was the incarnation of the god, and by eating its flesh, the worshipper received a little of the god's character and power. The play was written four hundred years before Christ, but many have pointed out the parallel with eating Christ's flesh in the eucharist' p. 24.
5 Albert Henrichs 'Loss of Self, Suffering, Violence: The Modern View of Dionysus from Nietzsche to Girard' pp. 205–40.
6 Rainer Friedrich 'Everything to Do with Dionysos? Ritualism, the Dionysiac, and the Tragic' in *Tragedy and the Tragic: Greek Theatre and Beyond* (ed.) M. Silk p. 258.
7 One thinks particularly here of the blood-feud. For a fascinating account of the workings of the blood-feud in Albania see Ismail Kadare's brilliant novel *Broken April* (HarperCollins 1990).
8 René Girard *Violence and the Sacred* p. 4.
9 Richard Seaford 'Something to Do with Dionysus' in *Tragedy and the Tragic: Greek Theatre and Beyond* (ed.) Silk p. 293.
10 Ibid. p. 284.
11 John Milbank *Theology and Social Theory* p. 393.
12 GM II: 3.
13 Hosea 6: 6: It is worth underlining that, as this reference suggests, hostility to the sacrificial mechanism is not to be understood in terms of, or taken to imply, the 'moral superiority' of the New Testament over the Old. See also Amos 5: 22.
14 Simone Weil *Gravity and Grace* p. 79.
15 René Girard 'Nietzsche versus the Crucified' in *The Girard Reader* p. 252.
16 Ibid. pp. 252–3.
17 GM II: 5.
18 GM II: 6.
19 GM II: 6.
20 GM II: 9.

21 GM II: 10.
22 GM II: 10.
23 R. W. Sharples *Stoicism, Epicureanism, and Scepticism: An Introduction to Hellenistic Philosophy* p. 107 The same example is used in A.A. Long's classic *Hellenistic Philosophy: Stoicism, Epicureanism and Scepticism* pp. 197–8.
24 Martha Nussbaum 'Pity and Mercy' p. 160.

8 Fear of the other

1 In order to distinguish between the various senses of scepticism, I will apply the convention of using the American spelling when referring to Cavell's particular use of 'skepticism'.
2 S. Mulhall (ed.) *The Cavell Reader* (Blackwell, 1996) p. 9.
3 Stanley Cavell *The Claim of Reason* p. 90.
4 Michael Fischer *Stanley Cavell and Literary Skepticism* p. 80.
5 Cavell *The Claim of Reason* p. 439.
6 Fischer *Stanley Cavell and Literary Skepticism* p. 140.
7 Wittgenstein *Philosophical Investigations* §287.
8 Cavell *The Claim of Reason* p. 470.
9 Thiele *Friedrich Nietzsche and the Politics of the Soul* p. 28.
10 EH p. 67.
11 GW 6: 36 (trans. PTG 18) see Thiele *Friedrich Nietzsche and the Politics of the Soul* p. 175.
12 D 73.
13 BGE 125.
14 Z p. 173.
15 Thiele *Friedrich Nietzsche and the Politics of the Soul* p. 30. Thiele is referring here to a passage in *The Gay Science* in which Nietzsche claims: 'We cannot look around our own corner: it is a hopeless curiosity that wants to know what other kinds of intellect or perspectives there might be.'
16 This is suggested by a passage in *Protestant Theology in the Nineteenth Century* (p. 137) in which Barth outlines a history of theological 'decline' beginning with Pietism and culminating in Nietzsche.
17 Barth *Protestant Theology in the Nineteenth Century* p. 114.
18 WP 768.
19 Luce Irigaray *Marine Lover of Friedrich Nietzsche* p. 34. Barth also makes the point about Nietzsche's failure to accommodate the female other. 'To this day Nietzsche has been much admired and honoured and loved. But he had no use for the fact; he could not love in return. Nothing is more striking than that he had no use at all for women.' Barth *Church Dogmatics* III/2 p. 234.
20 Stanley Cavell, *Themes out of School* (North Point Press, 1984) p. 61.
21 Barth *Church Dogmatics* III/2 p. 241.
22 Stanley Rosen *The Mask of Enlightenment: Nietzsche's Zarathustra* p. 181.
23 Cavell *The Claim of Reason* p. 109.
24 Cavell 'The Same and Different: The Awful Truth' *The Cavell Reader* ibid. p. 177.
25 Ibid. p. 176.
26 Rowan Williams *Open to Judgement: Sermons and Addresses* p. 230.
27 Ibid. p. 230.

Bibliography

Primary texts and abbreviations

References are either to page or to section (or sometimes both). I have preferred to refer to section, thus helping those using a different edition/translation of Nietzsche's work. If however, the section is too big, and thus the reference not specific enough, I refer to page. I have employed the following abbreviations:

AC   *The Anti-Christ* (Hollingdale trans.), Penguin, 1968.
BGE   *Beyond Good and Evil* (Hollingdale trans.), Penguin, 1973.
BT   *The Birth of Tragedy* (Kaufmann trans.), Random House, 1967.
CW   *The Case of Wagner* (Kaufmann trans.), Random House, 1967.
D   *Daybreak* (Hollingdale trans.), Cambridge University Press, 1982.
EH   *Ecce Homo* (Hollingdale trans.), Penguin, 1992.
GM   *On the Genealogy of Morals* (Diethe trans.), Cambridge University Press, 1994.
GS   *The Gay Science* (Kaufmann trans.), Random House, 1974.
HAH   *Human, All Too Human* (Hollingdale trans.), Cambridge University Press, 1986.
KSA   *Friedrich Nietzsche. Sämtliche Werke: Kritische Studienausgabe* (eds) Colli and Montinari, Walter de Gruyter and Deutschertaschenbuchverlag, 1967–77 and 1988.
NB   *Nietzsche Briefwechsel, Kritische Gesamtausgabe* (eds) Colli and Montinari, Walter de Gruyter, 1975–84.
PTG   *Philosophy in the Tragic Age of the Greeks* (Cowan trans.), Regency Gateway, 1962.
TI   *Twilight of the Idols* (Hollingdale trans.), Penguin, 1968.
UM   *Untimely Meditations* (Hollingdale trans.), Cambridge University Press, 1983
WP   *The Will to Power* (Kaufmann and Hollingdale trans.), Random House, 1967.
Z   *Thus Spoke Zarathustra* (Hollingdale trans.), Penguin, 1969.

Secondary literature on Nietzsche

Allison, D.B. (ed.) *The New Nietzsche: Contemporary Styles of Interpretation*, The MIT Press, 1985.
Ansell-Pearson, K. *Nietzsche contra Rousseau: A Study of Nietzsche's Moral and Political Thought*, Cambridge University Press, 1991.

Ansell-Pearson, K. *An Introduction to Nietzsche as Political Thinker*, Cambridge University Press, 1994.

Ansell-Pearson, K. *Viroid Life: Perspectives on Nietzsche and the Transhuman Condition*, Routledge, 1997.

Aschheim, S.E. *The Nietzsche Legacy in Germany, 1890–1990*, University of California Press, 1992.

Babich, B.E. *Nietzsche's Philosophy of Science: Reflecting Science on the Ground of Art and Life*, State University of New York Press, 1994.

Baeumer, M. 'Nietzsche and the Tradition of the Dionysian' in O'Flaherty, Sellner and Heln (eds) *Studies in Nietzsche and the Classical Tradition*, University of North Carolina Press, 1976.

Berkowitz, P. *Nietzsche: The Ethics of an Immoralist*, Harvard University Press, 1995.

Burgard, P.J. (ed.) *Nietzsche and the Feminine*, University Press of Virginia, 1994.

Chamberlain, L. *Nietzsche in Turin: The End of the Future*, Quartet Books, 1996.

Clark, M. *Nietzsche on Truth and Philosophy*, Cambridge University Press, 1990.

Clayton, J.P. 'Zarathustra and the Stages on Life's Way: A Nietzschean Riposte to Kierkegaard' in *Nietzsche Studien*, vol. 14, Walter de Gruyter, 1985.

Conway, D.W. 'Overcoming the Übermensch: Nietzsche's Revaluation of Values', *Journal of the British Society for Phenomenology*, 20, October 1989.

Conway, D.W. 'Genealogy and Critical Method' in *Nietzsche, Genealogy and Morality*, (ed.) Schater, University of California Press, 1994.

Conway, D.W. *Nietzsche and the Political*, Routledge, 1997.

Conway, D.W. *Nietzsche's Dangerous Game: Philosophy in the Twilight of the Idols*, Cambridge University Press, 1997.

Danto, A.C. *Nietzsche as Philosopher: An Original Study*, Columbia University Press, 1965.

Danto, A.C. 'Some Remarks on *On the Genealogy of Morals*' in *Reading Nietzsche* (ed.) Soloman, Oxford University Press, 1988.

Darby, T., Egyed, B. and Jones, B. (eds) *Nietzsche and the Rhetoric of Nihilism: Essays on Interpretation, Language and Politics*, Carleton University Press, 1989.

Deleuze, G. *Nietzsche and Philosophy* (H. Tomlinson trans.) The Athlone Press, 1983.

De Man, P. 'Genesis and Genealogy in Nietzsche's *The Birth of Tragedy*', *Diacritics*, Winter 1972.

Derrida, J. 'Nietzsche and the Machine: An Interview with Richard Beardsworth', *Journal of Nietzsche Studies*, vol. 7, Spring 1994.

Ferry, L. and Renault, A. *Why We are Not Nietzscheans*, (R. de Loaiza trans.) University of Chicago Press, 1997.

Gilman, S.L. (ed.) *Conversations with Nietzsche: A Life in the Words of his Contemporaries* (D.J. Parent trans.) Oxford University Press, 1987.

Golomb, J. (ed.) *Nietzsche and Jewish Culture*, Routledge, 1997.

Grundlehner, P. *The Poetry of Friedrich Nietzsche*, Oxford University Press, 1986.

Havas, R. *Nietzsche's Genealogy: Nihilism and the Will to Knowledge*, Cornell University Press, 1995.

Hayman, R. *Nietzsche: A Critical Life*, Phoenix, 1995.

Heidegger, M. *Nietzsche, vols 1–4* (D.F. Krell trans.) HarperCollins, 1991.

Heller, E. *The Importance of Nietzsche: Ten Essays*, University of Chicago Press, 1988.

Irigaray, L. *Marine Lover of Friedrich Nietzsche*, Columbia University Press, 1991.

Jaspers, K. *Nietzsche: An Introduction to the Understanding of his Philosophical Activity* (C.F. Wallraff and F.J. Schmitz trans.) Johns Hopkins University Press, 1997.

Kaufmann, W. *Nietzsche: Philosopher, Psychologist, Antichrist*, 4th edition, Princeton University Press, 1974.

Kellenberger, J. *Kierkegaard and Nietzsche: Faith and Eternal Acceptance*, Macmillan Press, 1997.

Klein, W. *Nietzsche and the Promise of Philosophy*, State University of New York Press, 1997.

Klossowski, P. *Nietzsche and the Vicious Circle* (D.W. Smith trans.) The Athlone Press, 1997.

Krell, D.F. *Infectious Nietzsche*, Indiana University Press, 1996.

Lampert, L. *Nietzsche's Teaching: An Interpretation of Thus Spoke Zarathustra*, Yale University Press, 1986.

Lea, F.A. *The Tragic Philosopher: Friedrich Nietzsche*, Methuen, 1977.

Long, A.A. *Hellenistic Philosophy: Stoicism, Epicureanism and Scepticism*, Duckworth, 1986.

Magnus, B., Stewart, S. and Mileur, J.-P. *Nietzsche's Case: Philosophy as/and Literature*, Routledge, 1993.

Magnus, B. and Higgins, K.M. (eds) *The Cambridge Companion to Nietzsche*, Cambridge University Press, 1996.

May, K.M. *Nietzsche and the Spirit of Tragedy*, Macmillan Press, 1990.

Morrison, R.G. *Nietzsche and Buddhism: A Study in Nihilism and Ironic Affinities*, Oxford University Press, 1997.

Nehamas, A. *Nietzsche: Life as Literature*, Harvard University Press, 1985.

Nussbaum, M. 'Pity and Mercy: Nietzsche's Stoicism' in *Nietzsche, Genealogy, Morality* (ed.) Schacht, University of California Press, 1994.

O'Hara, D.T. (ed.) *Why Nietzsche Now?*, Indiana University Press, 1985.

Owen, D. *Nietzsche, Politics and Modernity: A Critique of Liberal Reason*, Sage Publications, 1995.

Pasley, M. (ed.) *Nietzsche: Imagery and Thought*, Methuen, 1978.

Patton, P. (ed.) *Nietzsche, Feminism and Political Theory*, Routledge, 1993.

Pletsch, C. *Young Nietzsche: Becoming a Genius*, The Free Press, 1991.

Rosen, S. *The Mask of Enlightenment: Nietzsche's Zarathustra*, Cambridge University Press, 1995.

Sadler, T. *Nietzsche: Truth and Redemption, Critique of the Postmodernist Nietzsche*, The Athlone Press, 1995.

Salomé, L. *Friedrich Nietzsche in seinen Werken*, Carl Konegann, 1911.

Santaniello, W. *Nietzsche, God and the Jews: His Critique of Judaeo-Christianity in Relation to the Nazi Myth*, State University of New York Press, 1994.

Schacht, R. *Nietzsche*, Routledge and Kegan Paul, 1983.

Schacht, R. (ed.) *Nietzsche, Genealogy, Morality: Essays on Nietzsche's On the Genealogy of Morals*, University of California Press, 1994.

Schrift, A.D. *Nietzsche's French Legacy: A Genealogy of Poststructuralism*, Routledge, 1995.

Schutte, O. *Beyond Nihilism: Nietzsche without Masks*, University of California Press, 1984.

Silk, M.S. and Stern, J.P. *Nietzsche on Tragedy*, Cambridge University Press, 1981.

Simmel, G. *Schopenhauer and Nietzsche* (H. Loiskandl, D. Weinstein and M. Weinstein trans.) University of Massachusetts Press, 1986.

Smith, D. *Transvaluations: Nietzsche in France 1872–1972*, Oxford University Press, 1996.

Solomon, R.C. (ed.) *Nietzsche: A Collection of Critical Essays*, University of Notre Dame Press, 1980.
Solomon, R.C. and Higgins, K.M. (eds) *Reading Nietzsche*, Oxford University Press, 1988.
Stern, J.P. *Nietzsche*, Fontana Press, 1978.
Stern, J.P. *A Study of Nietzsche*, Cambridge University Press, 1979.
Strong, T.B. *Friedrich Nietzsche and the Politics of Transfiguration: Expanded Edition*, University of California Press, 1988.
Tanner, M. *Nietzsche*, Oxford University Press, 1994.
Thiele, L.P. *Friedrich Nietzsche and the Politics of the Soul: A Study of Heroic Individualism*, Princeton University Press, 1990.
Thomas, R.H. *Nietzsche in German Politics and Society, 1890–1918*, Manchester University Press, 1983.
Warren, M. *Nietzsche and Political Thought*, The MIT Press, 1988.
Westphal, M. 'Nietzsche as a Theological Resource', *Modern Theology*, 13: 2 April 1997.
White, A. *Within Nietzsche's Labyrinth*, Routledge, 1990.
White, R.J. *Nietzsche and the Problem of Sovereignty*, University of Illinois Press, 1997.
Winchester, J.J. *Nietzsche's Aesthetic Turn: Reading Nietzsche after Heidegger, Deleuze, Derrida*, State University of New York Press, 1994.
Young, J. *Nietzsche's Philosophy of Art*, Cambridge University Press, 1992.
Yovel, Y. 'Nietzsche and the Jews: The Structure of an Ambivalence' in *Nietzsche and Jewish Culture* (ed.) Golomb, Routledge, 1977.
Zuboff, A. 'Nietzsche and Eternal Recurrence' in *Nietzsche: A Collection of Critical Essays* (ed.) R.C. Solomon, University of Notre Dame Press, 1980.

Other works cited

Alison, J. *The Joy of Being Wrong: Original Sin through Easter Eyes* Crossroad Herder, 1998.
Altizer, T.J.J. *The Gospel of Christian Atheism*, Collins, 1967.
Altizer, T.J.J., Myers, M.A., Raschke, C.A., Scharlemann, R.P., Taylor, M.C. and Winquist, C.E. *Deconstruction and Theology*, Crossroad Publishing Co., 1982.
Auerbach, E. *Mimesis: The Representation of Reality in Western Literature*, Princeton University Press, 1968.
Augustine *Confessions* (R.S. Pine-Coffin trans.) Penguin, 1961.
Barth, K. *Church Dogmatics* T. and T. Clark, vols I/1, 1936 – IV/3.ii, 1962.
Barth, K. *Fragments Grave and Gay* (E. Mosbacher trans.) Fontana, 1971.
Barth, K. *Protestant Theology in the Nineteenth Century*, SCM Press, 1972.
Berry, P. and Wernick, A. (eds) *Shadow of Spirit: Postmodernism and Religion*, Routledge, 1992.
Bethge, E. 'The Challenge of Dietrich Bonhoeffer's Life and Theology' in *World Come of Age* (ed.) Ronald Grefor Smith, Collins, 1967.
Bettelheim, B. *The Informed Heart*, Free Press, 1960.
Blond, P. (ed.) *Post-Secular Philosophy: Between Philosophy and Theology*, Routledge, 1998.
Boeschenstein, H. *German Literature of the Nineteenth Century*, Edward Arnold, 1969.
Bonhoeffer, D. *Ethics*, SCM Press, 1955.
Bonhoeffer, D. *No Rusty Swords: Letters, Lectures and Notes from the Collected Works, Vol. I* (E.H. Robertson ed.) Fontana, 1970.

Bonhoeffer, D. *Letters and Papers from Prison: The Enlarged Edition* (E. Bethge ed.) SCM Press, 1971.

Bonhoeffer, D. *The Way to Freedom: Letters, Lectures and Notes from the Collected Works, Vol. II* (E.H. Robertson ed.) Fontana, 1972.

Buckley, M.J. *At the Origins of Modern Atheism*, Yale University Press, 1987.

Bultmann, R. *History and Eschatology*, Edinburgh University Press, 1957.

Carr, K.L. *The Banalization of Nihilism: Twentieth-Century Responses to Meaninglessness*, State University of New York Press, 1992.

Cavell, S. *Must We Mean What We Say? A Book of Essays*, Cambridge University Press, 1976.

Cavell, S. *The Claim of Reason: Wittgenstein, Skepticism, Morality, and Tragedy*, Oxford University Press, 1979.

Cavell, S. *Pursuits of Happiness: The Hollywood Comedy of Remarriage*, Harvard University Press, 1981.

Cavell, S. *The Cavell Reader* (ed.) Mulhall, Blackwell, 1996.

Chipp, H.B. *Theories of Modern Art*, California University Press, 1968.

Conrad, J. *Heart of Darkness*, Penguin Classics, 1983, p. 111.

Crossan, J.D. *In Parables: The Challenge of the Historical Jesus*, Harper and Row, 1973.

Cupitt, D. *The World to Come*, SCM Press, 1982.

Dawidowicz, L.S. *The War against the Jews 1933–45*, Pelican, 1987.

Dodds, E.R. *The Greeks and the Irrational*, University of California Press, 1951.

Dodds, E.R. 'The *Parmenides* of Plato and the Origin of the Neoplatonic "One"', *Classical Quarterly* 22, 1928.

Ebeling, G. *Luther: An Introduction to his Thought* (R.A. Wilson trans.) Fontana, 1972.

Fischer, M. *Stanley Cavell and Literary Skepticism*, University of Chicago Press, 1989.

Foley, H. *Ritual Irony: Poetry and Sacrifice in Euripides*, Cornell University Press, 1985.

Girard, R. *Violence and the Sacred*, (P. Gregory trans.) Johns Hopkins University Press, 1977.

Girard, R. *Things Hidden since the Foundation of the World* (S. Bann and M. Metteer trans.) Stanford University Press, 1987.

Girard, R. *The Girard Reader* (J.G. Williams ed.) Crossroad Publishing Co., 1996.

Goethe, J.W. von *The Sorrows of Young Werther*, (Hulse trans.) Penguin, 1989.

Gorringe, T. *God's Just Vengeance: Crime, Violence and the Rhetoric of Salvation*, Cambridge University Press, 1996.

Grunberger, R. *A Social History of the Third Reich*, Pelican, 1974.

Hahn, H.-J. *German Thought and Culture, from the Holy Roman Empire to the Present Day*, Manchester University Press, 1995.

Heidegger, M. *The Question Concerning Technology and Other Essays* (W. Lovitt trans.) Harper and Row, 1977.

Heidegger, M. 'The Self-Assertion of the German University' in *Review of Metaphysics* (Harries trans.) 38, March 1985.

Henrichs, A. 'Loss of Self, Suffering, Violence: The Modern View of Dionysus from Nietzsche to Girard', in *Harvard Studies Classical Papers*, 88, 1984.

Hope, N. *German and Scandinavian Protestantism 1700–1918*, Oxford University Press, 1995.

Jeremias, J. *New Testament Theology*, vol. 1, SCM Press, 1971.

Jüngel, E. *God as the Mystery of the World: On the Foundation of the Theology of the Crucified One in the Dispute between Theism and Atheism* (D.L. Guder trans.) T. and T. Clark, 1983.

Jüngel, E. 'Towards the Heart of the Matter' in *The Christian Century*, 1991.

Kearney, R. and Warner, M. *Heidegger's Three Gods*, Centre for Research in Philosophy and Literature, 1992.

Kerr, F. *Immortal Longings: Versions of Transcending Humanity*, SPCK, 1997.

Kundera, M. *The Unbearable Lightness of Being* (Heim trans.) Faber and Faber, 1984.

Kundera, M. *The Art of the Novel*, Faber and Faber, 1988.

Lasch, C. *The Minimal Self: Psychic Survival in Troubled Times*, Pan Books, 1985.

McGinn, B. *The Foundations of Mysticism: Origins to the Fifth Century*, SCM Press, 1991.

McGrath, A.E. *Luther's Theology of the Cross: Martin Luther's Theological Breakthrough*, Blackwell, 1985.

McGrath, A.E. *Iustitia Dei: A History of the Christian Doctrine of Justification*, Cambridge University Press, 1986.

McGrath, A.E. *The Making of Modern German Christology, 1750–1990*, Zondervan, 1987.

MacIntyre, A. and Ricoeur, P. *The Religious Significance of Atheism*, Columbia University Press, 1969.

McIntyre, J. *The Shape of Soteriology: Studies in the Doctrine of the Death of Christ*, T. and T. Clark, 1992.

Magee, B. *The Philosophy of Schopenhauer*, Clarendon Press, 1983.

Mazur, G.O. 'On Jüngel's Four-Fold Appropriation of Friedrich Nietzsche' in Webster (ed.) *The Possibilities of Theology: Studies in the Theology of Eberhard Jüngel in his Sixtieth Year*, T. and T. Clark, 1994

Milbank, J. *Theology and Social Theory: Beyond Secular Reason*, Blackwell, 1990.

Moltmann, J. *The Crucified God: The Cross of Christ as the Foundation and Criticism of Christian Theology* (R.A. Wilson and J. Bowden trans.) SCM Press, 1974.

Mulhall, S. *Stanley Cavell: Philosophy's Recounting of the Ordinary*, Oxford University Press, 1994.

Murdoch, I. *The Sovereignty of Good*, Routledge, 1970.

Nussbaum, M.C. *The Fragility of Goodness: Luck and Ethics in Greek Tragedy and Philosophy*, Cambridge University Press, 1986.

Nussbaum, M.C. *Love's Knowledge: Essays on Philosophy and Literature*, Oxford University Press, 1990.

Nussbaum, M.C. *The Therapy of Desire: Theory and Practice in Hellenistic Ethics*, Princeton University Press, 1994.

Oberman, H.A. *Luther: Man between God and the Devil* (E. Walliser-Schwarzbart trans.) Fontana, 1993.

Outler, A.C. 'Pietism and Enlightenment: Alternatives to Tradition', in Dupré and Saliers (eds) *Christian Spirituality III*, SCM, 1989.

Pernet, M. 'Friedrich Nietzsche and Pietism' in *German Life and Letters*, 48: 8 October 1995.

Pick, D. *Faces of Degeneration: A European Disorder c.1848–c.1918*, Cambridge University Press, 1989.

Rabinow, P. (ed.) *The Foucault Reader: An Introduction to Foucault's Thought*, Peregrine, 1986.

Raitt, J. (ed.) *Christian Spirituality: High Middle Ages and Reformation*, SCM Press, 1989.

Raschke, C.A. 'The Deconstruction of God' in *Deconstruction and Theology*, Crossroad, 1982.

Ricoeur, P. *Figuring the Sacred: Religion, Narrative and Imagination* (Pellauer trans.) Augsburg Fortress, 1955.

Robinson, E. *The Language of Mystery*, SCM Press, 1987.

Rose, G. *Judaism and Modernity: Philosophical Essays*, Blackwell, 1993.

Roth, J.K. and Berènbaum, M. (eds) *Holocaust: Religious and Philosophical Implications*, Paragon House, 1989.

Rubenstein, R.L. and Roth, J.K. *Approaches to Auschwitz: The Legacy of the Holocaust*, SCM Press, 1987.

Sanders, E.P. *Judaism: Practice and Belief 63 BCE–66 CE*, SCM Press, 1992.

Schopenhauer, A. *The World as Will and Representation*, Dover, 1958.

Schopenhauer, A. *Essays and Aphorisms*, Penguin, 1970.

Shanks, A. *Hegel's Political Theology*, Cambridge University Press, 1991.

Sharples, R.W. *Stoicism, Epicureanism and Scepticism: An Introduction to Hellenistic Philosophy*, Routledge, 1996.

Silk, M. (ed.) *Tragedy and the Tragic: Greek Theatre and Beyond*, Oxford University Press, 1996.

Taylor, C. *Sources of the Self: The Making of the Modern Identity*, Cambridge University Press, 1989.

Taylor, C. *The Ethics of Authenticity*, Harvard University Press, 1991.

Taylor, M.C. *Erring: A Postmodern A/theology*, University of Chicago Press, 1984.

Thielicke, H. *The Evangelical Faith*, vol. 1, T. and T. Clark, 1974.

Thielicke, H. *Modern Faith and Thought* (G.W. Bromiley trans.) William B. Eerdmans Publishing Co., 1990.

Tilley, T.W. *Postmodern Theologies: The Challenge of Religious Diversity*, Orbis, 1995.

Tillich, P. *The Shaking of the Foundations*, SCM Press, 1949.

Von Balthasar, H.U. *The Theology of Karl Barth*, Ignatius Press, 1992.

Wagner, R. *The Art-Work of the Future and Other Works* (Ashton trans.) Ellis Bison, 1993.

Ward, G. (ed.) *The Postmodern God: A Theological Reader*, Blackwell, 1997.

Webster, J.B. *Eberhard Jüngel: An Introduction to his Theology*, Cambridge University Press, 1986.

Webster, J.B. (ed.) *The Possibilities of Theology: Studies in the Theology of Eberhard Jüngel in his Sixtieth Year*, T. and T. Clark, 1994.

Weil, S. *Gravity and Grace* (E. Craufurd trans.) Routledge, 1963.

Weindling, P. *Health, Race and German Politics between National Unification and Nazism, 1870–1945*, Cambridge University Press, 1989.

Williams, R. 'The Suspicion of Suspicion: Wittgenstein and Bonhoeffer' in Bell (ed.) *The Grammar of the Heart: New Essays in Moral Philosophy and Theology*, Harper and Row, 1988.

Williams, R. *The Wound of Knowledge: Christian Spirituality from the New Testament to St. John of the Cross*, 2nd edition, Darton, Longman and Todd, 1990.

Williams, R. *Open to Judgement: Sermons and Addresses*, Darton, Longman and Todd, 1994.

Williams, S.N. *Revelation and Reconciliation: A Window on Modernity*, Cambridge University Press, 1995.

Young, F. *Sacrifice and the Death of Christ*, SCM Press, 1975.

Index

Ward, Graham 19–20
Warren, Mark 95–6
weakness 4, 7, 83, 93, 112, 129,
    147–8, 152, 154
weight 115–19, 163
Weil, Simone 90, 147
Weindling, Paul 92
Wesley, John 41
Westphal, Merold 20–1
Wiesel, Eli 22
Wilde, Oscar 68

will 51, 53, 102, 103, 108, 110, 161, 163
will to power 40, 94–6, 110
Williams, Rowan 37, 165–6
Williams, Stephen 15
Wittgenstein, Ludwig 13, 98, 107,
    156, 157–8
woman 36

Yahweh 5, 79–80
Young, Julian 1, 120, 121
Yovel, Yirmiyahu 133